Prolonged Connections

A hell of a deal
for a hell of a person

Steve

Social Demography

Series Editors   Doris P. Slesinger
James A. Sweet
Karl E. Taeuber
Center for Demography and Ecology
University of Wisconsin-Madison

Procedural History of the 1940 Census of Housing and Population
Robert M. Jenkins

Population Growth and Economic Development: Issues and Evidence
Edited by D. Gale Johnson and Ronald D. Lee

Thailand's Reproductive Revolution: Rapid Fertility Decline in a
Third-World Setting
John Knodel, Aphichat Chamratrithirong, and Nibbon Debavalya

Prolonged Connections: The Rise of the Extended Family in
Nineteenth-Century England and America
Steven Ruggles

Prolonged Connections

The Rise of the Extended Family in Nineteenth-Century England and America

Steven Ruggles

The University of Wisconsin Press

Published 1987

The University of Wisconsin Press
114 North Murray Street
Madison, Wisconsin 53715

The University of Wisconsin Press, Ltd.
1 Gower Street
London WC1E 6HA, England

First printing

Printed in the United States of America

For LC CIP information see the colophon

ISBN 0-299-11030-3 cloth, 0-299-11034-6 paper

To my noncoresident extended kin group

Contents

Preface   xvii

1   **The Rise of the Extended Family in the
    Nineteenth Century**   3

2   **The Economics of the Family:
    Some Theoretical Considerations**   13

    Traditional Sociological Interpretations   13
    The New Home Economics   16
    Exchange Theory   20
    Economic Theory and Levels of Analysis   22
    Economic Analysis and Nonmaterial Factors   23
    The Limitations of Economic Analysis   24
    Historical Interpretations   25
    Conclusion   27

3   **Evidence on the Economics of
     Extended-Family Structure**   30

     Economic Status and Extended-Family Structure   31
     Economic Dependence and the Extended Family   42
     Economic Exchange and Extended-Family Structure   47
     Conclusion   57

4   **Approaches to the Demography of the
     Extended Family**   60

     Theoretical Considerations   60
     Analytic Models of Extended-Family Structure   65
     Simulation Approaches   71
     The Socsim Demographic Microsimulation Model   74

5   **Analytic Strategies**   84

     Levels of Measurement and Residential Propensities   84
     The Whopper Assumption   89
     The Standard Propensities Approach   92
     Use of Hypothetical Rules with Momsim   102
     Conclusion   105

6   **Simulation Results**   106

     The Standard Propensities Results   110
     Hypothetical Rules and Stem-Family Structure   119
     Conclusion   125

Conclusion   127

**Appendix A: Notes on the Measurement of
                Historical Family Structure**   139

Family Extension versus Household Extension   139
Household Headship and Family Structure   140
The Unit of Measurement   142
The Effects of Intervening Variables   147

Appendix B: Data and Setting   150

**Appendix C: MOMSIM: An Individual-Level Model
                of Demography and Kinship**   156

General Characteristics of the Model   157
Input Data and Allocation Procedures   160
Strategy for Assigning Characteristics   169
Assumptions in Assignment of
    Individual Characteristics   172
Accuracy of the Life-History Allocations   174
Organization of the Model   175
The Piggyback Projection Model   181
The MOMSIM Adjustment Technique   182
Conclusion   184

**Appendix D: The Effects of Demography on
                Extended-Family Structure**   185

The 1900 Standard Propensities   186
Marital Patterns and Standard Propensities   191
Mortality, Fertility, and Standard Propensities   198
Analysis through Hypothetical Rules   203
Conclusion   206

**Appendix E: Marriage and Class Patterns of
                Extended-Family Structure**   208

Demography and Extended Families in Lancashire   208
Vertical and Horizontal Extension   211
Hypergamy and Horizontal Extension   214
Headship and Vertical Extension   216
Conclusion   219

Appendix F: Multivariate Analyses   220

Bibliography   237

Index   275

Figures

1.1. Percentage of Households Containing Extended Kin: England and America, 1600–1984   5

1.2. Mean Number of Extended Kin per 100 Households: England, 1650–1970   9

3.1. Percentage of Persons Residing with Extended Kin, by Occupational Class: Erie County, 1855–1915   34

3.2. Percentage of Persons Residing with Extended Kin, by Occupational Class: Lancashire Towns, 1871   37

3.3. Percentage of Persons Residing with Extended Kin, by Value of Farm: Erie County, 1855   38

3.4. Standardized Percentage of Persons Residing with Extended Kin, by Value of Dwelling: Erie County, 1855   40

3.5. Economic-Dependency Ratio of Extended Families, Including and Excluding Extended Kin, by Age of Family Head: Erie County and Lancashire Towns, 1871–1915   46

3.6. Percent of Migrants Residing in Extended Families, by Years Spent Locally: Erie County, 1855   55

C.1. Simplified Flowchart for Life-History Subroutine   170

C.2. Mean Number of Surviving Children, by Age of Mother: United States, 1900, and Simulated Population   176

C.3.   Percentage of Women with One or More Surviving Children, by
            Age of Mother: United States, 1900, and Simulated
            Population   177

C.4.   Example of Simulated Kin Group   179

D.1.   Percentage Ever Married, by Age and Sex: Marriage Runs   190

Tables

1.1.   Extended-Family Households for Localities in Which Time-Series Data Are Available   7

3.1.   Individuals Residing with Extended Relatives, Erie County, 1855–1915   35

3.2.   Effects of the Inclusion of Extended Relatives on the Family Economic-Dependency Ratio   43

3.3.   Effects of the Inclusion of Extended Relatives on the Family Economic-Dependency Ratio, by Occupational Class, Erie County, 1880–1915   44

3.4.   The Living Arrangements of Mothers and Working Women   48

3.5.   Living Arrangements and Multihousehold Dwellings, Erie County, 1855   52

3.6.   Ward Density and Percent Residing with Extended Relatives, Buffalo, 1855   53

5.1.   Percentage of Individuals with Available Kin of Selected Types, United States, 1900   94

5.2.   Percentage of Individuals Actually Residing with Kin of Selected Types, United States, 1900   94

5.3.   Propensities for Individuals to Reside with Kin of Selected Types, United States, 1900   95

6.1.   Basic Demographic Parameters for Simulation Runs: Preindustrial Run and Standard Population   111

6.2.   Preindustrial and Standard Simulation Runs: Measures of Family Structure, Assuming 1900 Standard Propensities   112

6.3.   Basic Demographic Parameters for Simulation Runs: Mid-Twentieth-Century Run and Standard Population   115

6.4.   Mid-Twentieth-Century and Standard Simulation Runs: Measures of Family Structure, Assuming 1900 Standard Propensities   116

6.5.   Basic Demographic Parameters for Simulation Runs: Exaggerated Third World Run and Standard Population   117

6.6.   Exaggerated Third World and Standard Simulation Runs: Measures of Family Structure, Assuming 1900 Standard Propensities   118

6.7.   Measures of Stem-Family Structure, Assuming Stem Hypothetical Rules and PRE Demographic Conditions   121

6.8.   Measures of Stem-Family Structure, Assuming Stem Hypothetical Rules: Combination Demographic Models   124

A.1.   Measures of Extended Family Structure for Hypothetical Populations, Assuming Constant Family Size   143

A.2.   Measures of Extended Family Structure for Hypothetical Populations, Assuming Variable Family Size   145

C.1   Proportion of Population Ever Married, by Age and Sex, United States, 1900   161

C.2.   Characteristics for a Hypothetical Kin Group   180

D.1.   Residential Propensities for Major Kin Groups in 1900   188

D.2.   Basic Demographic Parameters of Marriage Runs   191

D.3.   Marriage Runs: Measures of Family Structure, Assuming 1900 Standard Propensities   193

D.4.   Availability of Mothers   194

D.5.   Availability of Sisters   195

D.6.   Basic Demographic Parameters of Percent Marrying Runs   197

D.7.   Effect of Percent Never Marrying on Family Structure, Assuming 1900 Standard Propensities   197

D.8.   Basic Demographic Parameters of Spouse-Interval Runs   197

D.9.   Effect of Age Intervals between Spouses on Family Structure, Assuming 1900 Standard Propensities   198

D.10.   Basic Demographic Parameters of Mortality Runs   199

D.11.   Mortality Runs: Measures of Family Structure, Assuming 1900 Standard Propensities   200

D.12.   Basic Demographic Parameters of Fertility Runs   201

D.13.   Fertility Runs: Measures of Family Structure, Assuming 1900 Standard Propensities   202

D.14.   Measures of Stem-Family Structure, Assuming Stem Hypothetical Rules: Marriage Runs   204

D.15.   Measures of Stem-Family Structure, Assuming Stem Hypothetical Rules: Percent Marrying Runs   204

D.16.   Measures of Stem-Family Structure, Assuming Stem Hypothetical Rules: Mortality Runs   205

D.17.   Measures of Stem-Family Structure, Assuming Stem Hypothetical Rules: Fertility Runs   206

E.1.   Simulation Results, Assuming 1871 Standard Propensities   210

E.2.   Percentage of Extended-Family Members Residing in "Vertical" and "Horizontal" Families, Lancashire Towns, 1871   213

E.3.   Marital Status of Women over 35, Lancashire Towns, 1871   217

E.4.   Headship Patterns for Persons in Three-Generation Families, Lancashire Towns, 1871   217

F.1.   Multiple-Classification Analysis of the Probability of Residing in an Extended Family, Erie County, 1855   223

F.2.   Multiple-Classification Analysis of the Probability of Residing in an Extended Family, Erie County, 1855   225

F.3.   Multiple-Classification Analysis of the Probability of Residing in an Extended Family, Erie County, 1880   227

F.4.   Multiple-Classification Analysis of the Probability of Residing in an Extended Family for Women Aged 18 or Older, Erie County, 1880   229

F.5.   Multiple-Classification Analysis of the Probability of Residing in an Extended Family, Erie County, 1900   230

F.6.   Multiple-Classification Analysis of the Probability of Residing in an Extended Family for Women Aged 18 or Older, Erie County, 1900   231

F.7.   Multiple-Classification Analysis of the Probability of Residing in
           an Extended Family, Erie County, 1915   232

F.8.   Multiple-Classification Analysis of the Probability of Residing
           in an Extended Family for Women Aged 18 or Older, Erie
           County, 1915   233

F.9.   Multiple-Classification Analysis of the Probability of Residing in
           an Extended Family, Turton and Salford, Lancashire, 1871   234

F.10.   Multiple-Classification Analysis of the Probability of Residing
           in an Extended Family for Women Aged 18 or Older, Turton
           and Salford, Lancashire, 1871   235

Preface

Society is not as reasonable as social scientists like to think. We spend an awful lot of time trying to discern a system within the chaos and disorder, and sometimes we try too hard. We have constructed a vision of society as a marvelous self-adjusting machine, one in which every cog serves an essential purpose to the operation of the mechanism as a whole.

A few years ago, social scientists knew exactly what happened to the family during the nineteenth century: there was a shift from extended to nuclear family structure, which occurred because the nuclear family was functionally adapted to industrial society. We now have new evidence which shows that the opposite change took place: the frequency of extended families roughly doubled between about 1750 and 1900. So the old theory has been modified; the few scholars who recognize that there was an increase in the frequency of extended families now take the view that it was the *extended* family that was functionally adapted to early industrial society.

This book argues that we cannot explain the rise of the extended family by tinkering with functionalist theory. The nineteenth-century extended family was not a functional adaptation to new social conditions; the reasons people increasingly resided in extended families had little to do with any purpose the extended family may have served. Instead, the extended family should be viewed as an indirect consequence of changing social conditions.

To unravel the mystery posed by the high frequency of extended families in the nineteenth century, I round up the usual suspects: economics, demography, and culture.

Economic theory, I argue, does not work well for explaining changes in the family; when it comes to their relatives, people are seldom completely rational. Taking in relatives was not a strategy for economic survival under the harsh conditions of early industrial capitalism—on the contrary, extended kin typically imposed an added economic burden. If rational economic decision-making cannot explain residence in nineteenth-century extended families, then economic calculation was not the motive for the rise of the extended family. But that does not mean that material factors were irrelevant. Even if economics does not tell us why so many Victorians wanted to live in extended families, it can help explain how they were able to do so. As the century proceeded, more and more people were able to afford the luxury of supporting their dependent kin.

Demographic explanations turn out to be more important than economic ones, and they are the main focus of the book. There were few extended families before the industrial revolution primarily because most people had a shortage of living relatives. In the nineteenth century, rising life expectancy, together with falling age at marriage expanded the size of kin groups, and increased the opportunities to form extended families.

But demography is not the whole story. The rise of the extended family coincided with a revolution in attitudes to family life. The Victorians idealized family relationships far more than their ancestors had. They had an acute sense of obligation to kin, and were often willing to support relatives at great economic and psychic cost.

All three suspects, then, played a role in the rise of the extended family. Rising incomes allowed more people to choose economically disadvantageous living arrangements. And the increase of extended families was in part a byproduct of demographic change; at the very least, we can be confident that the rise of the extended family would never have happened without changes in the patterns of death and marriage. But if these economic and demographic factors can explain the increased opportunities to reside in extended families, they do not explain why people chose to take advantage of those opportunities.

When I say that the Victorians chose extended families, I do not want to overemphasize the role of individual agency. Social historians have become increasingly interested in the motives underlying the behavior of ordinary people. Many have stressed the rational elements of individual decision-making, and have regarded economic calculation as something admirable—as evidence that historical actors played an important role in shaping their own destinies. This has sometimes led to an implication that the pursuit of material gain is a good thing in itself.

The really interesting aspects of social behavior, it seems to me, are those that cannot be easily explained in terms of material selfishness. The nineteenth-century extended family rested partly on the earnest Victorian sense of duty. This is something larger, I think, than a calculated adaptation to new social conditions. Changing attitudes to the family in the early industrial period were a reflection of a fundamental shift in values. It would be difficult to ascribe that shift to individual agency. Nineteenth-century society was made by the people of the time, but they did so collectively and without conscious premeditation.

The text is devoted to explanations for the rise of the extended family in the nineteenth century, while the appendixes address a variety of related issues. For many readers, the most useful parts of my research will be found at the back of the book. There I discuss the measurement of family structure, new techniques for analyzing the demography of the extended family, the sensitivity of family structure to variation in demographic conditions, and the implications of demography for class differences in family structure. Although the appendixes are heavily methodological, they are not difficult; I have tried to make them as accessible as the main body of the book.

I have been working on this topic for over a decade, and along the way many people have given me help. I am fortunate in having a noncoresident extended kin group composed of experts in areas related to my topic. My sister Patricia gave me enormous help on microsimulation, economic history and social theory generally. My other sister Jo gave me critical advice on the computer programs and data structures used in this research. My parents provided me with a model of intellectual reasonableness. They have also shown great courage, consistently bucking the tide of economic orthodoxy. And—not the least of their accomplishments—they have done more than any others to advance the cause of microdata.

In its early stages, my work benefitted from the advice and criticism of the late David Glass and A.F. Thompson. My first exposure to formal demography came from Jim Sweet, who taught me to watch my denominators. He has remained an invaluable source of encouragement and assistance throughout. This book grew out of my dissertation, and it bears the influence of Michael Katz, my advisor in graduate school. My greatest debt is to my friend and colleague Miriam King, who was my chief consultant on demographic methods, microsimulation, social theory, the history of the family, and social history generally. She edited the entire manuscript several times over, ferreting out flaws of logic, content, style, and organization. The manuscript was also read at various stages by Michael Katz, Dan Smith, Jim Sweet, Maris Vinovskis, and Susan Watkins. Their advice saved me from committing a variety of statistical and logical sins.

Many others deserve mention. My former roommates—Roald Euller and Erica Flapan—consulted on computer graphics and mathematics, respectively. The criticism of Nancy Fitch and Roger Schofield of an early paper on the demography of the family helped to shape my approach to that problem. Lisa Duggan forced me to reevaluate my interpretation of the Victorian marriage market. Susan Cahn, Liz Faue, Werner Gundersheimer, Cindy Himes, Norris Lewis, Winston McDowell, Louise Merriam, Rosie Mestel, Alexander Riasanovsky, John Schroeder, and Nancy Shoemaker all helped with ideas, suggestions, or criticism. I am also grateful for the encouragement and support of my colleagues in the history department at Minnesota.

I received considerable help from institutions. The Roy F. Nichols Graduate History Society defended my funding during six years of graduate school. The now-defunct Green Lantern Eating Cooperative provided nutrition and moral improvement during long intervals spent in Madison, Wisconsin; Walsh's Tavern served the same functions in Philadelphia. I owe a great debt to the helpful staffs of two computing facilities, David Rittenhouse Laboratories of the University of Pennsylvania and the Center for Demography and Ecology of the University of Wisconsin. The latter, I am obliged to note, is supported by NICHD grant HD05876.

Minneapolis
November 1986

Prolonged Connections

"Taking the Census," from George Cruikshank et al., *The Comic Almanack: An Ephemeris in Jest and Earnest, Containing Merry Tales, Humorous Poetry, Quips and Oddities* (London, 1851; reprint 1912)

1 The Rise of the Extended Family in the Nineteenth Century

> I believe that more unhappiness comes from this source than any other—I mean from the attempt to prolong the family connection unduly and to make people hang together artificially who would never naturally do so. The mischief among the lower classes is not so great, but among the middle and upper classes it is killing a large number daily. And the old people do not really like it so much better than the young.
>
> Samuel Butler, *Note-Books* (ca. 1885)

The old myth of the extended family is the one we all grew up with. In olden days—before modernization, industrialization, and moral decay—people lived in extended families; now people live in nuclear families.[1] This view of the history of the family was first proposed in the nineteenth century, and by the 1950s it was safely cloaked in the protective language of science.[2]

Doubts about the old myth were first raised in 1963, when Peter Laslett and John Harrison published evidence that residence with extended relatives was rare in Clayworth, Nottinghamshire, during the seventeenth century. Subsequent research has shown that this village was not exceptional; only about 10 percent of households in English communities between 1650 and 1780 included extended kin.[3] The evidence for colonial

---

1. A family is defined here as any group of related people who reside together. A nuclear family is one which contains no relatives other than a husband, wife, and their children; an extended family includes other kin. Most of the evidence cited in this chapter refers to extended and nuclear *households* rather than families; the distinction between the two is discussed in appendix A.

2. The principal schools of thought are discussed in chapter 2.

3. Laslett and Harrison (1963). The subsequent research—based on analysis of local censuses for over a hundred localities—was mostly carried out by the Cambridge Group for the History of Population and Social Structure; their findings are described in Laslett and Wall (1972). These investigations have been sharply criticized; see especially Goubert (1977) and Berkner (1975). However, other studies, independent of the Cambridge Group, have arrived at the conclusion that only 10 percent or less of households included extended

3

America is scantier, because fewer listings of inhabitants are available. Nevertheless, the limited data do suggest that extended living arrangements were at least as unusual in eighteenth-century America as they were in England.[4] There are now few adherents to the myth that extended families predominated in the world we have lost.

Unfortunately, a new myth has replaced the old one. It is now commonly believed that American and English family structure has always been overwhelmingly nuclear. Thus the study of extended-family structure has been deemed irrelevant. If the frequency of extended families has remained unchanged for the past 300 years, and such living arrangements were always an aberration, then the significant developments in the history of the family must lie elsewhere. With this reasoning, several American social historians have criticized the study of extended family structure. For example, Robert Wells argues that such research "misses the point; one should not be concerned with whom an individual lived, but rather with the *quality* of relationships between kin."[5]

In fact, the frequency of extended families has not remained constant. The best evidence now available indicates that the frequency of extended-family households *increased* from the preindustrial period to the late nineteenth century.

Evidence about extended households from a wide variety of studies of both England and America is presented in figure 1.1.[6] This graph plots the

kin before 1780; see Glass (1965), Tranter (1967: 269–70), Pythian-Adams (1979), and the research described in Houlbrooke (1984: 20).

4. I know of only two colonial American figures which are strictly comparable to the English data, and both are based on small data sets from the late seventeenth century: there were 3 percent extended households in Bristol, Rhode Island, in 1689 (Laslett 1972a: 81), and 6 percent extended in Bedford, New York, in 1698 (Wells 1975: 132). Although we cannot generalize on the basis of data from two localities, it is noteworthy that these percentages are even smaller than has been found in the seventeenth- or eighteenth-century English localities. Moreover, the impression that extended families were rare in colonial America is bolstered by other kinds of evidence; see Demos (1968: 40, 44–45; 1965: 279), Greven (1966: 255), and Hecht (1973). A listing of inhabitants in Brumbaugh (1928: 113–14) suggests that some 10 percent of 978 families in six Maryland localities in 1776 contained extended kin.

5. Wells (1978: 526); see also D. S. Smith (1973b), Kobrin (1976: 127), Katz (1975: 9, 306–7). A notable exception is Chudacoff (1978: 179–205). The notion that the American family was "born modern" antedates the systematic study of extended-family structure (Furstenburg 1966), which perhaps helps to explain American historians' easy acceptance of the hypothesis of continuity.

6. To ensure comparability, only those researchers who explicitly define their statistics as the percentage of households containing extended kin are represented in figure 1.1; see appendix A.

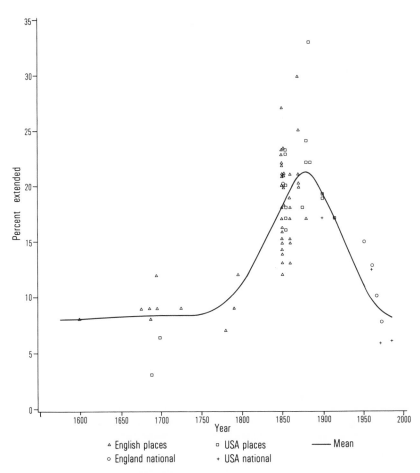

Figure 1.1. Percentage of households containing extended kin: England and America, 1600–1984. Sources: Laslett (1972), Armstrong (1974), Anderson (1971), Hareven (1971), Glass (1973), Smith (1970), Dupree (1979), Foster (1974), Glasco (1973), Pryor (1972), Blumin (1977), Brayshay (1980), Howlett (1983), Tranter (1967, 1973), Wall (1982), Wells (1975), General Register Office (1968), U.S. Bureau of the Census (1963, 1973, 1985), Agresti (1979). Figures for Lancashire, Erie County, and the U.S. in 1900 are based on data described in appendix B. For further details, see note 7

findings of twenty-seven separate studies of sixty-eight data sets drawn from localities and national samples in England and America between 1599 and 1984. According to these data, the percentage of households containing extended kin of the family head roughly *doubled* between 1750 and the late nineteenth century in both England and America.

Between 1850 and 1885, about 20 percent of households included extended kin.

During the twentieth century, this trend has reversed. In both America and England, the frequency of extended households has declined to levels even lower than in the preindustrial period. In England in 1971, only 7.7 percent of households included extended kin, while in the United States in 1984, the figure was 6.0 percent.[7]

The data presented in figure 1.1 may actually underestimate the increase in the frequency of extended families between the preindustrial period and the high Victorian era. The long-term comparison of statistics on household structure presents difficulties because the definition of what constitutes a "household" has not remained constant. If anything, however, changing definitions of the household probably result in *understatement* of the increase in extended living arrangements in the nineteenth century; preindustrial enumerators probably adopted a more inclusive definition of households than did their nineteenth-century counterparts.[8]

7. U.S. Bureau of the Census (1985: 6), Wall (1982: 83). Wall cites a figure of 20.2 percent extended households for England as a whole in 1851, based on a new national sample prepared under the direction of Michael Anderson. For additional twentieth-century data, see Great Britain, General Register Office (1968: 1–2), U.S. Bureau of the Census (1973: 276; 1963: 450). The twentieth-century American figures cited in the text and in figure 1.1 were adjusted to include primary individuals in the denominator.

The curve labeled "mean" in figure 1.1 is based on the averages of all data points over thirty-year periods, except that for the period before 1800 the curve was based entirely on the Cambridge Group data. The curve was smoothed with the SASGRAPH spline function; the same function was applied for the continuous graphs that appear in chapter 3 and appendix D.

8. We have quite a bit of information about the definition of the household in Victorian censuses, but the earlier period is more problematic. See, for example, P. Laslett (1972a: 23–28, 34–40), Wall (1972: 159–66), P. Laslett (1972b: 132–34), Tillott (1972), Anderson (1972b), Wright (1900), U.S. Bureau of the Census (1949: 18), Glick (1957: 210).

A great deal has been written about such problems of comparison, but it doesn't add up to much; we simply lack information on the criteria employed by precensus enumerators. Internal evidence, however, suggests that the preindustrial enumerators may have adopted a broader definition of the household than did the Victorian enumerators. In the nineteenth century, multiple-household dwellings were fairly common; investigators have found that between 10 and 40 percent of households shared premises with other households (cf. Anderson 1972a, Katz, Doucet, and Stern 1982). According to Peter Laslett (1972a), on the other hand, the preindustrial household was ordinarily "coterminous" with premises, broadly defined. Since a significant proportion of nineteenth-century multifamily dwellings contained kin who resided in different households, the narrow definitions used in the nineteenth century may have reduced the relative frequency of extended-family households.

Table 1.1. Extended-Family Households for Localities in Which Time-Series Data Are Available

Locality/Year	Percent Extended	Number of Cases
Puddletown, Dorset		
1724–25	9	154
1851	12	264
1861	15	257
1871	20	271
1881	17	248
Ealing, Middlesex		
1599	8	85
1851	13	248
1861	21	209
Cardington, Bedfordshire		
1782	7	180
1851	20	284
Corfe Castle, Dorset		
1790	9	272
1851	15	513
1861	15	297
Clayworth, Nottinghamshire		
1676	9	98
1688	8	91
1851	21	128
Chilvers Coton, Warwick		
1686	9	177
1851	16	570
Bilston, Staffordshire		
1695	12	192
1851	20	329
1861	13	264
Ardleigh, Essex		
1796	12	210
1851	14	366
Appledore, Devon		
1851	23	410
1871	30	488
Rhode Island		
1689[a]	3	72
1875	18	2,563
1960	15	31,488
Erie County, New York[b]		
1855	20	72,659
1880	24	13,778
1900	21	32,599
1915	19	63,452

Sources: P. Laslett (1972a: 61); Pryor (1972: 575); Tranter (1967: 269–70, 1973: 96–97); Howlett (1983: 42, 48).

[a]Bristol only.

[b]Percentage of persons in extended families; see appendix A.

For most of the localities shown in figure 1.1, we have information about household structure at only one moment in time. It might be objected that the localities represented in the earlier period might not be comparable to those of the late nineteenth century. Accordingly, table 1.1 provides figures for the few localities for which time-series data are available. The trend is unmistakable: in virtually every locality shown, extended family households were becoming increasingly common until about 1870 or 1880. In the words of Jean-Louis Flandrin, these data seem "to disprove, beyond question, the accepted notions regarding the supposed transition from the extended family to the nuclear family at the time of the Industrial Revolution."[9]

Similar conclusions are indicated by figure 1.2, which is based on recent research by Richard Wall. This graph shows that the mean number of persons listed as extended kin per 100 English households almost tripled between 1750 and 1850.[10] By 1970, this mean number of extended kin had returned to preindustrial levels.

Taken together, the evidence demonstrates that the high incidence of family extension in the second half of the nineteenth century was not a local phenomenon, nor even a national one. In both England and America, extended-family structure was more common in the high Victorian era than either before or since. The striking rise of the extended family in the nineteenth century provided the impetus for my research.

The data directly contradict the predictions of traditional sociological theory. The central question is straightforward: why did the frequency of extended families increase in the nineteenth century?

9. Flandrin (1979: 69).

10. Wall (1983b) also refers to a survey described in an unpublished essay apparently written around 1947, in which the mean number of extended kin appears to be *higher* than in the nineteenth century. This statistic is an anomaly; all the other figures from the twentieth century are substantially *lower* than the Victorian figures. If the figure for 1947 is accurate, it may reflect a short-term postwar housing shortage resulting from demobilization. Elsewhere (1982) Wall suggests that the peak frequency of extended families may have occurred around 1920. On the other hand, the data on Erie County and Puddletown shown in table 1.1 suggest a peak frequency of extended families in the 1870s or 1880s, and the figures from Bilston suggest an even earlier peak. At present we lack sufficient data to pin down the exact timing of change. Evidence compiled by Rudy Ray Seward (1978) for the United States as a whole in the period from 1850 to 1880 indicates that the frequency of three-generation families increased dramatically during that period, but Seward's figures are compromised by methodological difficulties (see Ruggles 1984). Even though the data are scattered, though, we can be reasonably confident that the peak frequency of extended families occurred sometime after the 1860s. At present, we also know that the peak occurred well before 1950. We will be able to narrow it down for the United States through tabulations of the new Public Use Samples for 1910 and 1940.

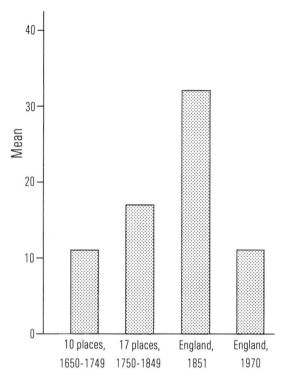

Figure 1.2. Mean number of extended kin per 100 households: England, 1650–1970. Source: Wall (1983: 500)

At the outset of my investigation I was convinced that the high fre-quency of extended families in the nineteenth century should be ex-plained in cultural terms. The Victorian idealization of home and family is well known.[11] Cultural historians have interpreted this reverence for family life as a sign of increasing isolation of the nuclear family from the outside world, in accordance with the old myth of the extended family. This view represents a selective reading of the evidence. It is true that our sources—diaries, letters, autobiographies, novels, and advice books—tend to stress the strength of bonds with parents, children, spouses, and siblings, rather than with more distant relations. But it is precisely these near relations that formed the basis of the Victorian extended family. The overwhelming majority of late-nineteenth-century extended families consisted of nuclear families with the addition of parents or siblings of the

11. See chapter 7.

husband or wife. Thus, extended families were formed as Victorians prolonged the family connections of childhood into their adult lives.

Social scientists, on the whole, are uncomfortable with the notion that ideas have a life of their own. Changes in the ways people think are generally regarded merely as symptoms of more fundamental structural change. By structural change I mean material change: the mode of production, economic relationships, and demographic conditions. My own prejudice is different. It seems to me that the way people think is as likely to dictate material structures as the other way around.[12] In the sphere of family relationships, bonds of emotion and obligation play an especially important role. I therefore proceeded with the assumption that it is more fruitful to conceive the family as a psychological unit than as an economic one.

In spite of this orientation, I chose to begin my research with an analysis of demographic and economic explanations for the rise of the extended family. Since the bulk of previous work on extended families has stressed demography and economics, I felt that it would be wise to start out by investigating whether these strictly material factors were sufficient to account for the high frequency of extended families in the late nineteenth century.

This task proved to be complicated—so complicated, in fact, that my analysis of demography and economics grew to encompass virtually the entire study. The realm of culture, like a poor relation, has been relegated to the back of the book. And my investigation of the demography and economics of extended families is still drastically oversimplified. What is worse, I have been totally unsuccessful at demonstrating the insignificance of the material sphere.

I have been unable to show that the effects of demography were trivial; to my dismay, I have shown the critical importance of demographic change to the rise of the extended family. Nor have I succeeded in dismissing the purely economic realm of explanation. But my interpretation remains reasonably consistent with my prejudices. Demographic and

---

12. Moreover, I find it equally plausible that social change arises from the internal development of systems of thought as from the internal development of material structures. For a sharply differing view, see Anderson (1980: 61–64). The distinction between systems of thought and material structures is artificial: the material and intellectual aspects of society are so intimately bound together that it is perhaps absurd to worry about which one is more fundamental. Still, if we are going to make any sense of the world we need to make some artificial distinctions; any sort of generalization requires the construction of categories. Although the division of society into things and thoughts oversimplifies, it does have intuitive appeal.

economic change may have had dramatic effects on extended families during the eighteenth and nineteenth centuries, but there is no evidence that these were functional adaptations to new material circumstances. Furthermore, the Victorian frame of mind can be seen as a necessary condition for the rise of the extended family; extended families were not merely an inevitable consequence of structural change.

The main thrust of social theory relating to historical change in family structure has been, broadly speaking, economic. My approach to the economics of the extended family is fairly circumscribed. In the following two chapters, I confine myself to arguing that existing economic theories of the family do not make a whole lot of sense and they do not explain residential behavior in the nineteenth century.

My primary focus is demographic. Between the early eighteenth century and the late nineteenth century, the demographic regimes of England and America were radically transformed. This demographic transition altered the biological opportunities for the formation of extended families. Demography works in mysterious ways, and so chapters 4 and 5 are devoted to the principles of demographic detection. The results of my demographic analysis appear in chapter 6.

Before turning to the analysis, a brief foray into methods is in order. Issues of measurement are central to the quantitative study of family structure, and we shall return to them again and again. My most practical contributions, perhaps, consist of innovations in the strategy of measuring family structure. With much reluctance, I decided against inserting a separate chapter on this topic, on the grounds that delving straight into a methodological discussion would drive away too many readers. Readers of hardier cast should turn straight to appendix A. For the rest of you, I shall briefly describe how my measures of family structure differ from those of other investigators.

First, and most important, measurements of family structure are made at the level of individuals rather than at the level of households. Thus, instead of measuring the percentage of households containing extended kin, I measure the percentage of persons residing with extended kin. As demonstrated in appendix A, measurement by households violates important principles of measurement and precludes critical statistical manipulation.

Second, this is a study of *family* structure, not of *household* structure. A family is defined as any group of related people who reside together. Families may consist of solitary individuals, and nonrelatives of the household head—such as boarders, lodgers, and servants—are considered to constitute separate families of their own.

Third, my classification of family structure does not depend on the culturally defined reference point—the head of household—provided by Victorian census takers. Instead, I have designated a single individual within each family to be the reference person for that family, on the basis of constant criteria. I call these individuals "family heads." The designation of consistent reference persons ensures that biologically identical families will be classified consistently. Thus, this strategy allows us to distinguish patterns of biological kinship from patterns of status and authority.

These decisions mean that few of my results are comparable to those of previous researchers. This is a significant liability, but a necessary one: as will become evident, much of my analysis would have been impossible if I had relied on traditional measures.

Enough of methods for now; we will encounter more than enough of them later. Let us first consider madness.

2 The Economics of the Family
Some Theoretical Considerations

> Economic theory may well be on its way to providing a unified framework for *all* behavior involving scarce resources, nonmarket as well as market, nonmonetary as well as monetary, small group as well as competitive.
>
> Gary S. Becker, "A Theory of Marriage" (1974)

> There is no more important prerequisite to clear thinking in regard to economics itself than is recognition of its limited place among human interests at large.
>
> Frank H. Knight, *The Economic Organization* (1933)

Economic explanation has occupied a central position in the analysis of family structure for some time. In 1855, for example, the conservative Frederic Le Play deplored the rise of the "unstable" family, which he attributed to the rise of manufacturing in the West. The materialist interpretation of the family received endorsement from a very different quarter thirty years later, with the publication of Engels' *Origin of the Family, Private Property, and the State*. Today, the importance of economic influences on the evolution of the family is rarely challenged. Even Edward Shorter, the most extreme exponent of the sentimental school of family history, views economic development as the prime mover in the making of the modern family.[1]

Traditional Sociological Interpretations
Le Play and Engels have their legacy in mainstream sociological theory. Structural-functionalists and modernization theorists assert that economic development is associated with a shift from extended to nuclear family structure. We now know that the opposite shift took place in the nineteenth century: the frequency of extended families increased during a period of rapid industrialization and modernization. But even if the traditional sociological interpretations try to explain something that never happened, they are worth a brief look because their functional approach has been highly influential.

---

1. Le Play (1855, 1871), Engels (1884), Shorter (1976).

13

The structural-functionalists argue that the extended family was the locus of productive activity in the preindustrial world, since it was the most efficient unit of economic organization. Hence, each member of the extended family—the elderly included—played a useful role in the family economy. When production shifted from family to factory, the family economy was destroyed. The new industrial system demanded a flexible and mobile family; the stripped-down nuclear family prevailed because it was functionally adapted to new economic realities. As part of this process, the elderly lost their productive role and became isolated from society and from the family.[2]

For modernization theorists, the influence of economic factors is less direct. Increasing economic and geographic mobility, the rise of individualism, the loss of traditional values, and the weakening of community ties reduced the value of extended kin. Like the structural-functionalists, modernization theorists point to a decline in the functional role of the aged. The accelerated rate of social and technological change is said to have undermined the utility of the elderly within the family by rendering their skills and knowledge obsolete. This problem was compounded by the high literacy characteristic of developed societies; use of writing reduced the need for the elderly to transmit knowledge and tradition. Moreover, modernization theorists argue that the increased proportion of older people in modern societies led to intergenerational competition for jobs and increased pressure for retirement. Thus, as a result of the various changes associated with modernization, the utility of the older generation declined and the traditional extended family disintegrated.[3]

2. The interpretation of the structural-functionalists is related to that of Engels (1884), who formulated the thesis that a free-contract system of labor dictated a free-contract system of family relations. This idea has been reworked and elaborated at great length to serve the purposes of conservative sociology. The best statements of the structural-functionalist interpretation appear in Parsons (1959) and Parsons and Bales (1965). Also, see Parsons' earlier work (1942, 1952), and Smelser (1959, 1967), whose analysis of nineteenth-century family structure is among the first historical studies in this field. For criticisms of the structural-functionalist approach to the family and industrial development, see Edwards and Jones (1973), Anderson (1976), Litwak (1965, 1970), Grieco (1982), Homans (1964), Greenfield (1961), Sussman (1959), Young and Wilmott (1957). As Harris (1967) and Pitts (1964) point out, some of the early criticisms may stem from a misreading of Parsons.

3. Much of this can be traced to W. Riehl, discussed in Leeuwen (1981), and F. Le Play (1871), discussed in Mogey (1955) and Laslett (1978). The range of ideas that fall under the rubric of modernization is very broad, and modernization theorists often contradict one another. Because it is difficult to pin down modernization theory, my portrayal of the distinctions between modernization and structural-functionalism is somewhat overdrawn; in fact, there is considerable overlap between the two perspectives. Compare Tönnies (1957), Nisbet (1967), Cowgill (1974a, 1974b), Cowgill and Holmes (1972), Burgess (1960,

An enormous quantity of scholarly energy has been devoted to criticism of structural-functionalism and modernization theories. I shall forgo the temptation to cast more stones on the mounting pile. These theories, after all, are not terribly relevant to the problem at hand; they cannot be invoked to explain the rise of the extended family in the nineteenth century. The sole reason I touch on the functionalist interpretations is to point out the basic economic motor of mainstream sociological theory.

According to both structural-functionalism and modernization the-

---

1963), Nimkoff (1962), Sheldon (1958), Palmore and Manton (1974), Fletcher (1963), Inkeles and Smith (1974), and Goode (1963a, 1963b). The critics of modernization are almost as numerous as its proponents, especially within the field of history. For a survey of the controversies, especially as they relate to the elderly, see Quadagno (1982); see also Bendix (1967), Smelser (1968), Grew (1978).

Although the arguments of the structural-functionalists and modernization theorists are similar, representatives of the two schools disagree on several key points. Structural-functionalists trace the change in family structure to the industrial revolution, whereas modernization theorists have cited a broad range of periods for the change. Modernization theorists have traditionally dated the transition prior to the industrial revolution—e.g., Tönnies (1957), Nisbet (1967)—but more recent theorists, particularly those specializing in social gerontology, argue that the change occurred much later—e.g., Cowgill and Holmes (1972). Recently, Achenbaum and Stearns (1978) proposed that although modernization in general occurred before 1780, it has only affected the elderly population during the last century. There are also differences in the perceived economic locus of the change. Structural-functionalists argue that the shift to nuclear families originated among the working class; modernization theorists generally believe that the changes began among the bourgeoisie and trickled down. Finally, structural-functionalists regard the adoption of nuclear-family structure as a positive adaptation, whereas modernization theorists often see the isolation of the nuclear family and the deterioration of the position of the elderly as sources of alienation and anomie.

There is scanty empirical support for either interpretation. To be sure, comparative analyses of family structure and the status of the elderly in societies at varying levels of development have found that complex families and high status for the aged are somewhat more frequent in developing countries than in Western capitalist nations; see Cowgill and Holmes (1972), Palmore and Manton (1974), Cohn (1982), Press and McKool (1972), and Shanas (1968). Other studies suggest that a more subtle model is needed; compare George and Pryor (1971), Pasternak, Ember, and Ember (1976), Winch and Blumberg (1968), Blumberg and Winch (1972), Nimkoff and Middleton (1960), Ogburn and Nimkoff (1955). There is evidence that the statistical relationship has more to do with the idiosyncrasies of the West than with level of economic development. Some investigations suggest that the status of the elderly is most precarious in those societies that face the harshest conditions, and that far from being taken into the family fold, the old are frequently abandoned. See de Beauvoir (1970), Simmons (1945, 1960). Furthermore, in Japan—a highly "modernized" society—the status of the old remains high (R. Smith 1961, Piovesana 1974, Palmore 1975), although there has been some simplification of family structure since 1935. Also, on the problems with assuming a transition from extended to nuclear-family structure, see Greenfield (1961), George and Pryor (1971), Taueber (1958), Goode (1964), P. Laslett (1972a).

ories, the frequency of extended families is a function of the utility of extended relatives—especially the elderly. This suggests that at some level the organization of the family is determined by the costs and benefits of alternative family structures.[4] Thus, the sociological paradigm implies that explaining historical change in the family is essentially an economic problem.

The New Home Economics

The analysis of economic decision making by families has achieved great technical sophistication with the rise of the new home economics during the past two decades. The mathematical tools of economic theory have for the first time been employed in the study of nonmarket behavior, such as childbearing, marriage, and the allocation of time within the family. The process of family decision making is cast in the form of analytic models. These models generally assume that at its inception each family develops a lifetime strategy for allocating scarce resources of time and money. The goal of the family strategy is to maximize satisfaction. Satisfaction need not be material; it can be based on tastes and preferences. Thus, the new home economics is an extension of formal economic analysis beyond the material sphere.[5]

The new home economists are just beginning to address the problem of family structure beyond the nuclear group and they have not been greatly

4. For structural-functionalists and modernization theorists, this mechanism can operate at the level of large groups or even the level of society as a whole. They see family systems not so much as the result of rational calculation, but rather as a product of social norms. These norms are constituted in such a way that they maximize social efficiency. The proposed mechanism for the establishment of social norms is not always clear. It is sometimes suggested that these norms evolve through a process of natural selection, as it were. If this were the case, one would expect norms to respond very slowly to changing conditions. Others—especially symbolic anthropologists—argue that the microlevel structures of society mirror those at the macrolevel, perhaps through a psychological mechanism, e.g., Douglas (1970). Under these circumstances, norms are not so much efficient as they are necessary. There are pitfalls associated with macrolevel analysis of causal mechanisms; one is almost forced to assume society-level motivation. The comments of Ryder (1974)—whose perspective differs greatly from my own—are revealing. The theoretical implications of level of analysis are discussed later in this chapter; see also Buckley (1968) and appendix A.

5. The most influential figure in this school is Becker (1964, 1965, 1974, 1976). The contributions to Schultz (1974) and Lloyd (1975) indicate the scope of the field. Also, see Schultz (1981) and Nerlove and Schultz (1970). Useful overviews of the new home economics include Nerlove (1974), Liebenstein (1977), and Sawhill (1978). For criticisms of the approach, see Blake (1968), and the comments of Ryder, Ashenfelter, Goode, Duncan, and Griliches, all in Schultz (1974).

concerned with historical change. They have nevertheless substantially influenced the study of extended families in the nineteenth century. The concept of family strategies—which was first articulated by these theorists—has been widely employed by social historians who are directly concerned with extended family structure.[6]

The models of the new home economists are static. They assume that families have perfect information before they make any decisions, and that the quality and quantity of information do not change over the life course. The criteria for optimal satisfaction are also assumed to remain constant. The members of each family, acting in unison, calculate the consequences of all possible decisions during their life course, and so determine their strategy for optimizing their psychological and material goals.[7]

There are a few problems with this scenario. Gary Becker's model of mate selection illustrates some of the difficulties. I am not entirely persuaded by Becker's contention that "at an abstract level, love and other emotional attachments, such as sexual activity or frequent close contact with a particular person, can be considered particular nonmarketable household commodities, and nothing much need be added to the analysis . . . of the demand for commodities."[8] This seems to me unsubtle.

6. Rozenzweig and Wolpin (1985) describe a model of intergenerational extension in an agricultural context. In his stimulating article, Liebenstein (1977) does briefly address historical change and extended-family structure (p. 61), but he does not incorporate these variables into a model. I do not pretend a thorough knowledge of the literature of the new home economics, nor am I qualified to evaluate some of the more technical aspects of the models. Nonetheless, this work must be explicitly discussed by historians; few of us actually read the new home economics, but as Sawhill (1978) correctly anticipated, the intellectual trickle-down has become a steady shower. The influence of "family strategies" on the work of historians of the family is discussed at the end of this chapter.

7. These points are implied by Sawhill (1978).

8. Becker (1974: 299). Because of his use of "bizarre" economic metaphors for "noneconomic" matters, Becker has been described as "that Kipling of the economic empire" (McCloskey 1983: 503). Models of mate selection are in some respects very close to the kind of model that would be required for analysis of extended-family structure. Unlike fertility or time-use models, marriage models are principally concerned with the determinants of coresidence. To create an extended-family model, one would need to develop new theory in several areas—such as the sorting mechanism—but much could simply be borrowed. I strongly doubt, however, that development of such a model is worth the effort. To date, marriage models have added little to our knowledge of family decision making. For example, Becker's marriage model arrives at four conclusions: first, "persons who care for each other are more likely to marry each other than are otherwise similar persons who do not." Second, sex ratio is related to the incidence of polygyny and more wealthy men are more likely to be polygynous. (As a minor point, Becker also argues that his model shows that polygyny increases the satisfaction of women.) Third, when people marry other people

Relationships between family members are often complex; individuals may have mixed feelings about one another that cannot be adequately encapsulated in an indifference curve.

Moreover, unlike other commodities, people are not always passive; selection of a spouse is not really comparable to selection of a refrigerator. The purchase of a refrigerator is straightforward: one buyer and one seller are involved in the exchange, and the choice between alternate refrigerators might plausibly depend on rational calculation of cost and quality. Mate selection proceeds on a very different basis: each prospective spouse is both a buyer and a seller, and both cost and quality are intangible and incalculable. Instead of merely selecting from an array of competing products, individuals must purchase one another. The optimal commodity might not allow itself to be bought.

Underlying the mathematical techniques of the new home economics is the requirement that aggregate satisfaction is maximized for the population as a whole. In the case of mate selection—or the selection of extended kin for coresidence—this assumption would not ordinarily be met, even in a world with rational behavior, perfect information, and perfect competition. This is because not all buyers in the marriage market have equal power to select their spouses. Since every buyer is simultaneously a seller, the desirability of buyers determines their options. The most desirable people will maximize their satisfaction and marry other desirable people. The leftover people are stuck with one another. It is easily demonstrable that this arrangement could not be expected to optimize overall satisfaction in the population.[9]

---

with similar genetic traits, this increases aggregate utility and aids the process of natural selection. Finally, couples with dissimilar members are more likely to divorce and if such persons remarry, they will find partners with more similar characteristics (p. 299). On the whole, Becker's equations have very orthodox opinions.

9. The point can be demonstrated by using Becker's own example. Becker contends that the optimal pairing of mates is such that no alternative match exists that would benefit both partners of any existing match. His example of this optimal sorting is a population of four people, two males (M1 and M2) and two females (F1 and F2). These four people can be sorted into marriages two ways, with the following results:

First,
F1 marries M1, yielding satisfaction of 8, and
F2 marries M2, yielding satisfaction of 7.
Total satisfaction = 15

Alternatively,
F1 marries M2, yielding satisfaction of 9, and
F2 marries M1, yielding satisfaction of 4.
Total satisfaction = 13

A major shortcoming of the new home economics as a tool for the analysis of family decision making is that interactions *among* family members are not adequately addressed. In general, there is an implicit or explicit assumption of a common household utility function.[10] This precludes the analysis of issues such as power, conflict, bonds of obligation, and altruism. The comments of Norman Ryder about a model developed by Robert J. Willis could serve as a critique of the entire approach:

> Willis has collapsed time to the instant of initial decision, he has defined the parents as subjects and the children as objects, he has denied the members the right to take satisfaction in the satisfaction of others, he has merged the husband and wife into a single utility function of the individual type—in short, he has dissolved the problems of family economics by dissolving the family.[11]

If we were interested only in the interaction of the family with the outside world, then it might make some sense to construct a combined utility function for all family members. But residence decisions depend on interactions between family members. When we turn to the internal dynamics of the family, we cannot adopt a single utility function—or a single family strategy—without making implicit assumptions about the

Becker argues that under these circumstances the first arrangement—the one that maximizes aggregate satisfaction—is the one that will take place. He reasons that F2 and M1 will not want to marry one another, because better alternatives are available to both of them. This is silly; in fact, F2 and M1 won't have any choice in the matter. The other couple, F1 and M2, have all the power, because they can increase satisfaction for anyone. And they will marry one another, because that is the arrangement that gives them the most satisfaction. Thus, F2 and M1 are stuck with each other, and total satisfaction is only 13, rather than the optimal 15. All is not fair in love and war.

Exactly the same problem would arise in a model of extended-family structure. Since both the extended relative(s) and the nuclear-family members have a voice in any coresidence decision, both are simultaneously buyers and sellers. Once again, this will mean that aggregate satisfaction is unlikely to be maximized.

One cannot help wondering how individuals are supposed to be able to make an a priori evaluation of the satisfaction they would derive from all possible marriages. After all, the chief component of spouse quality—emotional attachment—emerges in the process of bargaining itself. Thus, one is not able to evaluate the quality of alternative prospects until the preliminary negotiations are well underway and one has already made at least a partial commitment to buy.

10. Nerlove (1974). Ben-Porath (1977: 79) recognizes that "a full analysis would have to begin with individuals, the dynamics of their interrelationships," but like the others, he regards this as too difficult: "This is more than we can handle with ease. Let us, therefore, start by *assuming* that the family is indeed an institution that accommodates internal exchange and cooperation."

11. Ryder (1974: 77).

presence of power, guilt, altruism, or some other nonrational incentive that would lead a group of individuals to behave as one. In short, if we assume a single utility function for the family as a whole, then we must also assume a mechanism for achieving that solidarity. Guilt and power can be treated in economic terms only if we define being trodden upon as a form of satisfaction.

The problem is fundamental. As they stand, the models of the new home economics—the first attempts to analyze the internal dynamics of the family in mathematical terms—incorporate the hidden assumption that there are no internal dynamics at all.

Exchange Theory

Exchange theory addresses the problem of internal dynamics. In recent years, the sociological theory of economic exchange has been applied to the historical study of kinship and family. I refer here principally to the work of Michael Anderson, who has conducted the most sustained investigation to date of extended kinship relationships in the nineteenth century.[12] Anderson's interpretation is especially relevant for the present study because his primary goal was to explain the high frequency of extended families in Victorian Lancashire.

Anderson's version of exchange theory is nonmathematical but it is nonetheless formal. The main difference between Anderson's model and those of the new home economists is that Anderson's model operates at the level of individuals rather than the level of families. His central thesis is that kinship relationships occur and are maintained only when they are beneficial for all parties involved.

Anderson stresses the importance of personal needs and goals, and he acknowledges the social constraints and opportunities faced by individuals. He calls his approach a "structural-level actor-based perspective." Individuals, he writes, have goals, and they generally require assistance in order to attain them. Anderson argues that the choices between alternative forms of assistance are made in such a way that an individual maximizes his goal attainment in the long run. He describes this process in economic terms: those with "surplus resources" make an "investment" and reap "psychic profit."

Although Anderson recognizes the existence of affective goals and

---

12. Anderson (1971, 1972a, 1972b, 1976, 1977, 1978, 1980). Also, see Gouldner (1960), Blau (1964), Homans (1961), Thibault and Kelly (1959), Edwards (1969), Edwards and Brauburger (1973), Ekeh (1974), Huesmann and Levinger (1976), Osmond (1978), Nye (1978, 1979), and Reyna (1976). The best critique of Anderson is Katz (1975); compare the view of MacDonald (1981).

costs, his analysis concentrates on strictly economic factors. Particularly in the case of coresidence of extended kin, he suggests that "a very special set of hypotheses which consider only economic advantages and disadvantages may be appropriate." Among the working classes of Victorian Lancashire, distress from sickness, unemployment, old age, housing shortage, and the problems of working mothers and immigrants created "critical life situations." In such cases, Anderson argues, "kinship probably provided the main form of assistance." Because economic hardship was widespread and society was changing rapidly, kinship relationships "tended to have short-run instrumental overtones of a calculative kind."[13]

Even though material need was the primary reason people maintained kin relationships, extreme and unremitting poverty could also be their undoing; sustained neediness would preclude the reciprocation that is fundamental to exchange theory. All individuals who maintain relationships with family members must have economic needs or they would have no motive for maintaining the relationship. They must also, however, have a certain level of resources so they can reciprocate for the benefits received.

Anderson argues that the high frequency of coresidence of the elderly with their married children during the nineteenth century was brought about by an increase in the needs of young married couples. The elderly, particularly those who were widowed, had always been in economic need. However, before the nineteenth century there was little economic incentive for the younger generation to reside with elderly kin.[14] In the new industrial cities, young couples had more to gain by taking in older dependent relatives. A housing shortage forced many newlyweds to move in with their parents; even more important, the increase in the

---

13. Anderson (1971: 6–16, 170–75; 1978). Anderson's image of the calculating Victorian is reminiscent of Mr. Darling in J. M. Barrie's *Peter Pan* (1911: 2–4): "For a week or two after Wendy came it was doubtful whether they would be able to keep her, as she was another mouth to feed. Mr. Darling was frightfully proud of her, but he was very honorable, and he sat on the edge of Mrs. Darling's bed, holding her hand and calculating expenses, while she looked at him imploringly. She wanted to risk it, come what might, but that was not his way; his way was with a pencil and a piece of paper, and if she confused him with suggestions he had to begin at the beginning again. . . . 'Remember mumps,' he warned her threateningly, and then off he went again. 'Mumps one pound, that is what I have put down, but I daresay it will be more like thirty shillings—don't speak—measles one five, German measles half a guinea, makes two fifteen six—don't waggle your finger—whooping-cough, say fifteen shillings'—and so on it went, and it added up differently each time, but at last Wendy just got through, with mumps reduced to twelve six, and the two kinds of measles treated as one."

14. Anderson (1971, 1972b, 1978).

frequency of working mothers with small children placed a premium on child-care services, which could be provided by the elderly.

Like the models of the new economists, Anderson's model assumes rational behavior and (implicitly) perfect information. One may quarrel with these assumptions, but they are inescapable if one is committed to a theoretical economic interpretation. It is, after all, the nature of the beast. Anderson's theory is logical and internally consistent. If his model does not accurately predict observed behavior, then we must question its assumptions.

Economic Theory and Levels of Analysis

The notion that behavior is in some manner determined through the maximization of benefit is common to most mainstream social and economic theory. But there are important respects in which the main categories of theory differ. Above all, the theorists disagree about the level at which economic mechanisms operate. Traditional sociological theorists often stress the adoption of adaptive behavior by large groups or by society as a whole, the new home economists view the family as the decision-making unit, and exchange theorists focus on rational behavior at the individual level.

Individual-level measurement has a certain pragmatic appeal. As I point out in appendix A, there are sound statistical justifications for measurement by individuals and this approach offers a variety of methodological advantages. Moreover, as Nancy and Richard Ruggles have argued at length, it is both practical and convenient to gather, store, and analyze social and economic data at the micro level.[15]

But just because it is practical and convenient to analyze family structure from the perspective of individuals, we cannot assume that residential decision making actually *operates* at the individual level. Certainly, some individuals exert greater influence on family structure than do others; two-year-old children do not ordinarily have any choice about where they live. Even among adults the power to dictate living arrangements is unequally distributed. Nevertheless, when we observe complex extended families containing several adults, we may plausibly assume that more than one family member has influenced family membership.

Individual-level analysis of family structure does not assume that all family members have equal power to control residence decisions; on the contrary, such analysis provides the only possible means of investigating the structure of power relations within the family. We cannot assess the

15. Ruggles and Ruggles (1970).

influence of power relationships on living arrangements unless we concede that residence decisions are not made in a unitary way by an undifferentiated family.

I have argued that a chief limitation of the family-strategies perspective is its incapacity to address interactions among family members. Even if residence decisions are reached collectively they may be a product of bargaining and compromise. To comprehend the decision-making process we must ask how each member of a kin group could influence residence decisions and why each party might give active or passive consent.

Accordingly, I am persuaded that Michael Anderson's general approach to the economics of family structure—which combines individual-level analysis with the additional refinement of reciprocal interaction—is more sensible than the approaches of the new home economists or the mainstream sociologists. This is not to say that I find exchange theory to be plausible. Quite the contrary—exchange theory looks good only in comparison with the alternatives.

Economic Analysis and Nonmaterial Factors

Social and economic theorists also differ about the role of nonmaterial costs and benefits in the determination of living arrangements. Ironically, it is the economists who have placed the greatest stress on intangible motivations; some have argued that happiness, love, or any other source of satisfaction can be subsumed under utility. By contrast, the sociological theorists—including Anderson—emphasize factors that are economic in a narrower sense, such as income, housing, services, and the structure of employment.

It is certainly a good idea to consider nonmaterial motives for behavior if we wish to understand family structure. If we confine ourselves to studying the quest for material gain, then we limit our analysis to a narrow corner of human experience.

But economic theory does not actually allow us to investigate nonmaterial costs and benefits; these are merely postulated. Materially motivated behavior can allegedly be predicted by theory. The intangible motivations account for the residual between prediction and actual behavior; that is, nonmaterial forces are deemed responsible for whatever is left over. This is true by definitional fiat: utility is the goal of behavior and behavior maximizes utility. Since utility consists of both material and nonmaterial benefits, anything that is not explainable in material terms is necessarily a consequence of nonmaterial goals.

This catchall definition of utility makes it possible for the new home economists to avoid dealing with specific nonmaterial influences on residential behavior. If goals are assumed, the study of society is reduced to an analysis of tactics employed to achieve those postulated goals; the sources of motivation go unexplored. The new home economics does not, then, provide a framework for analyzing those influences on family structure that fall outside the traditional sphere of economics; the approach merely provides a label for behavior unexplained by material considerations. This is a limitation of economic analysis generally: it cannot fully explain the reasons people do the particular things they do, unless, in the end, all motivation has a material basis. Because economic approaches cannot really address nonmaterial influences on residence decisions, my remaining remarks are confined to economic theory in the narrow sense.

The Limitations of Economic Analysis

In sum, then, the most fruitful application of economic theory to extended family structure would seem to lie with analysis of the material costs and benefits of alternate living arrangements from the perspective of individual family members. But when we restrict ourselves to this narrow conceptualization of economic analysis, the limitations of the approach stand out in high relief.

We should ask ourselves, is it plausible that rational calculation which maximizes tangible gain is responsible for observed patterns of family structure? The two impossible assumptions—completely rational behavior and perfect information—should be constantly borne in mind.

The greatest weakness of classical economics is its assumption that people always behave rationally in order to maximize their own economic interest. This assumption is not valid even when the decisions are purely economic ones; people usually lack the information necessary to determine where their true self-interest lies and when adequate information is available, they are frequently unable to interpret it.

Decisions about the family are probably less often rationally calculated than virtually any of the other major decisions people make, except perhaps those related to religion. The family is as much a psychological construct as an economic one; emotional bonding, generational conflict, and social values no doubt influence residence decisions as much as the practical pursuit of material satisfaction does.

What is more, most people don't even know what they want from life; especially when it comes to their family relationships, they simply muddle through. Individuals have many conflicting motives, which they rarely scrutinize carefully. The hierarchy of incentives is constantly shifting;

short-term goals may rise briefly to the top, only to be shunted aside by changing circumstances or through an internal dynamic of their own. If we reduce the messy tangle of motivation and interpersonal relationships to a simplistic economic calculus, we can avoid dealing with some intractable issues. On the other hand, we may miss the opportunity to address some potentially crucial ones.

I doubt that extended kin are maintained solely for their material worth. Elderly dependents are a case in point. The sociological and economic interpretations regard the social position and treatment of elderly kin entirely as a consequence of their functional role in the family or in society at large. This is not plausible. The status of family members does not always hinge on their utility. No one, for example, would argue that the changing status of children in Western society has been entirely a function of their usefulness; in fact, it is well documented that as the treatment of children has improved during the past few centuries, their functional role has diminished.[16]

Because of its implicit functionalism, the economic paradigm also incorporates a conservative bias. The view that utility determines the position of individuals both within the family and in society as a whole is a subtle form of social Darwinism; it suggests that oppressed minorities are oppressed because they are not useful and that the rich are rich because they deserve to be. Furthermore, the terms employed to describe the economic motor—satisfaction, utility, benefit, even psychic profit—are loaded ones: they imply that society is a device for maximizing well-being. Intimidation and power are ignored and conflict is reduced to fair competition for scarce resources. In the perfect world of economic theory, the unpleasantness of the real world vanishes, and the status quo provides the greatest utility for the greatest number.

Historical Interpretations

In spite of the limitations of economic approaches to the analysis of family structure, historians have made extensive use of these theories. For the most part, historical studies incorporate the family-strategies perspective. Thus, like the new home economists, the historians stress the maximization of benefits by families rather than by individuals. John Modell, Tamara Hareven, Louise Tilly, and others argue that the family as a whole adopted the structure and employment pattern that was most

16. Aries (1962), Stone (1977a), DeMause (1974), Hunt (1970), Shorter (1976), Pinchbeck and Hewitt (1969).

beneficial for the group.[17] The economic motives of individual family members have received much less attention.

In the work of historians of the family, however, the distinction between family strategies and individual-level economic exchange is blurred. Historians are less rigorous than economists; they do not allow their theoretical models to overwhelm their good sense. According to Tilly's formulation of family strategies, for example, "families are conceived of as acting in a unitary way to make decisions." At the same time, however, she asks "who participates in making decisions as well as what concerns and constraints impinge upon them."[18]

Perhaps the main difference between the historians and the economists on family strategies is that the historians adopt a historical approach. They do not conceive of family adaptations in abstract terms; historical studies of family structure are set within a particular chronological and geographic context. Furthermore, among historians of the family there is near universal appreciation of the importance of specific economic circumstances and of how these circumstances vary with class, gender, ethnicity, and race.

Research into nineteenth-century family structure especially stresses the critical impact of urban poverty and the exigencies imposed by economic fluctuation and industrial employment. There is widespread agreement that family and kin provided the first line of defense against the hardships faced by the working class under early industrial capitalism.[19] The great strength of kin relationships in the nineteenth century is explained in precisely these terms. Thus, Barbara Agresti asserts that "within all stages of the life cycle, this percentage [of extended families] increased in response to economic difficulties" in at least one late-nineteenth-century American county. Similarly, Tamara Hareven argues that "the function of kin in modern industrial communities represented not merely an archaic carry-over from rural society but rather the development of new responses to needs dictated by modern industrial conditions."[20]

17. Modell (1978, 1979), Hareven (1982, 1978), Tilly (1979a, 1979b), Goldin (1981). Other historians follow Anderson's interpretation closely and stress exchange relationships above family strategies; see, for example, Darroch and Ornstein (1983, 1984), Dupree (1977), Agresti (1979). Anderson's (1980, 1985) comments on the family-strategies school of family historians are revealing.

18. Tilly (1979a: 202, 204).

19. For example, Modell (1978), Chudacoff and Hareven (1978, 1979), Anderson (1971), Dupree (1977), Brayshay (1980), Katz (1975), Goldin (1981). This hypothesis is applied to other periods as well; see R. M. Smith (1979).

20. Agresti (1979: 257), Hareven (1978: 177). Also see Hareven (1982: 101).

Marxist historians take a similar view. In general, they regard extended family structure as a defense against poverty. John Foster speaks of "sharing and huddling" among the impoverished extended families of industrial Victorian Yorkshire. According to Hans Medick, a new type of extended family emerged among rural industrial workers during the protocapitalist period "as a result of growing pauperization, increasing population pressure, of limited and congested living conditions and not least by the secondary poverty engendered by the family life cycle."[21]

Conclusion

Economic conditions provide the context within which residence decisions are made. They may preclude certain living arrangements and favor others, but they are not necessarily the crucial criteria on which decisions are based. A variety of family structures are usually feasible from a material point of view. Whenever this is true, nonmaterial motives can come into play. We should never ignore economics; it has far-reaching influence on every sphere of human activity. At the same time, there is no aspect of human behavior that is in its entirety the product of rational calculation for material gain. Incorporating the intangible within formal economic analysis is no solution; when economic theory overflows its bounds to encompass nonmaterial motives and processes, its usefulness is sharply diminished.

If we are interested in finding out why people do the things they do, we should beware of assuming in advance that human motivation can be reduced to rational calculation of maximum utility. If utility and rationality are broadly enough defined, they can be stretched to encompass the near-infinite variety of reasons for human behavior. But as we expand the economic metaphor, we reduce its meaning; in the end, we are left with the proposition that people do what they want to do.

Material circumstances have profound consequences for family structure. That is not at issue. Inheritance customs are one example and one could cite many others.[22] The critical question, as far as economic theory is concerned, is whether relationships within the family operate on the model of capitalist competition for scarce resources.

The capitalist mentality—the mentality that bases all decisions on rational calculation for material gain—is not the universal basis of human culture; it is merely an aspect of culture. Noneconomists call it greed.

21. Foster (1974: 91ff.), Medick (1976: 308); these sentiments are echoed by Levine (1977). See also Chaytor (1980) and Wrightson (1981).

22. On inheritance and family structure, see Berkner and Mendels (1978), Goody, Thirsk, and Thompson (1976), Anderson(1980), Flandrin (1979).

Greed must be counted among the most important of motives, but it is not the only reason people behave as they do. Jealousy, altruism, status anxiety, love, pride, and social obligations of all sorts can affect people's decisions. The relative importance of different motivations is not constant. In some contexts—such as the stock market or grain futures—the motive of greed clearly predominates, and economic models of decision making fit reasonably well. In the case of family relationships, I am convinced that the economic frame of mind generally plays a much smaller role.[23] Indeed, I believe I have yet to meet anyone who is entirely rational about his or her relationships with parents, spouse, siblings, or children.

Some readers may wonder why I have devoted so much space to economic theories of the family. After all, few historians of the family take the economic metaphor literally. But for all their limitations, economic theories and methods have enormous power of intimidation; wherever they have been introduced, they have acquired great prestige. As a result, a substantial proportion of scholarly energy in the social sciences is devoted to exegesis of the Received View. In some subdisciplines, the desire to illustrate the revealed truth of the gospel of greed has become all-consuming. Among social historians, things have not reached this pass, but even here some are not really satisfied unless they can argue that the invisible hand is the prime mover of social change.[24]

23. The focus on economic explanations for historical phenomena may be partly a result of projection: rational calculation for material gain is perhaps an especially characteristic mode of thought in late-twentieth-century industrial society and I suspect its influence is nowhere greater than among those who have been subject to graduate school in economics.

24. The proponents of "scientific" history—such as Benson (1966), Kousser (1984), and Barnes (1925)—have promoted the application of economic theory to historical studies. The recent popularity of quantification in historical studies may also help to explain the preeminence of economic thinking. There is considerable temptation when working with quantitative evidence to explain every aspect of social behavior in terms that we can measure, and economic factors are much easier to measure than cultural ones. This, in turn, because of the assumptions of economic theory, has meant that quantitative historical studies tend to attribute variation in family structure to rational agency.

Economists—and demographers too—are happiest when they can argue that people's values are fixed and only structural conditions change. It is, of course, logically conceivable that people's values and ideals regarding their families have been fairly constant during the past few hundred years, and that the changes we have witnessed in family structure have simply been a rational economic response to changing external material circumstances. My own feeling, as I think I have made clear, is that a cultural explanation is more plausible. But we have no rigorous theory of cultural change. For those of scientific bent, this state of affairs is uncomfortable.

Victorian doctrine on family life had little place for the gospel of greed. John Ruskin's vision of the Home, set down in 1865, has a decidedly pagan ring to it: "It is a sacred place, a vestal temple, a temple of the hearth watched over by Household Gods, before whose faces none may come but those they can receive with love."[25] For true believers of exchange theory or family strategies, this image must seem downright heathen.

25. Ruskin (1865: 99, section 68). Houghton's (1957: 343–44) analysis of this passage points to the appropriateness of the religious metaphor.

3 Evidence on the Economics of Extended-Family Structure

Everything in this crazy world
Whether happy, sad, or comic,
When you get right to the heart of it,
It's basically economic.

> Theme song of "It's Basically Economic"
> television program, WCAU-TV, Philadelphia

*Wealth! wealth! wealth! Praise be to the god of the nineteenth century!
the golden idol! the mighty Mammon!* Such are the accents of the
time, such the cry of the nation . . . there is nothing approaching to a
class of persons actuated by any other desire.

> John Sterling, *Essays and Tales* (1848)

The last chapter pointed to the theoretical flaws of the economic interpretation of extended-family structure; this chapter points to the empirical flaws of the economic approach. First, I assess the relationship between economic status and family structure, in order to test the thesis that
extended living arrangements were a response to material hardship. I
then discuss some evidence on dependence and family strategies. Finally,
I test the details of Michael Anderson's exchange theory.

My economic analysis is based on five individual-level samples of
census manuscripts, which together provide information about 200,000
individuals. Four of these samples are drawn from the state and federal
manuscript censuses for Erie County, New York—which includes the city
of Buffalo and the surrounding area—in 1855, 1880, 1900, and 1915.
Taken together, these samples comprise the longest time series of census
data currently available for any nineteenth-century locality. The fifth
sample is based on the 1871 census of two textile towns in Lancashire,
England. These towns resemble the community investigated by Anderson and are thus especially appropriate for testing Anderson's thesis that
the high frequency of extended families in the nineteenth century was a
result of reciprocal economic exchange.

The economic and demographic structure of the Lancashire towns differed markedly from that of Erie County. Nevertheless, as we shall see, patterns of extended-family structure in the American and English samples were closely parallel. This suggests that extended-family structure was not dictated primarily by local peculiarities. A description of conditions in each community appears in appendix B.

The reader should bear in mind that my measurements of family structure are unconventional in three respects, as indicated in chapter 1. First, family structure is measured in terms of the individual rather than in terms of the household. Thus, I assess the percentage of the population that resided with their extended relatives, not the percentage of households that contained extended kin. Second, I am concerned with family structure, not with household structure. A family is defined here as any group of related people who reside in the same household. Boarders, lodgers, servants, and other nonrelatives of the household head are considered to constitute separate families of their own. Third, since I am primarily concerned with biological relationships, I have designated standard reference persons for each family, instead of relying on the culturally defined head of household as determined by contemporary census takers.[1] The rationales for these measurement strategies are somewhat involved, so the discussion of these methodological issues is relegated to appendix A.

Economic Status and Extended-Family Structure

Historians have connected the high frequency of extended families in the nineteenth century to urban poverty and industrial working conditions. This explanation lacks empirical support. No one has established a relationship between economic hardship and extended-family structure for any part of nineteenth-century England or America. The evidence in fact indicates the opposite: members of the upper economic strata resided with extended relatives far more frequently than did members of the working class. Samuel Butler described the situation clearly: "the mis-

---

1. Individual-level measures of family structure are employed throughout this research. Measurement by households in misleading for two reasons. First, it effectively ignores boarders, lodgers, servants, and others who are unrelated to the household head. This distorts the extent of coresidence with kin, because the overwhelming majority of boarders, lodgers, and servants resided without relatives or with nuclear relatives only. For class comparison, it is especially important to consider the family relationships of nonrelatives, because boarders, lodgers, and servants were concentrated in the working class. Second, as argued in appendix A, the household is an inappropriate unit of measurement for investigations of family structure; it is far better to measure family structure by individuals.

chief among the lower classes is not so great, but among the middle and upper classes it is killing a large number daily."[2]

I have employed a variety of measures of economic status, each of which has advantages and liabilities. The most widely available measure is occupational status. The occupational listings in the census are a flawed indicator of economic rank, because Victorian enumerators were more concerned with type of business than with social hierarchy. For large segments of the work force—especially retailers, artisans, and the self-employed generally—the occupational listings are inadequate for precise occupational stratification.

I have therefore confined myself to a four-tiered classification of occupations; any greater precision muddles class with occupational sector. Ambiguous cases were classified on the basis of information from other sources: business directories, the census of manufactures, and newspaper advertisements.[3] The uppermost category—here termed the higher bourgeoisie—consists of professionals, rentiers, agents, and merchants; the lower bourgeoisie includes white-collar employees of business and government, master artisans, and the like.[4] Among the working class, skilled workers are for the most part those with artisanal titles, whereas unskilled workers consist largely of laborers. Those employed in agriculture are considered separately.

2. Butler (1912: 33). On historians' economic explanations for extended-family structure, see the discussion in chapter 2.

3. To resolve these ambiguities and classify workers in Erie County on the basis of their relationship to the means of production, Michael Katz and his associates turned to business directories, the manufacturing schedules of the census, and newspaper advertisements. My own occupational classification of the Erie County population is based on their research. It is impossible to devise an occupational classification system that will place everyone correctly relative to everyone else. Some of the problems are discussed by Katz (1981: 579–605), Katz, Doucet, and Stern (1982), Armstrong (1972a, 1978), Banks (1978), Bellamy (1978). My two upper categories—here termed the bourgeoisie—are equivalent to Katz's business class.

4. The use of the term "bourgeoisie" as defined here is somewhat problematic, but so are the alternatives. The term "upper class" is inappropriate, because the category includes many of middling status, including some labor aristocrats. On the other hand, "middle class" would seem to exclude the very rich. Terms like "entrepreneurial class" or "business class" have been used by others, but these terms imply a structural and theoretical role that I cannot verify; see Katz (1981). Family members were classified according to the occupation of the family head, except where the family head was not employed. In such instances, I used the occupation of the eldest employed member of the largest nuclear group in the family. Note that the family head is not necessarily the household head as listed in the manuscript census; to ensure comparability between groups and across time, I have designated standard reference persons for each family. See appendix A.

The frequency of extended living arrangements by class for Erie County is shown in figure 3.1.[5] The association between class and family structure is dramatic and unmistakable. In each census year, members of the working class were far *less* likely to reside with extended relatives than were the bourgeoisie. Moreover, within the working class extended-family structure was considerably less frequent among unskilled workers than among skilled workers. This pattern was not simply a consequence of structural differences between classes in age, sex, marital status, nativity, or duration of local residence. The basic relationship remains unchanged when these variables are controlled through regression analysis (see appendix F).

Although class differences in the frequency of extended living arrangements were significant in all census years, the extent of differences had diminished by 1915. The nineteenth-century class pattern of extended-family structure apparently continued to erode after 1915. By 1960, the relationship between class and extension had reversed: extended families were most frequent among the working class.[6]

The strong association between high economic status and residence in extended families is also evident when we employ alternate measures of social rank. Within the bourgeoisie, the presence of domestic servants may provide a better indicator of relative economic rank than occupa-

5. About a third of the information on occupation was missing for 1855. Rather than exclude these cases, I employed a "hot deck" imputation procedure. With such a large proportion of missing cases, exclusion can yield highly misleading results; imputing the missing values minimizes the probability of error. The procedure works as follows: when occupational data is missing, the computer assigns the occupation of the previous individual in the file who had the same age, birthplace, household status, sex, marital status, and years spent locally. If there is no previous individual with all the same characteristics, the program assigns the occupation of the next subsequent individual with the appropriate characteristics. Excluding individuals with missing data would yield correct results only if the occupations of such individuals were typical of the population as a whole. By imputing the missing data, we need not assume that the individuals with missing data were typical of the entire population; instead, we are assuming only that their occupations are typical of the population that has the same characteristics. Since the characteristics I used—including proximity within the file—are all highly related to occupation, the necessary assumptions for imputation are considerably more reasonable than the necessary assumptions for exclusion.

6. In 1960, the relationship between extended-family structure and economic status was more complex than in the nineteenth century. My tabulation of the 1960 Public Use Sample (PUS) of the U.S. federal census indicates that the highest frequency of extended living arrangements occurred among the working class, but extended families were almost as frequent among the upper-middle class. This bimodal distribution suggests that different mechanisms were operating to encourage extended living arrangements in different economic strata.

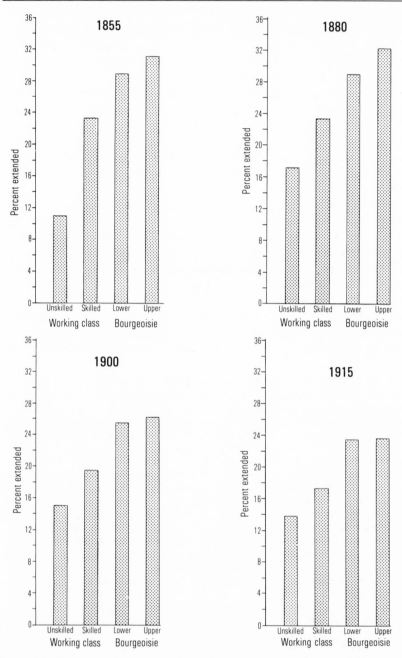

Figure 3.1. Percentage of persons residing with extended kin, by occupational class: Erie County, 1855–1915

Table 3.1. Individuals Residing with Extended Relatives, Erie County, 1855–1915
        (Farmers Excluded)

	Unskilled	Skilled	Middle Class[a]	With Servants
1855				
Percent extended	11.0	18.7	21.8	34.8
Number of cases	20,723	33,301	6,174	5,160
1880				
Percent extended	17.2	23.4	25.0	41.4
Number of cases	3,847	4,750	1,544	746
1900				
Percent extended	15.1	19.5	24.0	34.4
Number of cases	9,171	12,239	5,884	1,209
1915				
Percent extended	13.8	17.4	23.9	20.2
Number of cases	13,793	26,935	11,991	1,197

[a]Persons with "bourgeois" occupations who have no domestic servants.

tional title does, at least for the nineteenth century.[7] As table 3.1 demonstrates, the positive relationship between high economic status and extended living arrangements is even more pronounced when this criterion is employed for the Erie County data.

For the Lancashire textile towns, I adopted a different strategy of occupational classification. Instead of turning to other sources in order to clarify ambiguous occupational listings, I excluded from the analysis those groups whose status could not be readily identified. This was possible because much of the population worked in the mills. The job titles of factory hands were usually given with some precision, and thus it was possible to distinguish skilled workers unambiguously. Manual laborers were also included, on the grounds that their low status was beyond doubt. Finally, the bourgeoisie were identified by the presence of domestic servants in their households. Thus, artisans, shopkeepers, and transport workers were not included in the analysis.[8] Fortunately, in the

7. On the relationship of servants to income, see Mrs. Beeton's *Book of Household Management* (1861) and Armstrong's (1972a) data on the relationship of occupation to the presence of servants.

8. The status of laborers is unmistakable; they are near the bottom of the social hierarchy. For textile workers, economic status is a little more variable. Male factory operatives were near the top of the working class in terms of income, especially power-loom weavers and spinners. On the other hand, some of the female and children's textile jobs—such as piecers—were very poorly paid indeed; see Collier (1921). Since the classification system employed in this book is based on the occupation of the family head, most of the workers

Lancashire textile towns these groups represented a small proportion of the population.

Figure 3.2 gives the percentage of the population residing with extended relatives in Lancashire, broken down by occupational category. Although the occupational classification is not strictly comparable to the system employed for Erie County, the English figures bear a striking resemblance to the American ones; people residing in families with servants lived with extended kin almost three times as often as those in families headed by manual laborers. Once again, this basic relationship between economic status and family structure changes little when class differences in age, sex, marital status, and birthplace are controlled.[9]

Few of the residents of the Lancashire textile towns were farmers, but a substantial proportion of the Erie County population was engaged in agriculture. Farming families are excluded from the preceding figures for Erie County, because their occupation provides a poor measure of their economic status. As a group, farmers were slightly more likely to reside with extended relatives than were nonfarmers, but this difference is diminished when we control for such factors as nativity and length of residence.

For 1855, we can assess the economic status of farmers. Linking the state agricultural census for that year with the census of population allows determination of the relationship between family structure and value of farm. This relationship is illustrated in figure 3.3, which shows that the strong positive relationship between economic status and extended living arrangements that characterized the urban scene also existed among the farmers of Erie County.

One additional measure of economic status—dwelling value—is provided by the New York state census of 1855. Dwelling value has a number of advantages as a measure of economic rank. First, it is unambiguous;

who could dictate inclusion of a family in the textile category were male. I initially broke the textile workers into two categories, high status and low status. When it emerged that the two groups behaved almost identically with respect to family structure, however, I recombined the two. The occupational groups are hereafter referred to as "skilled" and "unskilled." The skilled category includes: weaver, finisher, piecer, carder, spinner, doubler, winder, tenter, cutter, cotton operative, bleacher, dyer, and so on. The unskilled category includes: general laborer, outdoor laborer, porter, navvy, construction laborer, warehouse laborer, road laborer. For the bourgeoisie, occupation is just as poor an indicator of status as it is for the working class; it is very often difficult to distinguish large manufacturers from artisans. Thus, I distinguished the bourgeoisie on the basis of presence of domestic servants. Servants whose occupation was apprentice or shop assistant, or who were employed by publicans or restauranteurs, could not determine inclusion of the family in the bourgeois category.

9. See appendix F.

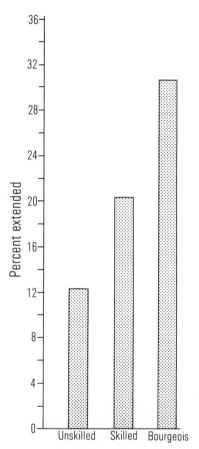

Figure 3.2. Percentage of persons residing with extended kin, by occupational class: Lancashire Towns, 1871

unlike more subjectively ranked variables—such as occupation—there is little chance of misclassifying dwelling value. Second, it is continuous, which allows considerably more subtle analysis than the four-category occupational-classification system. Third, since dwelling value is a measure of consumption, it may be a better indicator than occupational class of economic well-being; the occupational listings may have more to do with status than with material circumstances. Finally, the data on dwelling value seem to be reliable and consistent. The recorded amounts for dwelling value in the census suggest high accuracy; dwelling value was usually given in odd amounts, which points to accurate recording rather than rough estimation. There are also few missing data for this variable.

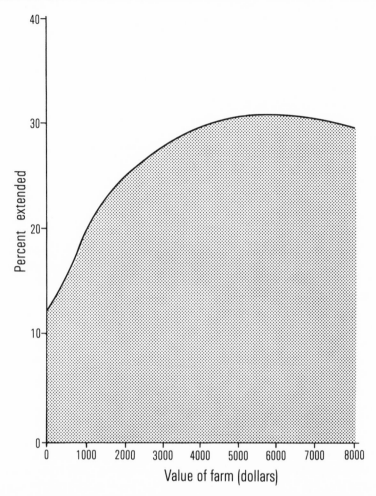

Figure 3.3. Percentage of persons residing with extended kin, by value of farm: Erie County, 1855

Despite these advantages, there are complications with the use of family dwelling value for analyzing the differences in family structure between economic strata. The problem results from the interrelationship between family structure and family size. Extended families tend to be larger than nonextended families and they thus require larger and more expensive dwellings. Accordingly, even if there were no relationship between economic status and extended-family structure, we would expect a positive relationship between dwelling value and family extension.

To compensate for this problem, direct standardization was employed to hold family size constant across dwelling values.[10] In fact, this strategy overcompensates for the problem. By eliminating differences in family size between economic strata, we necessarily understate the differences in family structure. Therefore, the standardized measure of family dwelling value yields a conservative estimate of the differences in family structure between economic strata; the true differences are almost certainly greater.

Bearing this in mind, consider the relationship illustrated in figure 3.4. The frequency of residence with extended kin is almost three times greater at the highest dwelling values than at the lowest. Considering the downward bias of the measurement technique, this striking relationship conclusively demonstrates a strong association between extension and economic well-being.

There is also evidence that the strength of kin ties beyond the household but within the neighborhood followed a similar class pattern. My investigation of neighborhood residence patterns for Erie County in 1855 is still in the preliminary stages, but it does permit some general conclusions. Analysis of the spatial distribution of surname frequencies indicates that members of bourgeois families were considerably more likely to have kin residing within a few blocks than were members of the working class. This evidence suggests that the statistics presented in this chapter are indicators of class differences in the strength of kin relationships generally, not just differences in the extent of kin relationships under one roof.

The finding that the bourgeoisie resided with extended relatives more frequently than the working class did should not surprise us. The few historians of nineteenth-century England and America who have broken down household structure by class have had similar results, but they have rarely stressed the point. Furthermore, evidence from other periods and places—in cultures as diverse as Renaissance Italy and twentieth-century China—suggests that extended families have usually been concentrated among the wealthy.[11]

10. I employed direct standardization just as one would if comparing the mortality of two populations with differing age structures. The standard population was taken to be the entire Erie County population. This technique allows us to estimate what the percentage of extended living arrangements at each dwelling value would be if the distribution of family sizes did not vary with dwelling value. Where dwellings contained more than one family, the value of the dwelling was distributed among the families in proportion to their size. Figures 3.3–3.5 were smoothed using the SASGRAPH spline function.

11. Roger Smith (1970), Wheaton (1975), Burch (1979), Anderson (1971), Katz (1975).

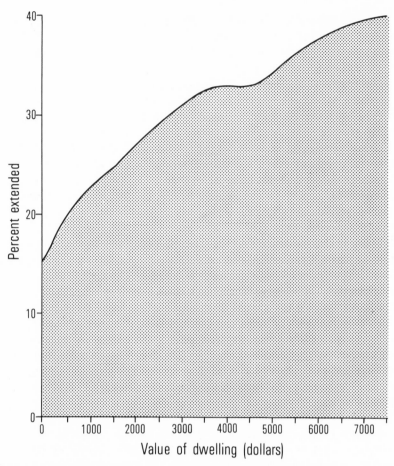

Figure 3.4. Standardized percentage of persons residing with extended kin, by value of dwelling: Erie County, 1855

Historians of the family have been influenced by contemporary class differences in family structure. The poor are now more likely than any other group to reside in extended families. The evidence from Erie County—which shows a pronounced weakening of the relationship between high occupational status and extended family structure between 1855 and 1915—reflects the beginnings of a twentieth-century reversal of the class pattern of extended-family structure. We are presented with a fascinating question for future research: what has occurred during the past seventy years to cause the concentration of extended living arrangements among the poor instead of among the rich?

An orientation toward history from the bottom up may also help to account for the prevailing assumption that extended living arrangements and strong networks of kin were a defense against economic hardship faced by the working class. The "new" social history has been more concerned with working-class behavior than with the behavior of elites. By earlier and subsequent standards, the frequency of extended families among the working class in Erie County and Lancashire was high. Because of our focus on the bottom of the social hierarchy, we have cast our explanations for the high frequency of extended families in terms of the precarious circumstances of Victorian working-class life.

In view of the interest in the lives of workers, our explanation of extended families as a consequence of economic stress is understandable. It is nonetheless wrong. Taking in extended kin in the nineteenth century was apparently a luxury—not a response to poverty. At the same time, because the rise of the extended family in the nineteenth century probably was not class specific, we should be wary of overstressing the importance of economic welfare per se. Instead, we should look for explanations—economic or otherwise—that can account for increases in complex living arrangements among both the working class and the bourgeoisie.

Those who are committed to the hardship thesis—that the high frequency of extended families in the nineteenth century was a response to adverse economic circumstances—might argue that the rationale for adopting extended-family structure was fundamentally different for the working class and for the bourgeoisie. According to this reasoning, the high frequency of extended families in the late Victorian era could have been a response to hardship *despite* the fact that extended living arrangements were especially common in the highest ranks. After all, most of the population was working class; the residential behavior of the wealthy may be irrelevant for explaining the high *overall* frequency of extended families in this period.

This line of argument would be more compelling if there were a bimodal distribution of extended-family structure with respect to economic status. That is, if those of very high and very low economic status resided in extended families more often than did persons of middling rank, we might suspect that there were entirely different reasons why working-class and bourgeois people resided with extended kin. The evidence on dwelling value, however, indicates that the frequency of extended families went up continuously with rising economic status.

It is, of course, possible that such a continuous relationship could arise from systematically different mechanisms at each level of the social hierarchy. As hardship pressures gradually declined with increasing economic resources, a variety of other motives—associated with higher economic status—could gradually come into play.

To test this scenario, we must look at the problem in greater detail. In particular, we must ask who gained and who lost through the adoption of extended-family structure: were complex living arrangements beneficial for the family as a whole or only for the extended kin themselves? Furthermore, we must investigate the specific economic circumstances associated with family extension. The sections that follow address these issues.

Economic Dependence and the Extended Family

If Victorian family structure was associated with high economic status instead of with hardship, this may be because taking in extended kin did not usually ameliorate the economic position of the family as a whole. In fact, taking in extended relations usually imposed an economic burden on nineteenth-century families. Most extended relations in nineteenth-century families did not earn wages, and those who did work typically had lower-status jobs than the family head.

The family economic-dependency ratio provides a means of estimating the economic contribution of extended kin. The economic-dependency ratio is here defined as the ratio of nonemployed family members to employed family members. A high dependency ratio is unfavorable; it means that a relatively small number of wage earners must support a relatively large number of dependents. If everything else remains equal, a low dependency ratio is economically advantageous. The reader should bear in mind that, because information on nonemployment is inferred from the occupational listings, the economic dependency ratio may be biased by incomplete reporting.[12]

---

12. For those who prefer equations, the family economic dependency ratio is defined as:

$$\frac{\text{number of nonemployed family members}}{\text{number of employed family members}} \times 100$$

The economic-dependency ratio is based on census listings of occupation. Where no occupation was listed, I assumed that the individual was not employed. This may not be justified; sometimes the information may simply have been omitted by the census taker. Moreover, the extent of omission may have varied by class or period. The measure does not, of course, take into account the relative wages of employed extended kin and employed nuclear-family members. Since the nuclear family usually included an adult male head of household and high-status jobs were usually held by such people, one might expect that the economic dependency ratio understates the relative burden of extended kin. But the ratio

Table 3.2. Effects of the Inclusion of Extended Relatives on the Family
Economic-Dependency Ratio (in Percentages)

	Lancashire, 1871	Erie County, 1880	Erie County, 1900	Erie County, 1915
Dependence declined	18.4	25.1	37.1	49.1
Dependence unchanged	5.6	21.0	14.6	5.4
Dependence increased	76.0	53.8	48.3	45.5
Total	100.0	99.9[a]	100.0	100.0
Number of cases	1,956	3,266	8,305	11,849

[a]Column does not sum to 100.0 because of rounding error.

To assess the economic consequences of extended living arrangements, the economic-dependency ratio of all members of extended families was compared with that of the nuclear members of extended families. These figures appear in table 3.2.[13] The data indicate that in nineteenth-century Erie County and in the Lancashire textile towns in 1871, only a small proportion of extended families benefited from the presence of extended relatives, at least in terms of the economic-dependency ratio. Especially in Lancashire and in 1880 Erie County, the addition of extended relatives was much more likely to raise the dependency ratio than to lower it. In Erie County, this pattern reversed between 1880 and 1915. By 1915, slightly more families benefited from than were hurt by the inclusion of extended kin.

---

also ignores wealth, which might conceivably work the other way around. For all these reasons, the figures based on the economic-dependency ratio should be interpreted with caution.

I should also note that the determination of which family members were extended and which were nuclear was, where feasible, based on the relation to household head as given in the census, rather than on the relation-to-family-head variable described in appendix A.

Kaestle and Vinovskis (1978) and Katz, Doucet, and Stern (1982) employed more elaborate work/consumption indices based on the age and gender composition of households. After considerable experimentation with these and with indices based on the U.S. poverty guidelines (Orshansky 1965), I decided to stick with a simple measure of the proportion employed. The more complicated measures strike me as rather arbitrary, and because they depend on the age and gender composition of the household, they are partly dependent on family structure.

13. The 1855 Erie County sample was excluded from the analyses of dependence because the family economic dependency ratio depends on occupational data, and the occupational data are not very complete in that census year. The "hot deck" imputation procedure used to correct for this problem (see note 5) is adequate for occupational stratification, but dependence figures would be misleading.

Recall that in Erie County between 1880 and 1915, the proportion of extended families among the bourgeoisie declined relative to the proportion among the working class. Thus, the twentieth-century pattern of extended-family structure—a low overall percentage of extended families, concentrated among the poor—was taking shape. The figures presented in table 3.2 suggest that the twentieth-century concentration of extended families among the poor may be related to a shift toward more economically adaptive extended families; between 1880 and 1915, the inclusion of extended relatives increasingly improved the family economic-dependency ratio.

Table 3.3 lends support to this interpretation. These figures show that in 1880, bourgeois extended families were substantially more likely to benefit from the inclusion of extended relatives than were working-class families. Among unskilled workers—the group with the greatest economic need—the economic-dependency ratio was improved by the pres-

Table 3.3. Effects of the Inclusion of Extended Relatives on the Family Economic-Dependency Ratio, by Occupational Class, Erie County, 1880–1915 (in Percentages)

	Unskilled	Skilled	Lower Bourgeois	Upper Bourgeois
1880				
Dependence declined	20.3	24.4	33.7	36.9
Dependence unchanged	27.8	23.2	18.4	12.6
Dependence increased	51.9	52.4	47.9	50.5
Total	100.0	100.0	100.0	100.0
Number of cases	661	1,070	386	309
1900				
Dependence declined	41.0	37.0	35.9	28.2
Dependence unchanged	10.7	8.5	6.5	12.7
Dependence increased	48.3	54.5	57.6	59.1
Total	100.0	100.0	100.0	100.0
Number of cases	1,380	2,382	1,410	416
1915				
Dependence declined	62.8	50.8	48.8	33.1
Dependence unchanged	3.4	4.0	4.9	5.3
Dependence increased	33.8	45.3	46.3	61.6
Total	100.0	100.0	100.0	100.0
Number of cases	1,898	4,687	2,862	241

ence of extended relatives only a fifth of the time. By 1915, the opposite class pattern of dependency prevailed: the bourgeoisie were *least* likely and the unskilled were *most* likely to benefit from residence with extended kin.

The 1915 pattern makes sense from an economic point of view: the people with the greatest economic need usually adopted extended-family structure only when this did not involve an additional burden of dependency. At the same time, wealthier people—who could best afford it—frequently supported dependent kin. By contrast, the nineteenth-century class pattern of dependence in extended families makes little economic sense: the poorest groups—who could least afford it—adopted the least beneficial extended-family structure, whereas the wealthy embraced the most beneficial extended living arrangements.

Even if the overall effect of extended kin was disadvantageous in the nineteenth century, taking in extended relatives might have provided a means of ameliorating the most economically strained phases of the life course. That is, when there were many dependents—such as young children—in the family, an employed relation who provided extra income would be taken in. At points of the life course when there were few dependents, on the other hand, an unemployed relative could be taken in with relatively little hardship. In other words, family extension could be a strategy for smoothing variation in the economic-dependency ratio over the life course.[14]

Figure 3.5 tests this hypothesis. For each census file, I have plotted the mean economic dependency ratio of extended families and of their nuclear members alone by age of the family head. The figures are expressed per hundred persons, so a dependency ratio of 100 indicates an equal number of nonemployed and employed persons, a dependency ratio of 200 indicates twice as many nonemployed as employed persons, and so on. If extended living arrangements did indeed provide a means of coping with economic hardship engendered by the life course, one would expect to find the curve for all members of extended families to be smoother than that for nuclear members of extended families.

In 1880, the presence of extended relatives did not have a significant effect on the economic-dependency ratio for families in which the head was between 20 and 45 years old. When the head was over 45 or under 20,

14. This hypothesis is proposed by Anderson (1980: 80, 81, 83); see also Hareven (1975). Katz, Doucet, and Stern (1982) tested the thesis that taking in kin usefully smoothed the life cycle of dependency, and their findings are consistent with my own.

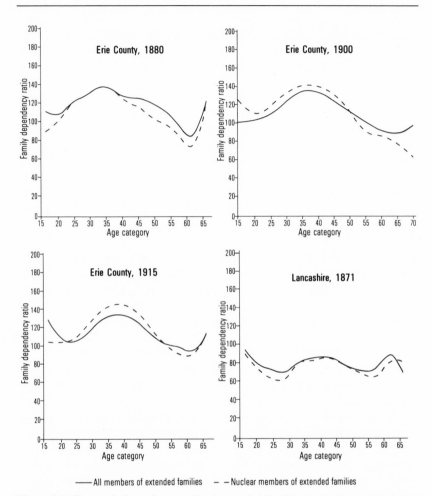

Figure 3.5. Economic-dependency ratio of extended families, including and excluding extended kin, by age of family head: Erie County and Lancashire towns, 1871–1915

the inclusion of extended kin significantly worsened the economic-dependency ratio. In a sense, the presence of extended kin did smooth the life course of dependence in 1880 Erie County, but only because such relatives significantly worsened the economic dependency ratio for families with very young heads and families at later points in the life course. In the lean years—when there were unemployed children still at home—the inclusion of extended kin had virtually no effect on the ratio.

In 1915, by contrast, the addition of extended kin usefully improved and smoothed the life course of dependence. The presence of extended relatives eased the economic dependency ratio during the middle years when such assistance was most needed. The negative effects of extended relatives were concentrated among the families with older heads, at a time of life when the pressure on the family budget was less severe.

In sum, the evidence on dependence consistently suggests that the model of family strategies has greater relevance for the twentieth-century extended family than for the nineteenth. Extended-family structure seems to have been economically dysfunctional in the nineteenth century, when the frequency of extended families was highest. In both Erie County and Lancashire, extended kin worsened the family economic-dependency ratio—especially for those groups that could least afford it—and the presence of extended kin did not ameliorate hardship associated with the life course. By 1915, all this had changed: extended kin improved the economic dependency ratio—especially for those who needed it the most—and the effects of extended kin were particularly beneficial during that phase of the life course with greatest economic strain. Ironically, the adoption of advantageous patterns of dependence in extended families occurred just as the frequency of extended families began to decline.

Economic Exchange and Extended-Family Structure

Anderson argues that "critical life situations" of economic exchange were responsible for the high frequency of extended families in the nineteenth century.[15] The evidence from Erie County and Lancashire suggests that he is wrong. In fact, these situations—the problems of working mothers, unemployment, housing shortage, migration, illness, and old age—for the most part discouraged the formation of extended families in Victorian Lancashire and Erie County.

Paramount among Anderson's explanations for the high frequency of extended families in the nineteenth century is the employment of women outside the home. According to his exchange theory, dependent extended relations were brought into the family fold in exchange for baby-sitting and housekeeping services while mother went off to the mill.

Table 3.4 shows the relationship between residence with extended relatives and employment of mothers with small children. In Erie County in 1880, working mothers with children under age 5 were *less* likely to reside in extended families than were either unemployed mothers with young children or working women without small children. This is prob-

15. Anderson (1971: 171).

Table 3.4. The Living Arrangements of Mothers and Working Women 18 Years or Older
(in Percentages)

	Mothers of Children under Five		Women with No Children under Five	
	Working	Nonworking	Working	Nonworking
Erie County, 1880				
Residing in extended family	16.9	32.2	19.1	32.9
Other living arrangements	83.1	67.8	80.9	67.1
Total	100.0	100.0	100.0	100.0
N	373	544	1,384	1,900
Erie County, 1900				
Residing in extended family	23.3	17.9	20.1	25.6
Other living arrangements	76.7	82.1	79.9	74.4
Total	100.0	100.0	100.0	100.0
N	94	2,955	2,828	7,013
Erie County, 1915				
Residing in extended family	69.8	20.0	16.5	25.2
Other living arrangements	30.2	80.0	83.5	74.8
Total	100.0	100.0	100.0	100.0
N	156	4,673	5,356	8,261
Lancashire, 1871				
Residing in extended family	32.6	20.9	13.5	31.0
Other living arrangements	67.4	79.1	86.5	69.0
Total	100.0	100.0	100.0	100.0
N	135	508	2,002	1,187

ably because families with working mothers of small children were often poor. If economic hardship was so great that the mother was forced to work, then the family perhaps could not afford to maintain an unemployed extended relative. On the other hand, if the extended relative was employed, then she or he could not provide child-care services.

Between 1880 and 1915, the relationship between mother's employment and family extension changed dramatically. By 1915, working mothers of small children were far more likely to reside in extended families than were either unemployed mothers of young children or working women without small children. This change toward a more economically functional form of extended family is consistent with the evidence on dependence presented above.

Despite an increase in female labor force participation in the United States as a whole between 1880 and 1915, there was no such increase in Erie County.[16] Moreover, the employment of mothers became increasingly rare during this period. By 1915, 97 percent of mothers with young children did not work, so the employment of mothers had only a marginal effect on the overall frequency of extended families.

In the Lancashire textile towns in 1871, unlike Erie County in 1880, the employment of mothers of young children was associated with extended-family structure. Nonetheless, this situation was not an important contributor to the high frequency of extended families in Victorian Lancashire. Despite the textile mills—which depended on female labor—the employment of mothers was relatively unusual.[17] Overall, working mothers with small children could be responsible for less than 1 percent of the Lancashire population residing in extended families.

Even this small percentage of extended living arrangements should not be entirely ascribed to an exchange mechanism. Anderson argues that extended kin were brought into the family because they were needed to take the place of a working mother. More often, however, mothers were probably able to work because there was already a coresident relative in the household available to perform baby-sitting and housekeeping chores. To the extent that the latter situation prevailed, the employment of mothers would have had no influence on the frequency of extended families.

Anderson also argues that the cyclical unemployment characteristic of industrial capitalism was responsible for the formation of extended families. By "huddling" in a single household, he asserts, kin were better able to weather these periodic crises. Furthermore, if only one relation was out of work, then support for the unemployed family member would be provided by kin, with the expectation of repayment at a later date.[18]

16. Smuts (1959). In Buffalo, the opportunities for employment of women were unusually low; see Katz, Doucet, and Stern (1982) and Yans-McLaughlin (1977). The overall average urban female labor-force participation in nineteenth-century England and America would fall somewhere between the Erie County and Lancashire figures, because the former was unusually low and the latter unusually high; see Tilly and Scott (1978).

17. The employment of women is probably understated by the census listings of occupation, but there is no reason to assume that the understatement of employment for mothers of young children was greater than that for other women.

18. Anderson (1971: 149–50).

This hypothesis can be tested using information on unemployment from the 1880 census. In that year in Erie County, 13 percent of those listed as unemployed resided in extended families, compared with 24 percent of the rest of the population. This pattern is essentially unaffected when the effects of age, sex, and marital status are controlled.[19]

In Lancashire there is no measure of unemployment per se, but we can test Anderson's hypothesis by using the occupational listings. Once we control for age, the percentage of extended living arrangements is virtually identical for working-age men with no occupation listed and for employed men.

Our evidence indicates that unemployment did not significantly contribute to the high frequency of extended families in the nineteenth century. This makes sense: the unemployed were unlikely to take in extended kin, because such kin were usually a burden. At the same time, unemployed persons were unlikely to be supported by their relatives; since unemployment was most frequent in the working class, the relatives of the unemployed were no doubt typically disadvantaged, with inadequate resources to support dependent kin.[20]

Overcrowding which resulted from housing shortage is also said by Anderson to have contributed to the high frequency of extended families in the nineteenth century. If we are taking an economic perspective, it makes sense to view housing as a perfect market. In this light, the problem is not so much an absolute shortage of housing, but rather an inability of the working class to afford housing within reasonable walking distance from their place of employment. To argue that the rise of the extended family resulted from a worsening housing shortage, we must also argue that the price increases for housing outstripped wage in-

19. Unemployment was drastically underreported by the census, but that should not create any difficulty for this analysis unless those for whom unemployment is indicated responded differently from the unemployed population as a whole in terms of their family structure. Unemployed people are necessarily adults. Since the age structure of extended families is older than the age structure of the entire population, when we standardize for age, the difference in family structure between unemployed people and for the whole population is *greater* than the unstandardized figures suggest. Gender, however, is a countervailing influence, since persons listed as unemployed tend to be male, and the proportion of females is greater for extended families than for the population as a whole.

20. Of course, individuals were doubtless assisted by their kin during times of unemployment, but there is no evidence that such assistance was generally reciprocal. Furthermore, such assistance does not seem to have taken the form of offers of housing.

creases, so that the working class was increasingly unable to afford rent payments.[21]

For Victorian Lancashire, I have no direct evidence on the interrelationship of family extension and housing shortage, but we can make an informed guess about the affordability of housing. The real income of working-class wage earners in England probably increased by at least 40 percent between 1800 and 1871.[22] No data are available on the average level of working-class rents, but it is possible that they rose faster than real wages. However, even at the end of the century, rent accounted for only 16 percent of working-class expenditures in York, which was a city with an acute housing shortage.[23] If this figure is representative, then rent increases must have consumed only a small portion of the increased income of wage earners, no matter how dramatic was the rise of housing costs during the course of the nineteenth century.

In brief, the argument that the rise of the extended family in the nineteenth century derived from housing shortage implies that housing was becoming increasingly unaffordable for the working class. Since incomes rose substantially and rent represented only a small percentage of working-class expenditures, it is doubtful that housing shortage was an important contributor to the rise of the extended family.

It is also questionable whether housing shortage was actually associated with extended-family structure. People who were forced into crowded accommodations did not necessarily cope with the problem by

21. A short-term lack of housing no doubt occurred in some areas of rapid urbanization and high in-migration. But this housing shortage would have been reflected in the cost of housing, assuming a market mechanism. Such a mechanism may not actually have operated very effectively; however, if we assume rational behavior and perfect information with regard to family residence decisions, it seems only fair to make similar assumptions about the housing market.

22. Mitchell and Deane (1962: 343). The debate over the standard of living in the industrial revolution is now moribund. Although disagreement persists on the overall impact of industrialization on the well-being of the working class in the first third of the nineteenth century, there is now general agreement that real per capita working-class incomes rose substantially over the course of the century as a whole. Some of the most important contributions to the debate are reprinted in A. J. Taylor (1975), but see also Deane (1965), Perkin (1969), Mathias (1968), Phelps-Brown and Hopkins (1956), and Deane and Cole (1968).

23. Rowntree (1902: 207). The housing shortage was not new in the nineteenth century; see Marshall (1926: 107). For discussion of the cost of housing as a proportion of working-class income in the United States, see the budget analyses of Modell (1979), Stern (1979), and Haines (1981).

Table 3.5. Living Arrangements and Multihousehold Dwellings, Erie County, 1855 (in Percentages)

| | Number of Households in Dwelling | | | |
	One	Two	Three	Four+
Residing in extended family	21.6	14.8	14.0	13.3
Other living arrangements	78.4	85.2	86.0	86.7
Total	100.0	100.0	100.0	100.0
Number of cases	99,771	13,176	5,680	7,788

taking in extended kin. The census provides no direct empirical evidence on housing shortage, but for Buffalo there are a variety of measures that are related to the problem.

The first measure of housing shortage is mentioned by Anderson himself, who suggests that the presence of multifamily dwellings is an indicator of housing shortage.[24] If this is reliable, then housing shortage was not associated with extended living arrangements. As table 3.5 shows, the more households in a dwelling, the lower the overall percentage of extended families.

Ward density is also measurable. If we assume, with Anderson, that housing shortage leads to overcrowding, and that overcrowding leads to high density, then ward density may be a usable indicator of housing shortage at the aggregate level. The relationship of extended living arrangements to ward density is shown in table 3.6. These figures indicate that there was virtually no association between density and the frequency of extended living arrangements at the ward level. In fact, the tiny correlation between the two variables is negative; if anything, high density was associated with nuclear-family structure.

A third indicator of housing shortage is dwelling value per person. If many people were crammed into a small space, then one would expect that dwelling value per person would be low. Contrary to Anderson's hypothesis, the percentage of persons in extended families at low dwelling values per person is much lower than that at high dwelling values per person.[25]

24. Anderson (1971: 33).
25. The relationship of dwelling value per capita to extended-family structure is essentially similar to the relationship of dwelling value per family to extended-family structure, once the latter has been standardized for differential family size; see figure 3.4.
The negative relationship between the indicators of housing shortage and family extension may partially reflect the fact that extended families were most common among the

Table 3.6. Ward Density and Percent Residing with Extended Relatives, Buffalo, 1855

Ward Number	Index of Density[a]	Percent Extended	Number in Ward
4	100	20.8	7,485
6	85	15.9	6,788
2	73	25.3	5,811
5	63	13.8	7,205
1	40	19.0	7,365
3	38	23.8	4,223
9	38	27.2	5,205
8	28	21.7	5,271
10	23	27.7	4,897
7	22	9.2	7,500
11	15	20.3	3,307
12	12	19.5	3,506
13	4	20.6	811
Total	—	19.6	69,893

[a]100 = Ward 4.

Finally, I should point out that housing shortage was principally an urban working-class phenomenon. Therefore, if crowding were a significant cause of family extension, one would expect that extended families would be most frequent among the urban working class. But city dwellers in Erie County between 1855 and 1915 were slightly *less* likely than residents of the Buffalo hinterland to adopt extended living arrangements, and as we have already seen, the working class was least likely to reside in extended families.

In sum, then, although we cannot measure housing shortage directly, every available indicator shows either no relationship or a negative relationship between housing shortage and extended-family structure. It

bourgeoisie and higher-status persons enjoyed less-crowded housing conditions. But this negative relationship does not seem to be purely a product of intervening variables, since it remains when we control for class, among other variables, in multivariate analysis. See appendix F.

The presence of boarders may also bear on the issue of overcrowding. If extended families were more often overcrowded than were other families, one would not expect them to take in boarders as frequently; such additional household members would only have aggravated the crowding. In fact, persons in extended families resided with boarders more frequently than did persons not residing in extended families. In 1855 in Erie County, for example, 17 percent of extended-family members resided with boarders, whereas only 14 percent of the rest of the population did so. The comparable figures for 1880 are 15 percent and 11 percent, respectively.

is not implausible that housing shortage actually discouraged extended-family structure; such a shortage might have meant that people were unable to find quarters large enough to house both their nuclear families and extended kin.

Anderson sees migration as another major source of extended-family structure in the nineteenth century. He argues that immigrants to Victorian cities faced a complex set of problems—including finding a place to live—and kin "were by far the most important source of assistance available to migrants."[26]

Analyzing the effects of migration on family structure poses several methodological and theoretical problems.[27] Although migration could—at least theoretically—encourage the coresidence of kin, it also drastically limits the range of kin available for coresidence.

The net effect of high migration in nineteenth-century Lancashire and Erie County was to discourage the formation of extended families. In every data set employed, it was those born nearest to their current place of residence who were most likely to reside with extended kin.[28] In Lancashire, nonmigrants lived in extended families 38 percent more often than migrants; in Erie County in 1855, the comparable figure is 65 percent. For the other data sets, only state or country of birth is available, but the same general pattern is apparent.

The evidence from Erie County also demonstrates that extended living arrangements were not even a common short-run living arrangement for migrants themselves. The 1855 census includes a variable indicating the number of years each individual had spent locally. As figure 3.6 indicates, those migrants who had arrived recently were *least* likely to reside in extended families. The longer the time people spent locally, the more frequently they adopted extended living arrangements. Once again, these conclusions stand when we control for the effects of intervening variables.

According to Anderson, problems resulting from illness also led to the formation of extended families. But illness cannot explain why extended living arrangements were especially prevalent in the late nineteenth century. Demographic data on life expectancy suggest that people were sick at least as often at the beginning of the nineteenth century as they

26. Anderson (1971: 152–60).
27. See note 1, chapter 5, for discussion of migration and family structure.
28. This is still the case when we control for the effects of intervening structural variables. See appendix F.

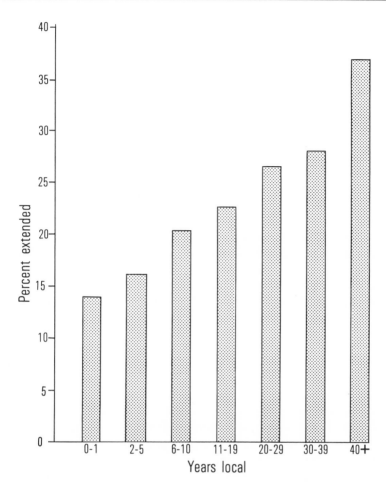

Figure 3.6. Percent of migrants residing in extended families, by years spent locally: Erie County, 1855

were at the end. True enough, health conditions among the working class of industrial cities worsened for a time, as the pace of urbanization outstripped improvements in sanitation. Yet, as was noted above, the urban working class was the group least likely to adopt extended family structure.

Moreover, census data suggest that illness was not significantly associated with the formation of extended families. Although we cannot measure total morbidity, we do have a crude measure of disability for 1855 Erie County. Only 12 percent of those who were listed as deaf, dumb, blind, or feebleminded resided in extended families, compared with 20 percent of the rest of the population.[29]

Of Anderson's six "critical life situations," only old age accounted for a significant proportion of extended families in the nineteenth century. In both Lancashire and Erie County, the majority of the elderly resided with extended kin. The benefits of coresidence, from the point of view of the elderly, are obvious. The great majority of those over 65 had no occupation. For old people without savings, the alternative to residence with kin was the almshouse. From the point of view of the younger generation, however, it is difficult to find an economic rationale for coresidence.

Anderson cites four material incentives for younger members of the working class to reside with elderly kin. First, sharing living quarters purportedly meant a reduction of rent. Of course, this would only be true if older kin had sufficient economic resources to contribute to rent payments. Since the aged were rarely employed, it is doubtful that many could add a significant sum, though a few working-class elderly may actually have owned their homes. Second, Anderson argues that sharing with an older person allowed young couples to avoid the expense of purchasing furniture. The census provides no measure of furniture; I have therefore not attempted to test Anderson's inheritance-of-furniture hypothesis. Third, if the younger generation included a working mother, the elderly person could provide valuable child-care and housekeeping services. The reasons this factor is unimportant are discussed above. Finally, according to Anderson, a housing shortage prevented many young couples from establishing a residence of their own.[30] Again, it is argued above that this factor did not increase the percentage of extended families in the nineteenth century.

Aside from the possible influence of furniture and home ownership, Anderson's argument that residence with elderly kin was beneficial for the younger generation is unpersuasive. Some of the elderly in the industrial towns may have been able to offer their children a house or furniture in exchange for maintenance. But we should keep in mind that a hundred years earlier many of the elderly had more substantial bribes to offer than "minimal scraps of furniture": land, agricultural tools, or perhaps a cow. Even with the more significant economic incentive of

29. Like unemployment, disability was almost certainly much underreported. As long as those whose disability *was* reported responded to that disability similarly to those whose disability was not reported, the analysis stands. As usual, the result is the same when intervening variables are controlled; see appendix F.

30. Anderson (1971: 141).

agricultural inheritance, extended families with elderly kin were much less frequent in the eighteenth century.[31]

More general theoretical considerations also contradict Anderson's hypothesis that coresidence with elderly kin became more desirable in the nineteenth century. As noted earlier, modernization theorists and structural-functionalists have pointed out a variety of ways in which the utility of the elderly to the rest of the family *declined* during the course of the nineteenth century. The breakdown of the family economy, rapid technological and social change, the rise of literacy, and increased intergenerational competition are said to have rendered the old obsolete. These hypotheses remain unproven, but one can make at least as good a case for reduced incentive to reside with the elderly as one can for greater incentive. It is quite plausible that the advantages of maintaining elderly kin were declining at the same time that family extension was on the rise.

Conclusion

There can be no question that economic considerations affected family residence decisions in the nineteenth century. Those who lacked resources frequently moved in with wealthier kin. The behavior of dependent extended relatives was rational and probably calculated; they had material benefits to gain.

---

31. Anderson (1971: 141). Of course, many persons may have maintained their parents in old age with the expectation that they in turn would be supported by their children. Such behavior is not, however, economic exchange. Rather, it is a reflection of social norms and bonds of obligation. If kin ties were merely rational economic relationships, such intergenerational obligations could not be maintained.

Anderson also suggests that the restrictions on poor relief in the nineteenth century reduced the institutional alternatives to residence with kin. However, although it is true that a larger percentage of the population was assisted under the Old Poor Law, fewer were probably institutionalized. Under the outdoor relief system, aid was not contingent on residence in a workhouse. Indeed, elderly who resided with extended kin were eligible. Thus, the economic resources available for exchange were augmented by poor relief before 1800. By contrast, in the latter part of the nineteenth century outdoor relief was no longer generally available. Workhouses were rare before 1700 and their increase during the eighteenth century continued well into the nineteenth. In fact, the setting up of new workhouses was a major goal of the New Poor Law. There were only 400 workhouses in 1802, when the population of England exceeded eight million; see Blaug (1963: 157). Although it cannot be proven, the available evidence supports the conclusion that the proportion of institutionalized elderly increased between preindustrial and high Victorian times. Thus, the availability of elderly kin for residence in extended families was probably reduced by changes in social-welfare policy. In America, the general direction of change in the poor-relief system was similar. See Marshall (1926: 2, 87, 96, 101, 127ff.), Roach (1978: 115ff.), Rose (1971: 143ff.), Ashcroft (1898: 132–37), Oxley (1974). On American poor relief, see Katz (1983).

There were rarely, however, mutual benefits, for most nuclear families gained little from taking in an extended relative. Thus, we cannot account for the high frequency of extended families in the nineteenth century in terms of reciprocal exchange. Nor should extended living arrangements be viewed as an adaptive family strategy; on the contrary, for many families the presence of dependent extended relatives was no doubt a heavy burden that jeopardized the material well-being of the family as a whole.

We must assume that the decisive power in forming an extended family did not rest in the hands of the poor relations. Those family members who exercised control over economic resources probably also exercised control over the coresidence of kin. Thus, if we acknowledge power relations within the family, we must acknowledge that the decisive impetus for the formation of extended families was neither economically rational nor calculative, at least from a strictly material point of view.

The rising frequency of extended families in the nineteenth century might simply have been a function of a rise in the proportion of people who could afford them.[32] Extended-family structure was associated with high economic status in both Victorian Lancashire and Erie County. Historians have generally viewed extended living arrangements as a response to economic adversity; the evidence presented here suggests that they should instead be regarded as a luxury. In this light, the adoption of extended living arrangements might be viewed as a by-product of rising incomes. But if the high frequency of extended families in the nineteenth century was a consequence of relative prosperity, one wonders why the frequency of extended families has declined in the twentieth century, and why nuclear family structure is sometimes associated with economic development.[33]

One can almost always come up with an economic explanation for practically anything if one is wedded to that perspective. I recall a conversation I had with a well-known economist. When I explained that the frequency of extended families increased in the nineteenth century, he said, "Of course! Incomes were rising, so more people could afford them." Why then, I asked, did extended families become less common in the twentieth century, as incomes continued to rise? "Obviously," he responded,

32. On changing incomes, see note 22.
33. Dahlin (1980: 99–107), Winch and Blumberg (1968); see also George and Pryor (1971: 201–6), Michael, Fuchs, and Scott (1980).

"more people could afford to live alone." While these two explanations may not be absolutely irreconcilable, they imply either an intervening change in values or a *very* complex economic mechanism.[34]

For those of us who lack faith in the existence of the economic Holy Grail, searching for alternative explanations may seem a more fruitful quest. I will therefore abandon this foray into the thicket of economics and plunge into the quicksand of demography.

34. A possible mechanism would be provided by Zitomersky's (1985: 23) hypothesis that extension is concentrated among those of "middling to precarious" economic status, and less frequent among the "comfortable" and among the "destitute." If most people in the eighteenth century were destitute, most in the nineteenth century were middling to precarious and most in the twentieth were comfortable, then the rise and decline of the extended family could be explained without great complication. Numerous economists have suggested this scenario to me, but I don't buy it: I have seen no evidence that extended families were concentrated among those of middling to precarious circumstances in any period.

4 Approaches to the Demography of the Extended Family

Historical demography is in high fashion these days.
Richard S. Dunn, *Sugar and Slaves* (1972)

We approached the problem modestly by examining the opinions of others, and found that men far wiser than ourselves had failed to agree.
Hans Zinsser, *Rats, Lice, and History* (1935)

In order to live with extended relatives, one must *have* extended relatives. The frequency and timing of births, deaths, and marriages in a population defines the biological context within which residence decisions are made. Accordingly, attempts to account for historical change in the frequency of extended families must weigh the influence of changing demographic conditions. But the authorities fail to agree on how one ought to go about the task of analyzing the historical demography of the extended family. This chapter surveys the various approaches people have taken.

Theoretical Considerations

It is now over twenty years since Marion Levy proposed a demographic interpretation of modernization and extended-family structure. Levy argued that a high frequency of extended families is impossible in premodern societies because of high mortality. Very short life expectancy prevents widespread residence in three-generation families; most people die before they become grandparents or shortly thereafter.

According to Levy, the extended family is often the *ideal* in premodern societies, even though a high frequency of extended families is precluded by demographic constraints. Thus, as mortality declines with modernization, the frequency of extended families may increase; with the removal of the demographic barrier, more people are able to achieve their ideal family type. But in Levy's eyes, an increase in extended-family structure associated with modernization would necessarily be confined to a short-lived, "transitional" phase. When extended-family structure becomes predominant, it leads to "sources of stress and strain which produce changes in the direction of less vertical and horizontal proliferation." In other words, when mortality declines sufficiently to allow a high frequency of extended families, societies tend to abandon the ideal of extended-family structure.[1]

Levy was attempting to predict the experience of contemporary Third World countries; he was not describing historical change in the West. In its broad outlines, however, Levy's interpretation fits neatly with the most recent evidence on family structure in England and America in the eighteenth and nineteenth centuries. As Levy's theory suggests, the frequency of extended families was low in the preindustrial period. As mortality declined, the frequency of extended families increased, but this increase was short-lived; in the twentieth century, the frequency of extended families returned to preindustrial levels.

At about the same time that Levy's work appeared, Peter Laslett published his findings that nuclear family structure predominated overwhelmingly in preindustrial England. The demographic explanation for the low frequency of extended families was immediately proposed, but Laslett insisted that the lack of extended families in preindustrial England was a consequence of cultural preferences rather than demographic imperative.[2]

The controversy over the relative importance of demographic imperative and cultural choice as determinants of preindustrial family structure has important theoretical implications. The interpretations of structural-functionalism and modernization theory, described in chapter 2, are sharply challenged by the new evidence on historical family structure. As noted, these sociological theories attempt to explain a decline in the extended family. If there was no decline in the extended family with industrialization and modernization, then it becomes pointless to develop such explanations. If, however, there had been an *ideal* of extended-family structure before the industrial revolution and that ideal disappeared by the twentieth century, then mainstream sociological interpretations of the evolution of the family could be rehabilitated. Instead of

1. Levy (1965: 49 et pass.); see also Levy (1970) and Levy and Fallers (1973). Levy's argument was published before it was widely known that the frequency of extended families was low in preindustrial England. P. Laslett's findings first appeared in Laslett and Harrison (1963), but these results were inconclusive, and they did not receive wide circulation. The results published in P. Laslett (1965a) and P. Laslett (1966) were more substantial.

2. On P. Laslett's early publication of his findings, see note 1. David Glass (1966), whose work is discussed below, was apparently the first to propose a demographic explanation for Laslett's findings.

explaining the decline of the extended family, sociological theorists could now explain the decline of extended-family ideals.

The demographic interpretation has received most of its support from advocates of the stem-family hypothesis. According to the stem-family hypothesis, it was usual in preindustrial Western society for one child to remain in his or her parents' household after marriage, while all other children left home to establish new households. This provided a mechanism for transmission of property and assured a steady supply of labor in the parents' old age. There are several variations on the stem-family hypothesis, but according to most interpretations it was generally the eldest male child who remained in his parents' household after marriage.[3]

The most eloquent efforts to reconcile the stem-family hypothesis with the statistical findings of the Cambridge Group can be found in the work of Lutz Berkner. Berkner stresses the developmental cycle of the stem family:

> A census taken at a given point in time takes a cross-section and gives a static picture of households and families that the historian and sociologist can sort out into types. We can count so many extended families, so many nuclear. But rather than being types these may simply be phases in the developmental cycle of a single family organization. There may be a normal series of stages that appear only rarely in a population because they last for only a short period of the family's cycle or in some cases do not appear at all. From this point of view, the extended family is merely a phase through which most families go.[4]

Thus, as Berkner points out, the stem-family hypothesis describes a cycle in which each household starts as nuclear, becomes a stem household—defined as a household containing parents and married child—

3. The stem-family hypothesis, introduced by Le Play (1871), has been highly influential among both historians and sociologists. For a highly partisan overview, see P. Laslett (1972a, 1978); also see Leeuwen (1981) and Mogey (1955). The classic application of Le Play's theory is Homans (1941).

There has been some suggestion that the interpretation of the stem family adopted by historians does not actually correspond to Le Play's interpretation; see Wall (1983a). Le Play (1871: 10) defined the stem family as follows: "One of the children, married close to the parents, lives in community with them and perpetuates, with their concurrence, the tradition of the ancestors. The other children set themselves up outside the family home when they prefer not to remain celibate within it." This definition is ambiguous in several respects, but it is roughly consistent with the usual definitions of historians. See, for example, Flandrin (1979), Stone (1977a), and Shorter (1976).

4. Berkner (1972b). See also Berkner (1975, 1976, 1977b).

upon the marriage of a child, and becomes a nuclear household again when both parents die. During the course of this cycle, a whole new crop of nuclear households is created by the siblings who do not remain in their parent's household after marriage. The new nuclear households will become stem upon the marriage of a child, and the whole process will be repeated.

Even if everyone in the population followed stem-family organizational rules, in a society characterized by late marriage, early death, and relatively high fertility the proportion of observed stem households at any one time would necessarily be low.

This scenario implies a considerably more complex mechanism of demographic constraints on extended-family structure than Levy had proposed. High mortality is not the only possible demographic constraint on the frequency of extended families. Berkner's interpretation points to the importance of marriage age as a determinant of the frequency of extended families. In natural fertility populations, age at marriage is the most important influence on generation length. Generation length— along with life expectancy—is a principal determinant of the extent of overlap between generations. If people tend to bear children late in life, then few three-generation families may occur even where mortality is not exceptionally severe.

The much-heralded preindustrial pattern of late marriage in the West necessarily dictated long generations. Therefore, late marriage may have been just as important as high mortality in producing a demographic constraint on the frequency of three-generation families in preindustrial England and America. By the same reasoning, a decline in marriage age during the eighteenth and nineteenth centuries could have been a major source of increase in the frequency of extended families.[5]

The stem-family hypothesis also introduces a mechanism whereby fertility could influence the frequency of extended families, although Berkner is not explicit on this point. Because of the rule that only *one*

5. Hajnal (1965), Outhwaite (1973). On declining marriage age, cf. Wrigley (1968), Levine (1977), Wrigley and Schofield (1983), Glass (1973: 192), and Great Britain, General Register Office (1841–1881), which provides data on the percentage of marriages occurring before age 21.

Geographic comparison lends support to the thesis that age at marriage had important consequences for extended-family structure. The European marriage pattern was confined to northwestern Europe; in eastern and southern Europe, marriage occurred much earlier. There is mounting evidence that family structure was substantially more complex in the South and East. See Hajnal (1982), Czap (1978), Mitterauer and Kagan (1982), P. Laslett (1977a: 15–16), Mitterauer and Sieder (1982: 37), Berkner (1972a), Plakans (1973, 1975), McArdle (1974).

child will remain in his or her parents' household after marriage, all other children must create new nuclear households upon marriage. Thus, it is not simply generation length and mortality that dictate the frequency of stem households in a population that obeys stem-family rules; the level of fertility is also important, because it dictates the number of "extra" children who must form independent nuclear households. High fertility, then, could contribute to a low observed frequency of stem households.

Berkner's argument also points to some important new theoretical wrinkles. First, it shows that extended-family structure could have had a critical *functional* role in a society that had few extended families. Second, it suggests that the majority of the population might have experienced stem-family living arrangements at some point during their lives, even if only a small minority resided in stem households at any one time.

Berkner tested the stem-family hypothesis using evidence from eighteenth-century Austria. He found that a relatively small proportion of households contained both parents and married children. But of those households with very young heads, whose parents would be most likely to be alive, a majority were stem or extended.[6]

This does not, as Berkner seems to suggest, necessarily mean that a majority of households went through a stem phase. Households with very young heads, aged 18 to 27, were atypical. Marriage generally occurred late, and Berkner's data suggest that most people did not become household heads until they reached their thirties. Those who became heads unusually early had greater demographic opportunities to form stem households than most people did.

Furthermore, the very young heads may have been atypical in other respects. It is likely that those with the greatest family resources were able to marry soonest, and wealthy people were probably best able to become household heads unusually early in life. Berkner's data indicate that stem households were almost three times more common among peasants with large landholdings than they were among peasants with little land. If both stem-family structure and early headship were associated with property holding, then Berkner's finding may not have great relevance for the population as a whole. In other words, Berkner's evidence for the stem-family hypothesis may be simply a by-product of intervening variables.

Even if Berkner's case is unproven, however, it remains plausible. But the stem-family hypothesis cannot be tested through the use of statistics

6. Berkner (1972b).

generated directly from the census or lists of inhabitants. Similarly, we cannot directly measure the extent to which the *increase* of extended families in the nineteenth century should be ascribed simply to demographic change.

These issues are not, however, insoluble. The problem is a technical one: we must construct a statistical model to evaluate the effect of demographic factors on family structure.

Although the problem is simply technical, it is nonetheless complex. The remainder of this chapter reviews previous attempts to grapple with the problem of accounting for demographic effects on extended-family structure. First, I discuss analytic approaches to the demography of the extended family. Second, I introduce the methodologies of microsimulation and macrosimulation. Third, I describe and criticize the major previous microsimulation model for the historical study of extended family structure, the socsim model developed by K. W. Wachter and E. A. Hammel. Chapter 5 and appendix C outline my own approach to the problem, which is based on a new demographic microsimulation model.

Analytic Models of Extended-Family Structure

When Levy presented his demographic interpretation of the evolution of family structure, he called for the development of demographic models to aid in understanding the relationship between demography and the extended family. His observation that "actual construction of the demographic models involved appears to be an interestingly complex matter" has proven to be a gross understatement.[7]

The earliest studies of the effects of demographic conditions on family structure were all based on analytic models. These models are limited in a variety of respects, but they set the stage for subsequent research.

Analytic models in demography are an expression of assumptions in mathematical terms. Such models are composed of equations that define the relationships between variables. In the demography of the family, the dependent variables of the equations are characteristics of the household or family, and the independent variables are demographic conditions, principally fertility, mortality, and nuptiality.

The use of analytic models for studying the demography of the family began with A. J. Lotka in 1931, but the earliest serious analysis of the influence of demography on the extended family was undertaken by

7. Levy (1965: 51). See also Fallers (1965).

Ansley Coale. This model appeared in conjunction with Levy's theoretical work.[8] Coale's model is simple and elegant, but it does not address the problem of *frequencies* of extended families. Instead, Coale focuses on the mean size of households under various household-formation rules. Coale's model is not very useful for the present purpose. To estimate the constraining effect of demography on extended-family structure, one would need to know the *percentage* of extended families that would result from a given set of assumptions; mean size of families is not immediately relevant.[9]

Laslett's first publication of his findings that extended families were rare in preindustrial England sparked several more relevant models. The first attempt came from David Glass, who devised a simple analytic model to illustrate the point that three-generation households would be infrequent in a population with high mortality.[10] The structure of the model is crude: Glass assumed that all parents have six children, all born when both parents are aged 30, that all six children have a first child at age 25, and that life expectancy at birth is 25. Glass used binomial expansion to calculate the ratio of surviving parents to surviving children at the time those parents become grandparents—that is, when the parents are 55 and the children are 25. This is the peak moment of overlap between generations; if the children were any younger, there would be no grandchildren, and if they were any older, more of the grandparents would have died. Given these conditions, Glass calculates that only 27 percent of the 25-year-old children would be able to reside with their parents. Implicit in this model is the assumption that only one of several married siblings will reside with a given set of parents, in accordance with the stem-family hypothesis.

Glass's model was the first attempt to measure the influence of demography on the frequency of three-generation families, and several subse-

8. The model assumes constant demographic conditions: very high mortality (life expectancy at birth of 20), early marriage (all women marry at 15), and high fertility (gross reproduction rate = 3.25). Coale shows that if one assumes household formation rules that maximize the frequency of three-generation families, then family size is about 75 percent larger than if one assumes that everyone resided in nuclear families (Coale 1965). Earlier work on the demography of the family includes Lotka (1931), Fourastie (1959), and Kunstadter (1963).

9. Nevertheless, Levy found comfort in Coale's findings, for reasons that are not altogether clear. A modification of Coale's technique, by Thomas K. Burch (1970), was reprinted in conjunction with Peter Laslett's (1972a) main theoretical statement in 1972. It is ironic that Laslett—whose views differ markedly from those of Levy—also found comfort in the results.

10. Glass (1966).

quent models adopted the same basic form. But the model is not very useful. The demographic assumptions are unrealistic; as Glass himself points out, "Life is not like that." Moreover, the model makes no provision for parents-in-law, and it therefore ignores roughly half of potential three-generation families. On the other hand, Glass implicitly assumes that all grandparents have at least one surviving child, and thus he overestimates the proportion of grandparents that could reside with their children. It should also be kept in mind that Glass was not trying to measure the frequency of three-generation families at a single moment in time; rather, his model is intended to estimate the proportion of families that would *ever* go through a three-generation phase. As it happens, the 27 percent figure is probably not far off from the overall percentage of stem families at one moment in time that would result from Glass's assumptions if the various problems with his technique were corrected. But this is just good luck; the biases resulting from the three problems tend to cancel one another out.[11]

In 1969, E. A. Wrigley described a technique that seems to be a modification of Glass's approach.[12] Although the two techniques are similar, Wrigley's approach is more sophisticated. This model accounts for the possibility of residence with parents-in-law as well as with parents. Furthermore, the measurement of three-generation overlap is taken at the mean age of couples instead of the age at which the maximum frequency of vertical extension occurs.

Wrigley assumes that the mean age of married couples is 40, and that the mean age of their parents is 72. He also implicitly assumes that the average probability that a parent of a married person will be alive is equivalent to the probability of surviving from age 40 to age 72. This would not necessarily be true; probability of parental survival depends on the age distribution of married persons and the shape of the mortality curve. Wrigley is really assuming, therefore, that *all* married couples are 40 and *all* of their parents are 72. The model further postulates that married couples have between one and nine children, all born when the couples are aged 32, that everyone marries at 27, and that life expectancy at birth is 32.5.

Wrigley's residence rules are somewhat different from those of Glass; he assumes that widowed parents of the eldest generation always reside with their children, but married ones never do. The latter rule is rather odd, since it contradicts the stem-family model of extended-family forma-

11. See chapter 6.
12. Wrigley (1969); see also Wrigley (1978).

tion. The model employs binomial expansion to measure the proportion of married couples who could reside with their widowed parents or parents-in-law. Under the demographic conditions outlined above, that figure comes out to be 29 percent. Wrigley regards this result as "too crude to be a realistic guide," and he is right. Although this sort of approach may suggest the order of magnitude of three-generation families under a given demographic regime, the author has no means of estimating the extent to which the simplifying assumptions lead to erroneous results.[13]

Historians have taken the results of these models much too seriously and they have often misinterpreted their meaning. Referring to Glass's model, as sophisticated an observer as Lawrence Stone wrote that "owing to the demographic attrition of old people in pre-modern societies, the proportion of conjugal families with grandparents still alive at any one time could never have been more than about twenty-seven percent." In a similar vein, Michael Katz and his associates write that Wrigley "calculated that taking early modern mortality into consideration, no more than 15 [sic] percent of households would ever have three generations present at any time." And Berkner alludes to both Glass and Wrigley with his statement that "two theoretical calculations of family composition under preindustrial demographic conditions estimate respectively that only 27 or 29 percent of the families could contain three generations."[14]

Such sweeping conclusions are completely unjustified and they badly misrepresent Glass and Wrigley. At best, the authors' findings suggest that in a society characterized by late marriage and early death, the maximum frequency of three-generation families might be substantially constrained. If these techniques actually prove anything, it is that analytic models at the household level are an awkward technique for the study of the demography of the extended family.

In spite of their limitations, these early back-of-the-envelope techniques for estimating the frequency of three-generation families set the terms for subsequent analysis of the influence of demography on historical family formation. They established the principle that the effects of demography can be assessed in the context of household formation

13. Brian Bradley and Franklin Mendels (1978) have published a minor modification of Wrigley's approach, but the impact of their refinement is small. Unlike Wrigley, however, Bradley and Mendels seem to place considerable confidence in the model. See also Mendels (1978).

14. Stone (1977a: 24), Katz, Doucet, and Stern (1982: 422), Berkner (1972b: 407). The 15 percent figure quoted by Katz, Doucet, and Stern is in error. Another example of misinterpretation—this time of Coale's model—appears in Wheaton (1975: 609–10).

"rules," e.g, that married siblings do not reside with one another. Such rules allow us to focus on the specific combinations of kin of greatest theoretical interest. All subsequent household-level models of extended-family structure have relied on hypothetical rules.

A major limitation of the techniques discussed so far is that they are exclusively concerned with *vertical* extension—that is, with the size or frequency of three-generation families. They ignore horizontal extension, which results from the presence of siblings, aunts, uncles, nephews, nieces, or cousins of the head or head's spouse. These kin types are responsible for a substantial proportion of extended living arrangements in most populations for which data are available, including preindustrial and nineteenth-century England and America.

It might seem that it is less important to understand the effects of demography on horizontal extension, since in almost any population the majority will always have some sort of living horizontal kin available for coresidence. In fact, demographic conditions are perhaps even more important as a determinant of horizonal extension than they are as a determinant of vertical extension. This is true because in practice the bulk of horizontal extension is confined to kin who possess a narrow set of demographic characteristics.

Coresident horizontally extended kin tend to be "unattached individuals." Unattached individuals are defined as adult bachelors and spinsters, widows, widowers, and orphans. In the United States in 1900, 95 percent of horizontal extension was a consequence of unattached horizontal kin.[15] In addition, horizontally extended kin are typically concentrated in certain age groups; in nineteenth-century England and America, most were in their twenties and thirties. And not all types of horizontally extended relations are likely to coreside; in Western experience the main types of horizontally related kin have been siblings, siblings-in-law, nephews, and nieces.

Those horizontally extended relatives that are likely to reside in extended families thus constitute a small subgroup of all horizontally extended relations. Moreover, the availability of such high-risk horizontally extended kin for residence in extended families is highly sensitive to demographic conditions. For example, the frequency of unattached individuals in a population is a function of age structure, marriage age,

15. That is, 95 percent of horizontally extended families would appear as nuclear families if all unattached family members were removed; this measure ignores headship. (See the definitions of "family" and "family head" in appendix A.) This is based on my tabulation of the 1900 Public Use Sample.

marriage and remarriage rates, mortality, and age intervals between spouses. Demographic change could lead to dramatic change in the pool of unattached horizontally extended kin available to reside in extended families. Therefore, in order to assess the effects of demographic factors on extended family structure, we need to look at horizontal extension as well as vertical extension.

The focus of analytic models on vertical extension is partly a consequence of the preoccupation of historians with the stem-family hypothesis. Horizontally extended families are simply considered less interesting. The use of hypothetical household formation rules also discourages modeling horizonal extension. The rules are not empirically derived; rather, they are based on theories of stem-family formation. Since we have no theory of horizontally extended family formation, any set of rules for analyzing horizontal extension would be arbitrary.

Another reason horizontal extension has been ignored is the logistical difficulty of assessing frequencies of horizontal kin through analytic techniques. In recent years, demographers have made considerable progress in this area.[16] To date, however, no analytic method has been devised for estimating the frequency distribution of horizontal kin broken down by their demographic characteristics. As noted, coresidence of horizontal kin is highly dependent on their characteristics. Thus, current analytic methods are inadequate for developing a model of horizontally extended family structure.

Analytic models are an inexpensive and tidy approach to the study of many demographic problems. As may be apparent, however, they are

16. Although historians have so far given little attention to horizontal extension, some statistical progress in this area has been made by demographers. In 1974, Goodman, Keyfitz, and Pullum described an analytic method that allows estimation of the mean number of extended kin of both vertical and horizontal types that would be available under a given demographic regime. Unlike the techniques developed by the historical demographers, this method was not explicitly concerned with living arrangements. Because of this, the Goodman-Keyfitz-Pullum approach can reveal only the *mean number* of relatives of a given type; it is not capable of estimating the *percentage* of persons with relatives of a given type. Thus, like Ansley Coale's work described above, this model is inappropriate for analyzing the frequency of extended families in real populations. See Goodman, Keyfitz, and Pullum (1974), and their "Addendum" (1975). More recently, Thomas Pullum (1982) derived estimates of the frequency distribution of horizontally extended kin, but he was unable to break those kin down by their age and marital status. Pullum suggested that it might be possible to incorporate such refinements in an analytic model, but because of the complexity involved microsimulation might be a more appropriate approach. Some additional analytic calculations of the demography of kinship include Fourastie (1959), Immerwahr (1967), and Anderson (1972a).

not well adapted to assessing the effect of demographic conditions on historical family structure. To avoid unmanageable complexity, analytic models must make simplifying assumptions. The necessary oversimplifications of analytic models have proven to be a problem even for the study of human fertility. The problem of the extended family is much more complex. We must go beyond estimating the frequency of three-generation overlap or the mean number of certain kin types. To assess the effects of demographic constraints on extended-family structure, we need to know the detailed characteristics of *all* kin available for residence in a family. These data should be in the form of frequency distributions rather than means. Moreover, we should have these figures broken down by characteristics of the family head and his spouse, and also by combinations of kin.

No one has invented an analytic model capable of such feats, and it is doubtful that anyone will.[17] The problem is simply too complex to be efficiently resolved with analytic methodology. Fortunately, alternative methods are available.

Simulation Approaches
During the American Civil War, a Captain Fox was wounded. To occupy himself during his recovery, he derived estimates of *pi* by repeatedly throwing a needle of known length across a standard grating and counting the proportion of times that it fell through.[18]

This was a sort of microsimulation. Captain Fox conducted a series of random trials. The outcome of any one trial provided little new information, but the combination of many trials could yield accurate results.

The broadest definition of simulation includes all attempts to mimic reality. The term has been applied to models of such diverse phenomena as the outbreak of World War I and the process of photosynthesis. But a demographic simulation is a fairly specific kind of model. It is a procedure for allocating demographic events—births, deaths, and marriages—to hypothetical individuals or groups. A simulated population is thereby constructed, the characteristics of which should correspond to the characteristics of a real population that shares the same demographic rates. The simulation approach allows us to measure characteristics of a hypothet-

17. On the limitations of analytic techniques, see Sheps (1969), Barrett (1977), De Vos and Palloni (1984), and De Vos and Ruggles (1986). See also Pullum's comments (1982: 564).
18. Dyke and MacCluer (1973).

ical population that may be difficult or impossible to measure for real populations.[19]

Simulation models fall into two general categories, macrosimulation and microsimulation. Microsimulation, like Captain Fox's experiment, can be viewed as a series of trials. Demographic events are assigned to individuals in order to build up life histories. When sufficiently many individuals have been created, a microsimulation model generates summary statistics.

The allocation of vital events to individuals is governed by predetermined probabilities. The means by which a microsimulation model assigns vital events to hypothetical individuals has been described by Nancy and Richard Ruggles:

> In applying mortality data, for example, the probability of a specific individual's death was based upon the age, sex, and race of that individual, and whether the death actually occurred was determined by this probability and by the generation of a random number. Thus, if the probability of death for a specific individual was determined to be 4 chances in 1,000, a random number from 1 to 1,000 was generated, and if this happened to be 4 or less, a death was considered to take place. By applying this method of generating changes, a complete life process model was simulated for each individual in the sample.[20]

As Gigi Santow points out, this process has the advantage that "nonstationary probabilities can be introduced and analyses can be as detailed as required 'since the output resembles a complete set of data from an ideal survey.'"[21]

19. For descriptions of simulation approaches, see Olinick (1978), Dyke and MacCluer (1973), Sheps (1969), Menken (1981), Santow (1978), and Hammersley and Handscomb (1964).

20. Ruggles and Ruggles (1970).

21. Santow (1978:5). A simple historical application of Monte Carlo simulation was carried out by Herve LeBras (1973), who calculated the proportion of persons at various ages who would having living parents, grandparents, and great-grandparents under varying demographic conditions. Because LeBras considered only ascendant kin, the problem is greatly simplified; the frequency of ascendant kin is essentially a function of mortality and generation length. Other historical microsimulation models include SOCSIM (discussed below), CAMSIM (described in P. Laslett 1984), and my own model MOMSIM (described in chapter 5 and appendix C). These are the only microsimulations devoted to analysis of extended-family structure, although Howell's (1979) model, called AMBUSH, is concerned with extended kin relationships. Demographic applications of microsimulation include Horvitz (1969), Rossi (1975), and Gilbert and Hammel (1966).

Because of the random element, microsimulation is also known as Monte Carlo simulation. Like Captain Fox's tossing of needles, demographic microsimulation models are subject to random error. To minimize this error, it is necessary to generate large populations. There is a trade-off, however—the larger the simulated population, the more expensive the model becomes to run.

The other form of demographic simulation—macrosimulation—works differently. Macrosimulation is a sort of compromise between analytic techniques and microsimulation. Instead of allocating characteristics to individuals, macrosimulation operates at the level of groups. A population is broken into subgroups based on such characteristics as age, sex, and marital status. Over a given time period, a portion of the members of each subgroup will die, give birth, or marry. Death results in removal from the population; other demographic events, such as marriage, result in shifting individuals between subgroups. As time proceeds, all individuals are shifted into *older* subgroups, and the youngest subgroups are filled with newborn babies. Thus, the population is projected over time.

Unlike microsimulation, macrosimulation models provide determinate solutions; there is no random element. It is possible to avoid the random factor because macrosimulation is based on groups rather than on individuals. Suppose that according to a predetermined probability, we know that 10 percent of the population with a given set of characteristics will die in a given period. In a macrosimulation model, we can simply select the subgroup that has the appropriate characteristics and reduce its size by 10 percent. There is no need to determine *which* members of the subgroup will die, so there is no need to introduce randomness. By contrast, because microsimulation constructs *individual* life histories, the random element is essential.

The only real advantage of macrosimulation relative to microsimulation is that the former provides determinate solutions by avoiding the need to introduce random error.[22] As noted earlier, however, we can obtain high accuracy using microsimulation if we generate a sufficiently large number of cases. In effect, then, macrosimulation offers savings of computer time.

There are, on the other hand, major limitations of macrosimulation that outweigh its cost advantages. Like analytic models, macrosimulation generally requires simplifying assumptions that compromise accuracy. Furthermore, if many characteristics of the population must be taken into account—such as characteristics of extended-family members—then the

22. Bongaarts (1981).

number of subgroups required multiplies rapidly and the model becomes unwieldy. By contrast, in a microsimulation model the number of characteristics employed may be increased dramatically without greatly altering the structure or complexity of the model.

Because of the limitations of macrosimulation, it is chiefly employed for simple problems. The most promising macrosimulation model of the family devised to date was developed by John Bongaarts.[23] This model can generate distributions of nuclear-family size and children surviving over the course of a woman's reproductive years, but it cannot be employed for the study of extended-family structure. Although it is likely that more sophisticated macrosimulation models of family relationships may be developed in the future, the technique will never be as powerful or as flexible as the microsimulation approach.[24] My own analysis focuses on microsimulation, since it is the most effective technique currently available for addressing the problem of extended-family structure.

I have developed a microsimulation model specifically to assess the impact of demography on historical extended-family structure; this method is described in appendix C. The only previous microsimulation model designed for this purpose is SOCSIM, developed by Kenneth Wachter and E. A. Hammel.[25] From both a methodological and a theoretical perspective, the SOCSIM model is extremely important. I have therefore devoted the rest of this chapter to discussion of this model.

The SocsIM Demographic Microsimulation Model

On a sunny afternoon in June of 1971, Peter Laslett, Kenneth Wachter, and Eugene Hammel met by accident in Bishop's Hostel of Trinity College, Cambridge. It might seem that these three would have little to talk about; the first is an historian, the second a statistician, and the third an anthropologist. During casual conversation Laslett explained his hypothesis that the people of preindustrial England overwhelmingly preferred to reside in nuclear rather than extended families.

This took Wachter by surprise; although Laslett had published his first findings eight years before, they had not yet found much of an audience outside a small circle of social historians. As the discussion proceeded, the alternative hypothesis was raised that the observed low frequency of stem households in preindustrial England might simply have been a function of demographic conditions. In other words, as Berkner had

23. Bongaarts (1981). See also Watkins and Menken (1984) and Ryder (1975).

24. As shown in appendix C, macrosimulation can be *combined* with microsimulation. This approach offers the efficiency and accuracy of macrosimulation together with the flexibility of microsimulation.

25. Wachter, Hammel, and Laslett (1978).

argued, stem-family structure might have predominated among those with the demographic opportunity to reside in stem families.[26]

It happened that the three scholars were uniquely qualified to address this problem statistically. Hammel, a student of kinship structures in Latin America, was already exploring the use of simulation models for the analysis of kinship; Laslett had access to the best available historical data on both household structure and demographic rates; and Wachter had the technical expertise to carry through the task. And so Wachter, Hammel, and Laslett became collaborators on what was to become a major undertaking: the development of a microsimulation model to measure the effects of demographic conditions on household structure in preindustrial England.

Seven years after their meeting at Bishop's Hostel, Wachter, Hammel, and Laslett published their results in a volume entitled *Statistical Studies in Historical Social Structure*. They concluded that Laslett had been correct all along: "any resort to demography for the sake of reconciling a theory of stem-family formation behavior with such low levels of occurring complex households appears unjustifiable."[27]

Unlike Laslett's earlier work, this volume was subjected to little close scrutiny. The methodology was daunting; besides *Statistical Studies*, two other volumes and several articles were required simply to document the microsimulation model and classification systems employed by the project. Not only historians but also demographers were impressed with the work; the team of researchers seemed to have demonstrated conclusively that Laslett was right and Berkner was wrong.[28]

In fact, the results of Wachter, Hammel, and Laslett's study are ambiguous at best. The research strategy has serious flaws, and the findings that do emerge are consistent with Berkner's interpretation that stem-family structure was preferred. This is not to deny the considerable merits of the work; it was the first study of its kind and it represents an impressive technical achievement. My own methodology has benefited critically from the authors' pioneering labor. But the conclusions based on this early effort are nonetheless misleading.

The authors employ the socsim microsimulation model to analyze household structure in preindustrial England. Socsim is a modification of an

26. Ibid., preface.
27. Ibid.
28. Ibid., Hammel and Wachter (1977), Hammel and Deuer (1977), Hammel et al. (1976). Favorable interpretations by demographers include Bongaarts (1981); Michael Anderson (1980: 32) also gave strong support. Virtually the only critical response came from Fitch (1980).

early version of the demographic microsimulation POPSIM, which was developed to study population growth.

Wachter and Hammel attempt to model not only the effect of demography but also the effect of residence decisions. The model is designed to simulate the living arrangements of the inhabitants of a preindustrial English village of a few hundred souls. Individuals are assigned to households according to a set of hypothetical rules governing residence decisions.

Hypothetical rules in microsimulation are a means of specifying the behavior of the simulated population.[29] Unlike the probabilities used to specify demographic behavior, however, such rules are not empirically determined. There are a variety of ways that hypothetical rules have been used in simulation models.[30] The strategy employed by the SOCSIM modelers consists of devising rules to represent behavior predicted by a particular theory, as a test of that theory. By this means, simulation can be used to disprove theory through counterfactual argument: if the results of the simulation do not correspond to conditions in an observed population, and the fundamental demographic aspects of the model are correct, this proves that the theory—as expressed in the rules—must be incorrect.

Thus, hypothetical rules are not always intended to describe reality; rather, they are hypotheses that are plugged into a model to see what

29. We have encountered hypothetical rules before, in the analytic models of Coale, Glass, and Wrigley. The SOCSIM rules are very different, however, both in terms of their complexity and in terms of their underlying philosophy. In the previous analytic models, the rules do not affect the basic demographic functioning of the system; instead, they define which aspect of the system is to be measured. For example, Glass measures the ratio of married persons to living persons of the previous generation and Wrigley measures the ratio of married couples to widowed parents and parents-in-law. These sorts of rules are to some extent neeessary; one must always make decisions about what one is going to measure relative to what. My own application of hypothetical rules, described in chapter 5, is closer to that of Glass and Wrigley than it is to Wachter and Hammel.

30. In some cases, one may want to devise rules that are deliberately different from reality. For example, one may incorporate hypothetical rules designed to reflect a proposed government policy, in order to see what the effect of such a policy would be; see Orcutt et al. (1976). Alternatively, one may attempt to devise realistic rules that mimic actual behavior as closely as possible. If a simulation incorporating such rules produces aggregate results similar to those directly calculated from an observed population, then this suggests that the rules were actually followed. But we should bear in mind that hypothetical residence rules do not actually allow one to prove hypotheses. Even if a simulation model incorporating supposedly realistic hypothetical rules produces results that correspond closely to a real population, there is no guarantee that the hypothesis is correct; alternative rules almost always exist that could produce similar results. This point is made by Michael Anderson (1980: 35).

effect they have. This is potentially a useful technique for historians since it allows them to conduct a sort of "experiment" in the past.

There are, however, pitfalls. It is difficult to disprove social theory by using hypothetical rules. Social theorists do not ordinarily state their hypotheses so clearly and specifically that these hypotheses can be directly translated into programming instructions. Thus, it is up to the person designing the simulation to interpret any social theory he or she wishes to test. In a sense, then, investigators using hypothetical rules in microsimulation can only disprove social theory of their own creation.[31]

In their attempt to test the stem-family hypothesis, Wachter and Hammel "grew" a population subject to observed preindustrial demographic rates; in the process they applied hypothetical rules governing residence decisions that favored the formation of stem families. They reasoned that if their simulated population showed a greater percentage of stem households than the real preindustrial English population, then demographic constraints could not be the cause of the low percentage of stem households observed in the real population.

In its simplest form, the stem-family hypothesis states merely that one child remained in his or her parents' household after marriage while the rest left home to establish new households. This information is not sufficient to allocate people to households in a microsimulation. For example, where there is more than one child, one must specify which one stays behind after marriage and at what age the others leave home.[32] There is no agreed-upon version of the stem-family hypothesis that covers these situations.

To make a convincing case to historians and sociologists that they had fairly represented the stem-family hypothesis, Wachter and Hammel constructed three sets of hypothetical rules that produce a range of

31. Another problem is that if the rules are kept simple, they will almost inevitably produce results very different from any real population and so "disprove" the theory in question. Simple rules rarely describe behavior realistically because they cannot accommodate variations between different kinds of individuals; a fair test of social theory would have to employ more complicated rules. But complex rules reveal little since it is difficult to determine which aspects of the rules produce the results; see my discussion of this problem below.

32. The rules must also account for every other situation that can crop up. For example, the rules must specify what happens if a child who stays behind is childless or dies before his or her parents. Socsim actually attempts to model entire preindustrial communities. Because of this, it also incorporates hypothetical rules governing such matters as who can marry whom. Further details concerning the rule systems and how they are incorporated into the model can be found in Hammel and Wachter (1977: 113–14) and Hammel et al. (1976).

variation in stem-family frequencies consistent with a variety of interpretations of the hypothesis.[33] According to the first set of rules—called
"primonuptial"—the first child to marry remains in the parents' household after marriage; according to the second set of rules—called "primoreal"—the oldest son remains; and according to the third set—the "ultimonuptial" rules—the last married child remains. Under all three sets of
rules, the other children cannot leave their parents' household until they
are dead or married. Furthermore, according to the rules, if both a
prospective bride and a prospective groom are required to remain in their
parents' household after marriage, that marriage is prohibited.

Space does not permit a detailed critique of the rule systems, but I will
point out a few general problems. Wachter and Hammel adopted the
household as their unit of measurement. Thus, their denominator is the
total number of households in the population; their numerator is the
number of stem households. Accordingly, their measure of the percentage of households that take a stem-family form at any one time is as
dependent on their rules for formation of *nonstem* households as it is on
the *stem*-household formation rules.

As the SOCSIM rules are structured, they not only maximize the proportion of stem households, but they also minimize the proportion of other
households. For example, there is no mechanism for the formation of
solitary households except through the death of all household members
but one; it is impossible to form a new solitary household. Indeed, the
only way new households can be formed is through marriage, and the
model minimizes the frequency of marriages.

SOCSIM is a *closed* model. This means that there is no provision for
migration; marriage partners for members of the simulated population
must be found within the population or the marriage cannot take place.
By contrast, in an *open* simulation model, marriage partners are created
as they are needed. Since marriages cannot take place if there is no
suitable partner within the village, and since the population size runs
about 200, many people in the simulated population must be prohibited
from marriage altogether; it is impossible, in SOCSIM, to marry someone
from the next village. The authors of the model provide no measure of
marriage rates produced by the model, but I suspect that they are unrealistically low.[34]

33. The extent to which these rules fairly represent the stem-family hypothesis is open to
question; see Nancy Fitch's thoughtful review essay (1980).

34. For discussion of the differences between closed and open simulation methods, see
Sheps (1969) and Horvitz et al. (1969).

The procedure for rejecting marriages is described in the following passage from the technical description of SOCSIM. This selection provides some indication of the complexity of the rules:

> If the marriage search has failed—that is, if every potential groom whose JSCOR 6 IRB is prohibited by HOUSHLD from marrying the bride searching for a groom, one additional chance is provided. The program calls HHGROOM(J) again with FWA = J for the male whose JSCOR is the smallest of all those scores greater than IRB, if such a male exists. This is the "best available" of the males rejected by the bride's "choosiness index" . . . If this best available male is still rejected, and if MONTH 5 HHPR ≠ 0, the program prints the message, "No SUITABLE GROOM FOUND."[35]

It is not really fair to quote a passage from a technical description out of context, but it serves to make an important point. One cannot understand the rules of SOCSIM without understanding the entire program. The description of the rules goes on for many pages. In part, this testifies to the excellent documentation of the program. The amount of space devoted to the rules is, however, in large part a consequence of the almost incredible detail of the rules.

The complexity of these rules leads to several difficulties. First, such complexity makes it difficult, if not impossible, for historians to understand thoroughly the way the SOCSIM model actually works. Understanding the rule system thoroughly requires a substantial investment of time even for those well versed in computer programming and microsimulation techniques. This is one reason the SOCSIM model has not been subjected to the kind of rigorous criticism it deserves.

Second, without experimentation it is impossible to know the relative importance of the various provisions of the rule system. Thus, one has no means of determining whether the flaws in the system have significant effects. More generally, one has no means of determining *which aspects* of the rule system produce the overall results.

Third, complex rule systems are necessarily rather arbitrary. Historians and sociologists have rarely devoted more than a few sentences to describing the behavioral rules of the stem-family hypothesis. Since it takes the best part of a volume to describe fully the SOCSIM hypothetical rules, most of the detail is necessarily invented by the authors of the model.

Wachter and Hammel would have been wise to heed the advice of

---

35. Hammel et al. (1976: 57).

Jacquard and Leridon regarding microsimulation models: "If it is too complicated, there is a risk of misintepretation, or to be more exact, of losing sight of important points (or even, if carried to the extreme, of even losing sight of the problem itself) . . . For example, it is illusory to include a variable about which nothing is known."[36] Socsim quickly loses sight of the problem; it is hypothetical rules that take center stage, not demographic conditions. Indeed, in the socsim model, demography is to some extent *dictated* by the hypothetical rules.[37] The central problem that sparked the development of socsim was the effect of demography on historical household structure; in the end, however, socsim is primarily concerned with the effect of rules on household structure.

Even if we took on faith that the socsim rules accurately describe the stem-family hypothesis, the results of the model would be ambiguous. Wachter and Hammel's three sets of rules yield such a broad spectrum of stem-household frequencies that in the end their model reveals little. Assuming for women a life expectancy at birth of 40 and a mean age at marriage of 25, the simulation produces (on average) anywhere from 16 percent to 45 percent stem families at any one time, depending on which version of the hypothetical stem-family rules is applied.[38]

The Cambridge Group has found that in sixty-four English settlements before 1822, an average of 13.2 percent of households appeared as stem families.[39] Thus, if the simulation is accurate and the data from these communities are representative, somewhere between 29 percent and 83 percent of the households that could have appeared as stem households actually did so.[40]

36. Jacquard and Leridon (1974).

37. This occurs because marriage (and thus fertility) can depend on household structure and household structure depends on the rules. The authors' relative lack of concern with the effects of demography is reflected in their choices of unrealistic demographic parameters for their model.

38. Wachter, Hammel, and Laslett (1978: 44, exhibit 4.1).

39. Ibid., p. 74, exhibit 5.3. Actually, in their terms, this is the figure for MLN plus XLN households, which is a slightly more conservative definition of stem households than they employ for their simulation runs; the true percentage of stem households by their definitions would be marginally higher.

40. Wachter and Hammel also allowed their demographic rates to vary, since they were unsure of their accuracy. Overall, if we wish to cover the full range of possible variation in both demographic rates and stem-family rules, their results suggest that between 27 percent and 88 percent of potential stem families actually existed. Ibid., p. 44, exhibit 4.2. The range would have been even greater if the authors had applied the full postulated range of demographic variation to each of the three sets of hypothetical rules. Strictly speaking, one cannot simply divide the percentage of extended households observed by the percentage produced by the simulation to find the "propensity" of households to be stem families,

Wachter, Hammel, and Laslett use their results to argue that demography was not a major constraint on the formation of stem households, since all versions of the simulation produced a higher frequency of stem households than typically existed in English communities.[41] This position is untenable. Let us make an analogy to the analysis of voting statistics. Suppose that 13 percent of the total population voted for a particular candidate, and only 16 percent of the total were eligible to vote. It would be absurd to argue that the restrictions on suffrage were not a major constraint on the percentage of the total population voting for the candidate.[42] But this is exactly the argument made by Wachter and Hammel about stem households. According to their figures, 13 percent of households adopted the stem-family form, and as few as 16 percent were eligible to do so under the most restrictive rule system of the model. If it were an election, 13 percent out of a population at risk of 16 percent would be called a landslide.

Because Wachter and Hammel do not view their problem in terms of the population at risk, they have missed the point. They claim to have shown that demographic constraints were not the principal reason for the low frequency of stem households that have been found in preindustrial England. In fact, their evidence implies the opposite: even assuming the hypothetical rules that most favor their case—those producing the greatest frequency of stem-family households—Wachter and Hammel's results indicate that demographic constraints more than halved the overall percentage of stem-family households. When all three sets of hypothetical rules are taken into account, the socsim evidence is apparently consistent with the interpretation that a majority of individuals who had the option of residing in stem households actually did so.[43]

Beyond the issue of absolute constraints, the authors view socsim as a means of revealing the sensitivity of household structure to variation in specific demographic factors. For each of their three sets of hypothetical

---

because as I point out in appendix A, the total number of households is dependent on household structure. Accordingly, in order to measure propensities we must measure household structure in terms of the individual. Further discussion of these matters appears in chapter 5 and appendix C.

41. Ibid., pp. 64, 80–85, 89.

42. The problem is elucidated if we view it in terms of the population at risk. See appendix A.

43. This might be true even if less than half of the stem households that could exist actually did exist; it all depends on the relative size of stem households compared with other households. Stem households were probably significantly larger than other households because they cannot consist of solitaries and must include nonnuclear relatives. This issue is discussed in chapter 6 and appendix A.

residence rules, Wachter and Hammel ran their model subject to a variety of demographic conditions. They conclude from this analysis that differing demographic conditions lead to only small differences in household structure, and that marriage age has greater influence on household structure than either fertility or mortality.

It might seem that holding the rules constant and allowing the demographic factors to vary would isolate the influence of demography from the influence of residence rules. However, this requires an implicit assumption that is not justified for historical studies of household structure: we must assume that the hypothetical residence rules are realistic. Models that depend on residence rules can only reveal the effects of demography on household structure within the context of a particular set of residence rules; thus, they are confined to the study of the interaction between rules and demography. If the criteria employed by the simulation model for the formation and dissolution of households are not the same as the criteria employed by the real population, then we cannot assume that the effects of demographic variation on household structure will be similar in the model population and the real population.

An example will serve to clarify this point. Let us assume that we are interested in analyzing households consisting of parents who reside with their married children. We postulate the hypothetical rule that such households are formed upon the marriage of a child, in accordance with the stem-family hypothesis. Suppose that the real population does not follow the stem-family rules and such households are formed when elderly widowed parents move in with their married children, after they can no longer maintain a household of their own. Under these circumstances, a simulation model based on our hypothetical rule will show that residence of parents with married children is quite sensitive to age at marriage; the earlier children are married, the longer the period of coresidence. By contrast, in the real population the relationship of marriage age to household structure would be substantially weaker, because the marriage of children would not lead directly to the formation of households containing parents with married children. Furthermore, the role of mortality would be smaller in the simulation than in the real population, because mortality is the most important determinant of widowhood. Thus, since the mechanism postulated by the hypothetical rules is unrealistic, our model cannot accurately assess the impact of demographic factors.

Residence rules are almost inevitably unrealistic, since the real world is simply too complex to encapsulate in a computer program. Consequently, a simulation model based on hypothetical rules is a poor device for analysis of the effects of demography on historical household structure.[44]

The socsim demographic microsimulation program is probably the most complex statistical model ever created for the study of historical social structure. But heavy artillery is not the most effective technique for catching mice. The next chapter proposes a better mousetrap.

44. If the problems posed by unrealistic rules could somehow be overcome, we would still be faced with a second assumption. By varying the demographic rates while we hold the rules constant, we are implicitly assuming that demographic factors have no effect on residence rules. In reality, of course, a dramatic shift in demographic conditions—such as the Irish potato famine—would almost certainly influence norms governing residence decisions. More subtle demographic variation probably also affects residence rules. To achieve realistic rules under varying demographic conditions, therefore, we must also allow the rules to vary.

Thus, we face Catch-22. On the one hand, we must hold the rules constant in order to isolate the role of demography. On the other hand, we must allow the rules to vary if we wish them to be realistic enough to accurately capture the effects of demographic variation. This problem—which is shared by my own approach—is further discussed in chapter 5 and appendix C.

5 Analytic Strategies

This is not an age for mysteries, except where the mysteries properly belong. I am certain that married life, in its relation to the family and civilization, presents no very great mystery. Its facts and laws can be studied and known. It requires neither great philosophical skill nor scientific training to understand them.

John B. Robins, *The Family: A Necessity of Civilization* (1896)

"You may place considerable confidence in Mr. Holmes, sir," said the police agent loftily. "He has his own little methods, which are, if he won't mind me saying so, just a little too theoretical and fantastic, but he has the makings of a detective in him. It is not too much to say that once or twice, as in the business of the Sholto murder and the Agra treasure, he has been more nearly correct than the official force."

A. Conan Doyle, *The Adventures of Sherlock Holmes* (1891)

Like the little methods of Mr. Holmes, my analytic strategies are perhaps too theoretical and fantastic. But if we are to unravel the mysteries of the extended family in the nineteenth century, we must adopt unconventional principles of detection.

This chapter is limited to the minimum information necessary to understand the demographic results presented in chapter 6. I describe my principal strategies of analysis and point out the most egregious of the assumptions of my demographic model. I do not, however, say much about the model itself; those who wish to understand more of the sordid details must turn to appendix C. But first, let me introduce some conceptual issues and explain my general approach.

Levels of Measurement and Residential Propensities

Patterns of coresidence between kin are largely determined by the availability of kin. Thirty-year-old women, for example, rarely reside with their married daughters. This is not because 30-year-old women have any special aversion to living with their married daughters, but rather because very few 30-year-olds *have* married daughters.

Demography affects family structure by determining the characteristics of the pool of available kin. Our concern, then, is with those demographic factors that can determine entry into or departure from the kin group. Thus for the most part I have limited my discussion to demography in the narrowest sense; specifically, as employed here, demography refers to those variables most directly connected with the frequency and timing of births, deaths, and marriages.

Births, deaths, and marriages are not the sole demographic determinants of family structure. Variables that fall within a broader definition of demography—such as race and migration—also exert considerable influence on the family.[1] Furthermore, the most interesting determinants of family structure—at least from the perspective of social historians—are not the demographic ones. Living arrangements are profoundly affected by residence decisions based on economic and cultural considerations, such as family economies, inheritance systems, and social norms. To uncover the ways in which these things affect family structure, we must distinguish the basic demographic context in which residence decisions are made. If we are interested in family structure because it provides a means of assessing social behavior, then it is crucial that we determine what kinds of living arrangements are demographically feasible.

It is convenient, then, to divide the determinants of family structure into two categories. First, there are the demographic factors, narrowly conceived. These include all those variables than can affect the frequency and characteristics of living kin available for coresidence. The second category consists of everything else; it encompasses all influences on family structure that are not a function of the pool of available kin. Hereafter, I refer to this second category as "residential preferences." This term should not be taken to imply volition; in certain cases, residen-

---

1. I distinguish "narrow" demographic variables from other social variables not because they have different causes, but rather because they determine the membership of the kin group. Once the demographic events of birth, marriage, and death have occurred, the range of potential family members with whom each individual could reside is fixed, and cannot be influenced by the individual (except perhaps through murder, which is itself a demographic event in the narrow sense). Migration and race effect the pool of living kin only because they affect demographic behavior in the narrow sense; see note 5 in appendix C. Migration is in a different category from race, however, since the act of migrating may make it logistically impossible for an individual to reside with certain relatives. Nevertheless, there are several reasons for considering migration separately from births, marriages, and deaths. First, the act of moving is itself a residence decision; moving between cities or between countries may prevent coresidence, but then, moving down the block has the same effect. Second, we lack sufficient historical data on the processes of migration to incorporate it into a demographic model without seriously compromising accuracy. Finally, the consequences of migration for family structure can be directly studied using cross-sectional data; there is really no need to resort to the sorts of methods described in this essay.

tial preferences as defined here may be beyond the control of the individuals involved.[2]

The realm of demography is important principally because it gets in the way: we need to isolate the effects of demography on family structure chiefly in order to get a handle on the nondemographic sources of residential behavior. Ideally, one would want to measure what family structure would be like in the absence of demographic constraints; that is, one would want to measure residential preferences.

Previous demographic models have not attempted to measure residential preferences. The models of extended-family structure described in the last chapter are based on hypothetical residence rules; they *assume* a theoretical set of residential preferences at the outset. Such an approach can reveal only the combined effects of demographic conditions and hypothetical rules. If we want to distinguish demographic effects from economic and cultural influences on family structure, we cannot begin with highly stylized assumptions about people's preferences. Instead, we should attempt to describe residence "rules" empirically.

Why, then, have previous models started out with a set of assumptions about residential preferences? Once again, the issue of measurement rears its ugly head. Hypothetical rules in models of extended-family structure are necessitated by the convention of measuring residential patterns at the level of households. One cannot create hypothetical extended households without having some means of allocating individuals to households. This means that one must make some sort of assumptions about individual residential preferences. Households don't make residence decisions; people do. And it is impossible to assess individual-level residential preferences using household-level data.[3]

Individual-level measurement allows us to estimate residential preferences without knowing the mechanisms of household formation in advance. Daniel Scott Smith has proposed that family structure should ideally be measured according to the "propensity" of individuals to reside with their relatives.[4] "Propensity" is defined as the extent to which individuals who have the demographic possibility of residing with a given set of kin actually do so. For example, instead of measuring the percent-

2. For example, two relatives cannot reside together if one of them resides in jail. But residence in jail could be considered to be a residential preference on the part of the government.

3. See appendix A.

4. D. S. Smith (1981).

age of the population that lives with their grandchildren, we can measure the percentage of grandparents who live with their grandchildren.

The use of propensities allows us to measure family structure relative to the population at risk of residing with a given set of kin. This automatically accounts for the main effects of demographic factors.[5] Demography affects family structure by determining the structure of the kin group; measurement by residential propensities means measurement relative to the pool of available kin. This gives us a strategy for filtering out the effects of purely demographic factors so that we may uncover residential preferences based on economic and cultural considerations.

By restricting ourselves to the population at risk of residing with a given set of kin, we shift our focus away from an experiential description of residential patterns. If we wish simply to describe the living arrangements of people in the past as a means of reconstructing daily life, then measurement by propensities is not desirable; we should instead measure the overall percentage of the population residing in each type of household. If we wish to go beyond experiential description and analyze residential decision making, then we must isolate the overarching effects of demography on the kin pool.

Smith does not suggest a practical means of measuring living arrangements in terms of propensities and it is not a simple task. The measurement of residential propensities requires knowledge of the potential living arrangements of each individual. We must know in particular what kinds of relatives existed—both inside and outside the household—with whom each individual could reside. Although historical sources tell us much about family structure within the household, they generally provide little direct evidence about kin relationships outside the household. Thus, to take Smith's example, we ordinarily have no direct means of measuring the percentage of elderly who were grandparents, and we therefore cannot measure the propensity to reside with grandchildren. Meaningful interpretation of data on family relationships within the household requires information about kin groups generally.

---

5. The simple form of residential propensities does not *fully* account for the direct effects of demography on family structure for two reasons. First, propensities do not account for the possible effects of having particular combinations of kin. These could be important, for example, in a society in which stem-family rules were actually followed. Second, residential propensities only take the *existence* of relatives of particular types into account; they do not control for any additional effects of having multiple kin. A further potential problem is that family structure itself may affect demographic conditions; see Burch and Gendall (1970). My application of residential propensities has some additional wrinkles that circumvent these problems to some extent; see the discussions in note 10 and in appendixes C and D.

Even though we cannot directly measure the availability of kin in most historical contexts, we can infer a great deal about kin groups as long as we know enough about demographic conditions. To draw such inferences, we need to construct a demographic model of kinship.

Because my own model was primarily designed for the calculation of residential propensities, it is essentially a model of kinship rather than a model of household structure. Given a specific set of demographic conditions, the model can estimate the proportion of individuals of each age, sex, and marital status who would have living kin or combinations of living kin of specific types. The types of kin generated by the model include maternal and paternal grandparents, parents, parents-in-law, aunts, uncles, aunts-in-law, uncles-in-law, spouses, siblings, siblings-in-law, cousins, children, children-in-law, nieces, nephews, nieces-in-law, nephews-in-law, and grandchildren. These relational categories can be further broken down by age, sex, and marital status.

By themselves, these figures on frequencies of available kin are of little use. To assess the effects of demographic variation on extended-family structure in the past, it is necessary to boil down the raw figures on availability of kin into a form that is conceptually accessible and that focuses on those kin relationships that are empirically or theoretically most significant.

I have adopted two strategies for analyzing the relationship between the availability of kin and historical family structure. First, I employ a technique that I call "standard propensities." This approach allows estimation of what the effects of demographic variation on family structure would be if residential preferences were held constant. The second strategy involves the use of hypothetical rules. Despite my strong reservations about hypothetical rules, they can play a useful role as a supplementary analytic technique. My implementation of hypothetical rules differs both conceptually and methodologically from that of previous microsimulators.

These two analytic strategies are described in this chapter. A detailed description of my demographic microsimulation model—which is called MOMSIM—can be found in appendix C. This description is long and complicated, and I sympathize with those who would rather avoid it. But nothing about it is conceptually very difficult and I have avoided the use of technical language wherever possible. Above all, my goal has been to impart a profound sense of the mushiness of statistical speculation. Appendix C is essential reading for anyone who wishes to understand fully how my results were derived. It is also advisable for those who entertain notions that this sort of history is scientific.

There are many potential sources of error in demographic models of kinship, but one stands out above the rest. It is important enough that it should be addressed here in the text, rather than buried in an appendix. Accordingly, we will take a brief excursion before the discussion of strategies.

The Whopper Assumption

Microsimulation works by creating life histories for a hypothetical population on the basis of predetermined probabilities. The procedure for assigning life-course events to individuals involves a variety of assumptions that are, in varying degrees, unrealistic. A discussion of these assumptions appears in appendix C.

When demographic models are used for the study of kinship, there is an additional assumption and this one is a Whopper. The life history of each individual in a kin group is assigned independently of all the other individuals in the group. This implies that the characteristics of one member of a kin group are entirely uncorrelated with the characteristics of other members of the kin group. This is almost certainly wrong. Members of the same kin group, in a real population, will generally share many of the same characteristics—what one might term a demographic family resemblance. For example, family members often belong to the same ethnic group, class, and religion and they frequently reside in the same part of the country. For these reasons, members of the same kin group are probably more similar to one another in demographic behavior than they are to persons randomly selected from the population as a whole. For example, a kin group in which the members are poor will probably experience systematically higher mortality than a kin group with wealthy members. Similarly, some kin groups belong to ethnic groups that tend to marry young, so members of such kin groups would tend to marry younger than the rest of the population.

The principle holds for all demographic characteristics: one would expect greater homogeneity within a kin group than within a group of similar size comprised of individuals selected randomly from the population. The members of some kin groups in the real population will consistently experience more severe mortality, later marriage, or lower fertility than general population. Such shared characteristics would tend to minimize the availability of kin. Conversely, members of other kin groups in the real population would consistently have characteristics that maximize the frequency of kin. Within a demographic model, on the other hand, there is no reason for some kin groups *systematically* to favor the availability of kin, and other kin groups *systematically* to minimize the frequency of kin; any differences between kin groups are entirely the product of random variation.

The assumption that the characteristics of members of a kin group are uncorrelated should not lead to error in the aggregate number of kin of any particular variety. However, the model will produce less variation in the frequency of kin of any particular type than would occur in a real population. For example, one would expect that a smaller proportion of the simulated population would have many grandchildren—say, two or more—than in a real population with the same demographic characteristics. In addition, one would expect that in the simulated population there would be a smaller proportion of persons with very few grandchildren—say, fewer than one—than would be found in the real population. On average, the two effects would tend to cancel out, so the mean number of available grandchildren estimated by the model should still be quite accurate.

But as I have pointed out before, for the analysis of the effects of demography on historical family structure the mean number of kin of a given type is much less important than the frequency distribution. In particular, we must determine the proportion of the population that has *one or more* kin of a given type available for coresidence.

Accordingly, the assumption of independence in the demographic characteristics of different members of a kin group could have serious consequences. To the extent that exaggerated homogeneity of characteristics yields exaggerated homogeneity of kin frequencies, the model will tend to underestimate the proportion of individuals having unusually few available kin of a given type. In other words, the model probably *overestimates* the proportion of the population who have *one or more* available kin of a given type.

The adverse effects of this assumption are particularly serious for those kin types most likely to occur in combination. For example, the error should not affect the proportion of the population with a living mother, since it is only possible to have one mother and her chance of being alive depends entirely on her own characteristics. By contrast, it is possible to have many grandchildren. If grandchildren in a given kin group behave homogeneously with respect to mortality, then the odds are greater that all will have died or that all will survive. Put another way, in a real population the standard deviation of the number of available grandchildren would be greater than in the simulated population.

There are two special cases of the Whopper Assumption that have special relevance for assessing the effects of demographic constraints on the frequency of three-generation families in preindustrial Europe. First, the Whopper Assumption implies that age at marriage is unrelated to age of parental death. Since the preindustrial pattern of late marriage was probably at least partly a consequence of people waiting to receive their inheritance before they married, we would expect a strong correlation between marriage age and parental longevity.[6] Such a correlation would minimize the average interval between marriage and parental deaths. It would reduce the aggregate amount of time spent after parental deaths and before marriage, and it would also reduce the aggregate amount of time spent after marriage and before parental deaths. Therefore, if those who married early tended to have parents who died young and those who married late tended to have long-surviving parents, the overall overlap between the marriage of children and the death of their parents would be minimized. Since demographic models must assume that there is no correlation between age at marriage and parental longevity, they almost inevitably overestimate the potential for formation of three-generation families.

The second special case of the Whopper Assumption has to do with the mortality of husbands and wives. The Whopper Assumption implies that the death of one partner in a marriage is entirely unrelated to the death of the other. Although I know of no data on this for the preindustrial period, there is ample evidence for a correlation of spouses' longevity in the twentieth century and there is no reason to believe that this is a new phenomenon.[7] A correlation between the life expectancy of husbands and wives is important because it only takes one living member of the eldest generation to form a three-generation family. If the men and

6. That a positive correlation existed between marriage age and parental longevity in the preindustrial West is now a commonplace; see Ohlin (1961), Habakkuk (1953), Wrigley (1978), D. B. Smith (1978), D. S. Smith (1973b), Russell (1948), Greven (1970), Hajnal (1982), Berkner (1972b), Goody, Thirsk, and Thompson (1976). Recently, Levine (1982) has proposed the revisionist argument that there was an *inverse* relationship between marriage age and parental longevity in preindustrial England, but his analysis is badly flawed. Levine's findings are mainly a by-product of chronological change. The failure to control for change over time is exacerbated by Levine's omission of crucial categories of marriages. A simple back-of-the-envelope calculation using Levine's data together with model life-table survival rates can illustrate the point that he would probably have found a strong positive association between paternal longevity and marriage age if he had focused on marriages before 1750 among people who had living fathers until they were at least 14 years old.

7. A related violation of the Whopper Assumption is suggested by Walling's (1904: 83) comment, that the offspring of remarriages "are generally vitiated in blood, sickly and predisposed to all morbific agencies." This implies a positive correlation between the mortality of individuals and the mortality of their parents' former spouses.

women who survived long enough to form three-generation families tended to be married to one another—and therefore concentrated in a small number of families instead of randomly dispersed throughout the population—the maximum frequency of three-generation families would be reduced. To the extent that they occurred in combination, the long-surviving members of the eldest generation would be "wasted."

We cannot tell how badly these two special violations of the Whopper Assumption would distort the predictions of a demographic model of kinship. But these examples serve to underscore my comments about the Whopper Assumption in general. Any estimates of the availability of kin derived from a method depending on the Whopper Assumption are likely to be inflated, and probably substantially so. Since all techniques devised to date incorporate the Whopper Assumption, all of them probably underestimate the effects of demography on family structure.

The greater the detail with which we measure kin types, the fewer the problems that will crop up as a result of assuming no systematic rela- tionships between the characteristics of different members of the same kin group. This is because the probability that a category of kin will occur in combination is reduced if categories of kin are defined narrowly. For example, the odds are generally high that an individual will have multiple living siblings, but the odds of having multiple widowed sisters between 45 and 49 years of age are always low. If there is never or almost never more than one individual within a given category of kin, the problems I have been discussing are largely circumvented. This is one advantage of classifying kin simultaneously by their age, sex, type, and marital status.

The severity of this problem also depends on the strategy employed to relate the availability of kin to actual living arrangements. If one is using the technique of standard propensities (discussed below), any small errors in the model are largely irrelevant, as long as such errors are consistent; the reasons for this will be made clear presently. On the other hand, any simulation technique that depends on hypothetical rules will probably overestimate the proportion of the population capable of resid- ing with extended kin. This caution applies equally to my own use of stem rules, described below, and to the socsim model discussed in chapter 4. The Whopper Assumption, of course, applies not only to my own model but also to all demographic models of the family.

The Standard Propensities Approach

I have already introduced the concept of residential propensities. The reader will recall that propensities are a technique for measuring family structure relative to the population demographically capable of adopting particular living arrangements. For example, the propensity to reside with grandchildren is the proportion of grandparents who reside with grandchildren. Residential propensities can help us to distinguish residential preferences from the strictly demographic determinants of family structure. This section describes how residential propensities can be calculated with the momsim demographic model and explains how they can be applied in the analysis of the long-term effects of demographic change on extended-family structure.

If we possess detailed information about the living arrangements and demographic conditions of a population, my simulation model allows us to calculate detailed residential propensities. The calculation of propensities for specific types of kin is illustrated in tables 5.1 through 5.3. Table 5.1 is a fragment of output produced by the model; it shows estimates of the availability of sisters and grandsons of family heads in the United States in 1900. I chose the United States in 1900 because excellent data on both demographic conditions and living arrangements are available. These figures represent the approximate percentage of persons in 1900 who had extended kin of particular types available for coresidence.[8]

From the census we can measure the proportion of persons in 1900 who resided in families that actually contained particular types of extended kin. These figures are contained in table 5.2. Note that all the figures are low, especially those for married and widowed sisters and grandsons.

Table 5.3 shows the propensities to reside with specific types of sisters and grandsons—that is, the percentage of persons who could have resided with an extended relative of the indicated type who actually did so. These figures were derived by dividing table 5.2 by table 5.1.

The figures in table 5.3 show that there is a great deal of variation in residential propensities with individual characteristics. For example, the propensity to reside with elderly spinster sisters is several hundred times as great as the propensity to reside with elderly married sisters. Because of this, propensities calculated for broad classifications of kin—which do not break down relatives by their age, sex, marital status, and type—are not very useful. But detailed residential propensities constitute a revealing index of residential preferences. A fuller set of residential propensities for 1900 is presented and discussed in appendix D.

Ideally, one would want to calculate detailed residential propensities

8. Note that relationships are classified according to relationship to family head; see appendix A. Bear in mind that "family head," as employed in this work, is not a census classification but simply a means of designating standard reference persons in order to describe biological relationships. The classification in table 5.1 assumes constant propensities to reside with family heads who have a given set of characteristics; see note 12.

Table 5.1. Percentage of Individuals with Available Kin of Selected Types, United States, 1900

Age of Sisters	Sisters of Head		
	Single	Married	Widowed
0–9	1.44	0.00	0.00
10–19	8.34	1.13	0.07
20–29	8.17	15.62	0.84
30–39	4.26	29.72	2.92
40–49	1.65	29.50	4.29
50–59	1.74	16.26	5.11
60–69	0.36	6.40	4.16
70+	0.10	1.36	1.85

Age of Grandsons	Grandsons of Head		
	Single	Married	Widowed
0–9	10.66	0.00	0.00
10–19	5.34	0.13	0.00
20–29	1.28	1.03	0.00
30–39	0.05	0.43	0.00

Table 5.2. Percentage of Individuals Actually Residing with Kin of Selected Types, United States, 1900

Age of Sisters	Sisters of Head		
	Single	Married	Widowed
0–9	0.067	0.000	0.000
10–19	0.418	0.000	0.000
20–29	0.657	0.078	0.087
30–39	0.472	0.067	0.081
40–49	0.375	0.034	0.066
50–59	0.188	0.037	0.074
60–69	0.121	0.070	0.032
70+	0.066	0.000	0.041

Age of Grandsons	Grandsons of Head		
	Single	Married	Widowed
0–9	2.580	0.000	0.000
10–19	1.015	0.009	0.000
20–29	0.154	0.027	0.000
30–39	0.006	0.000	0.001

Table 5.3. Propensities for Individuals to Reside with Kin of Selected Types, United
States, 1900 (in Percentages; Table 5.2 Divided by Table 5.1)

Age of Sisters	Sisters of Head		
	Single	Married	Widowed
0–9	4.65	0.00	0.00
10–19	5.01	0.00	0.00
20–29	8.04	0.50	10.31
30–39	11.08	0.22	2.80
40–49	22.75	0.11	1.53
50–59	10.81	0.23	1.47
60–69	33.74	0.10	0.79
70+	65.71	0.00	2.26

Age of Grandsons	Grandsons of Head		
	Single	Married	Widowed
0–9	24.21	0.00	0.00
10–19	19.01	6.89	0.00
20–29	12.05	2.61	0.00
30–39	11.62	0.00	1.45

for a variety of times and places before the late nineteenth century in order to assess changing patterns of residence decisions. In fact, this is impossible. Our knowledge of family structure in the period before 1850 is based on tiny "censuses" of local populations. These data sources do not usually provide detailed demographic characteristics—age, sex, and marital status—at the individual level. Moreover, the number of cases involved is too small to calculate meaningful residential propensities. We can deal with the problem of random error within the microsimulation by generating a large hypothetical population, but there is not way to cope with random variation in the real population. But even if we cannot calculate preindustrial propensities, my method offers an alternate strategy for the analysis of the effects of long-term demographic change on family structure.[9]

To distinguish the role of demographic change from the role of changing residential preferences, we must isolate the independent effects of each of these two factors. Demographic conditions and residential preferences

9. The files of the Cambridge Group might be used to construct very rough residential propensities, but since these data for the most part do not include information on age, much variation would be missed. In practical terms, detailed and reasonably accurate residential

change simultaneously. Together, they produce the observed changes of family structure. By asking how demographic change affects family structure, we are implicitly asking how family structure would have changed if residential preferences had remained constant, but demographic conditions had varied.

The residential propensities from 1900 can be employed as *standard* propensities. By standard propensities, I mean a set of residential propensities that are used to define a constant relationship between the availability of kin and residential patterns. By combining a set of standard propensities with data on availability of kin corresponding to alternate demographic conditions, we can infer—at least approximately—the influence of demographic changes. Thus, standard propensities can be used as a yardstick for assessing the independent role of demography in determining residence patterns.

Standard propensities allow us to calculate what aggregate family structure would have been like under varying demographic conditions if residential propensities had been constant and had conformed to those of the standard population. With the MOMSIM model, we can calculate the availability of specific types of kin under differing demographic conditions. As demographic conditions change, so does the distribution of available kin of different types. In terms of extended-family structure, some types of kin—such as widowed mothers—are much more important than others—such as cousins. To assess the overall effect of changing availability of kin on the frequency of extended living arrangements, we can adopt a standard set of weights that reflect the relative importance of each kin type in the standard population. This is the purpose of standard propensities. They can be viewed as a means of systematically weighting specific kinds of kin to derive meaningful summary measures of the effects of demography on family structure.

The use of standard propensities to evaluate the effects of varying demographic conditions on family structure is analogous to the use of a price index to assess inflation. A price index is a summary measure of the

propensities cannot be constructed except on the basis of individual-level census data that includes a variable on relation to head.

By way of consolation, let us bear in mind that calculation of detailed residential propensities for the preindustrial period would not directly tell us whether or not demographic change could explain the rise of the extended family in the nineteenth century. Residential propensities provide a measure of family structure with the demography removed. By themselves, the propensities cannot tell us about the role of demography. We need to put the demography back in and boil down these detailed figures into a form that is conceptually accessible and that focuses on those kin relationships that are most significant.

prices for a group of commodities. Prices do not change uniformly, and not all commodities are equally important. To compare the general level of prices across time, we adopt a standard set of weights for different commodities according to their relative importance. The imposition of a standard set of weights is unrealistic, since the relative importance of different commodities is constantly changing. But the distortion is inescapable. In the real world, both the distribution of prices and the distribution of consumption of commodities are in constant flux. If we did not adopt a standard set of weights reflecting the relative importance of different commodities, we would be unable to disentangle the effects of changing prices from the effects of changing consumption patterns.

My technique is also comparable to the use of direct standardization of age structure to compare death rates between populations. To distinguish the effects of differences in the age distribution from the effects of differences in the level of mortality, we make the counterfactual assumption that the populations have an identical age distribution. We choose a "standard" population and weight the age-specific mortality rates by the proportion of the standard population in each age category. If the standard age distribution is inappropriate and the populations differ radically in their age pattern of mortality, direct standardization can yield highly misleading results. Standardization does not, therefore, uncover the pure differences of mortality with the intervening factor of age structure removed. But it does at least allow us to see what the general magnitude and direction of mortality differences would be if age structure could be held constant.

The same limitations apply to the use of standard propensities for analyzing the effects of demographic change on family structure. To isolate the role of demography we must assume constant propensities. Just as in the case of price indices or direct standardization, however, there is a catch: residential propensities were not really constant. The distribution of residential propensities is no more likely to remain constant than is the distribution of prices. Whenever substantial changes in the relative importance of specific types of kin have occurred, any standard set of weights may be misleading. Moreover, the propensities themselves are to some extent a function of demographic conditions.[10] These

10. Consider, for example, a society in which it was the norm for one child—but no more than one—to reside with his or her parents after marriage. Such behavior would be consistent with stem-family rules. In such circumstances, we would expect the propensity to reside with parents to decline if fertility increased and vice versa. Where such problems are known to exist, they could be handled through the use of conditional propensities, although

are a potential sources of bias. We should bear in mind, however, that the same potential error exists whenever social scientists hold one or more variables constant in order to assess the independent effects of another variable.

Unless we adopt some kind of standard, we have no means of disentangling the relative importance of changing availability of kin and changing propensities to reside with specific types of kin. By holding propensities constant and allowing the availability of kin to vary, we can at least begin to get a handle on the problem.[11]

this would further complicate an already overelaborate technique. The difficulty could be minimized simply by employing alternate standard-propensities populations, e.g., by first combining the residential propensities of population A with the demographic characteristics of population B, and then combining the demographic characteristics of population A with the residential propensities of population B. This approach is analogous to the use of alternate standard-age distributions when directly standardizing demographic rates. Such a strategy cannot be employed, of course, unless the residential propensities corresponding to all the populations being compared are known.

Given our limited state of knowledge about the historical demography of the family, the partial dependence of residential propensities on demographic conditions does not seriously compromise the method. All of our measures of historical living arrangements and demographic conditions are highly approximate, and what we really need to evaluate the role of demography is a set of weights reflecting the approximate importance of different kin types. It is much more important that unmarried kin have tenfold the residential propensities as married kin than it is that propensities to reside with elderly parents may be affected by fertility. As we begin to map the patterns of residential propensities in different times and places, we will be in an increasingly better position to generalize about the ways in which demography affects propensities.

An additional potential problem stems from the fact that living arrangements may be influenced by the *number* of living kin as well as by the existence of one or more kin. For example, a person with ten surviving siblings may have a greater chance than a person with only one surviving sibling of living with one or more siblings. But this is probably not a major factor, compared with the influence of the availability of *any* kin of a specific type. In 1900, elderly women with multiple surviving children were not substantially more likely to reside with a child than were elderly women with only one surviving child. This phenomenon was noted by D. S. Smith (1979a). If we found that the *number* of kin of any type was a principal determinant of living arrangements, then a more complex tabulation procedure might be required. However, because of the great detail of momsim's main table (see appendix C), multiple kin of a particular type are available relatively rarely, so the number of kin is a moot point.

11. It might seem at first that we should do the opposite, that is, hold the availability of kin constant and allow the residential propensities to vary. After all, our main interest is residential decision making, not the availability of kin. The goal is to *eliminate* the effects of demographic variation so that we can understand the nature of changing residence decisions. If we could hold demographic conditions constant, then we could assess how family structure would have changed if there had been no demographic change.

As noted, however, we cannot allow the propensities to reside with specific types of kin to

My strategy is to calculate what the distribution of family types *would be* in a population that shared the same *propensities* as the U.S. population in 1900, but which had a different set of demographic conditions. This is practical since even though we lack sufficient data to calculate detailed propensities for the period before the nineteenth century, we can mimic with a moderate degree of accuracy the demographic regimes of a broad range of historical periods. We also have empirically observed measures of aggregate family structure since at least the seventeenth century. By comparing *actual* family structure to the *hypothetical* family structure that would have resulted if residential propensities had been constant, we can infer the extent to which residential propensities must have changed.

The procedure for calculating what family structure would be like if we combined the standard propensities from the United States in 1900 with demographic conditions corresponding to a different time and place is fairly straightforward. First, we calculate the residential propensities for the standard population, as described above. Next, we run the model using alternative demographic parameters. The simulation results provide data on the proportion of persons with available kin of each type, age, sex, and marital status under the alternate demographic conditions. These figures are then multiplied by the corresponding standard propensities from 1900. This yields the proportion of the population that would have resided with each specific type of kin if propensities had remained constant.[12]

---

vary since we lack sufficient data to calculate propensities in most historical periods. As an alternative, we could invent hypothetical propensities, but there would be little point to this exercise. Any assumed system of propensities would necessarily be arbitrary, and we would end up demonstrating only the self-evident fact that different propensities yield different family structures when demography is held constant. This is, in effect, the conclusion of the SOCSIM modelers. The strategy brings us no nearer to the goal of accounting for the effects of demographic change on family structure.

Demography is much better understood than residential decision making and it seems to operate more systematically. For purely pragmatic reasons, then, the most sensible approach is to hold residential propensities constant and measure the effects on family extension of alternative demographic regimes.

12. In addition to assuming that propensities to reside with kin remain constant, we must also postulate that propensities to reside with family heads who have a given set of characteristics remain constant. This allows us to estimate a hypothetical proportion of persons under alternative demographic circumstances who would reside with a family head of each age, sex, and marital status. Let me reiterate that family headship, as used here, is simply a means of designating a consistent reference person within a family; see appendix A.

The proportion of persons residing with family heads of each age, sex, and marital status

I have devoted considerable space to discussion of the limitations of hypothetical rules as a strategy for understanding the interaction of demography and family structure. Let us consider the points of similarity and difference between hypothetical rules and standard propensities. Hypothetical rules are simply a means of systematically describing a theoretical set of residential preferences. Given a constant set of residence rules, one can vary the demographic parameters of a model to see how family structure would be affected. Standard propensities are also a means of describing residential preferences, and the strategy of analysis is similar. But the propensities are not designed to maximize any particular type of family, such as three-generation families. Standard propensities may be viewed as a sort of probabilistic set of residence rules. But unlike hypothetical rules, standard propensities are empirically based.

The adoption of any standard set of residential preferences is a distortion. The more stylized the assumed standard is, the greater will be the risk of misleading results. This generalization holds for the examples of

---

is assumed to be

$$\frac{\text{PFS}_{\text{asm}} \times \text{PA}_{\text{asm}}}{\text{PS}_{\text{asm}}}$$

where PFS_{asm} is the proportion residing with family heads of a given age, sex, and marital status in the standard (1900) population, PA_{asm} is the proportion of persons of each age, sex, and marital status in the alternate population, and PS_{asm} is the proportion of persons of each age, sex, and marital status in the standard population. This has the effect of holding patterns of headship constant, just as other residential propensities are held constant.

One additional calculation is needed to present the results of the standard-propensities technique. The procedure described in the text for calculating family structure under standard propensities yields a large table that shows the percentage of persons who would have resided with extended kin of each type, age, sex, and marital status if the propensity to reside with such kin were the same in 1900 but demographic conditions were different. Since the table consists of hundreds of cells, it is too complex for convenient analysis. We must therefore aggregate the table into broader categories of kin. This requires knowing the extent to which different *combinations* of kin are likely to occur. Some combinations never occur; for example, one cannot reside with both a married mother and a widowed mother of the family head. Other kin types *usually* occur in combination; for example, where a married mother is present, there is generally a married father as well. I have assumed that the propensity for different kin types to occur in combination remains constant. In other words, the likelihood of combination differs from the 1900 standard population only to the extent that the availability of kin is different. To carry through the aggregation of results obtained from the use of standard propensities, we simply add up the percentage of persons residing with any general category of kin and then deflate the total by a factor representing the proportion of combinations for that category in the standard population.

This footnote constitutes proof of the assertion that "writing a family history can be an interesting and exciting experience, one that stimulates enthusiasm for history as few other endeavors do" (Kyvig and Marty 1978: 9–10).

price indices and standardization of demographic rates as well as for the standardization of residential preferences.

In fairness, hypothetical rules are not intended to be realistic. Rather, they are designed to test specific hypotheses about residential behavior. These hypotheses assume uniform behavior with regard to residence decisions. Real populations are not so consistent. The use of hypothetical rules can provide insight into the interaction of demography and family structure, but only in the abstract context of unrealistic residential preferences. If our goal is to assess the impact of demographic factors on family structure in the real world, our description of standard residential preferences should be as realistic as possible.

Using standard residential propensities to analyze the effects of demography on family structure also has an important practical advantage. Any flaws in the model that produce proportional systematic errors in the estimates of available kin will cancel out. For example, suppose that MOMSIM always *overstates* the availability of grandchildren by 20 percent. This would result in standard propensities for residence with grandchildren that were *understated* by 20 percent. The two errors cancel out; the error in standard propensities would correct for error in the availability of grandchildren under alternative demographic regimes.

Given the various assumptions of the microsimulation model discussed above and in appendix C, there can be no doubt that the estimates of availability of kin produced by MOMSIM are inaccurate. But how inaccurate are they? There really is no means of finding this out; if we could directly measure the availability of kin, there would be no need for the model. Fortunately, one would expect that most sources of error would be systematic. In other words, errors probably would be in the same direction and of roughly proportional magnitude, regardless of the demographic parameters employed. Thus, the use of standard propensities will tend to minimize errors in the model.

One point should be made absolutely clear: standard propensities are no panacea. The calculation of detailed residential propensities requires an enormous quantity of accurate data, and such data are currently unavailable for periods before the mid-nineteenth century. Moreover, as noted, changing demographic conditions can *cause* changes in residential propensities. I do not contend that standard propensities allow us to determine the long-term effects of demographic change on extended-family structure. We can only indirectly infer the ways in which residence decisions changed by comparing results produced through use of standard propensities with empirical measures of historical family structure. I have no doubt, however, that generalizations based on analysis with standard propensities will be more realistic than will generalizations based on an elaborate set of hypothetical rules. Moreover, if we are ever going to understand much about residential behavior we will have to attempt measuring residential decision making. My use of residential propensities is intended as a first step in that direction.

For all their limitations, standard propensities are a powerful analytic device. The utility of the method is best illustrated by example, and such examples will be forthcoming soon enough: most of the next chapter and appendix D are devoted to the analysis of results derived using standard propensities. But before I can unveil the products of my grand design, I must explain one alternative analytic approach.

Use of Hypothetical Rules with Momsim

From the perspective of extended-family structure, not all types of relatives are equally important. Momsim generates detailed statistics on the availability of a wide variety of kin of each age, sex, and marital status. To analyze historical family structure effectively, we need to focus on those types of kin that were most likely to reside in extended families. Standard propensities provide a means of weighting different types of kin according to their relative importance. From a theoretical perspective, however, it may sometimes be more appropriate to concentrate exclusively on the availability of specific combinations of kin.

The use of hypothetical residence rules can be a means of narrowing the scope of our analysis to focus on the most theoretically important combinations of kin. As employed here, hypothetical rules are merely a means of assessing the frequency with which certain combinations of kin would appear in a population. Unlike those of socsim, the hypothetical rules in momsim have no effect on the demographic mechanics of the model; indeed, most individuals in the simulated population are not even grouped into residential families. Instead, the rules are simply a system for choosing strategic numerators and denominators for measuring available kin.

This is not to say that the rules employed in momsim have nothing in common with those employed in socsim. In fact, the momsim rules have many of the same problems as the socsim rules. But I have avoided some of the greatest shortcomings of socsim.

Like the socsim rules, the momsim hypothetical rules are designed to assess the demographic potential for residence in stem families. In particular, they measure the proportion of the population that would have resided in stem families if certain family-formation rules were obeyed. But because measurement is carried out at the level of individuals, it is unnecessary to devise rules to classify the household structure of individuals who could *not* reside in stem families. This fact eliminates one of the most problematic aspects of the SOCSIM rules (see chapter 4).

The example of the SOCSIM microsimulators has persuaded me of the importance of keeping rules simple. Rules cannot be made realistic and should not be designed to mimic reality with great subtlety and detail. If residence rules are so complex that they might conceivably approach reality, then it becomes impossible to know which aspects of the rules produced the results.

We should view hypothetical rules instead simply as a means of measuring the frequency of certain select combinations of kin. We have then already implicitly abandoned the notion of modeling the way that society actually works. From this perspective, the importance of clarity far outweighs the advantages of subtlety.

Like the SOCSIM modelers, I have devised three sets of stem-family rules. The main system of rules—or Rule System 1—is designed to approximate the mainstream interpretation of the stem-family hypothesis. These rules are as follows:

1. The eldest living son remains in his parental family after marriage.
2. If there are no surviving sons, the eldest daughter remains.
3. Other children leave their parental family when they marry or when they reach age 21, whichever comes first.

The implementation of these rules is simple. The program determines if there is a living parent with an eldest married son in each kin group. If there are no sons, the program checks for a living parent with an eldest married daughter. If either of these combinations of kin exists, the kin group contains a stem family. The members of the stem family consist of the spouse and any living parents of the married son or daughter, together with those unmarried siblings and children of the son or daughter who are younger than 21. If there are married members of any kin group who are not part of a stem family within their kin group, the program subjects them to the appropriate risk of marrying *into* a stem family.[13]

This classification procedure allows construction of age-specific rates of

13. The risk of marrying into a stem family is based on a probability distribution calculated in a previous run of the model. This distribution indicates the probability that married persons of each age will be married to eldest married sons (or eldest married daughters with no male siblings) with at least one living parent. The situation occasionally arises that an eldest married son marries an eldest married daughter without brothers. When this occurs, the couple is assumed to reside with the son's parents, and the second-eldest married daughter gets a chance to form a stem family.

residence in stem families. With the help of the piggyback projection model described in appendix C (to calculate the age distribution), these rates can be converted into estimates of the overall percentage of the population that would reside in stem families if the rules were actually followed.

Rule Systems 2 and 3 are designed to provide more generous estimates of the maximum frequency of stem families. Rule System 2 is the same as Rule System 1, except there is no preference for sons over daughters. This means that the duration of marriage is maximized, which tends to maximize the number of grandchildren. Rule System 3 is the same as Rule System 2, except that the unmarried siblings and children of the married son or daughter remain in their parents' household for their entire lives. Rule System 3 is closest to SOCSIM's hypothetical rules.[14]

The figures produced by MOMSIM's hypothetical rules have limited utility. They measure only one narrow aspect of the availability of kin. Moreover, like the statistics produced by SOCSIM, the estimates of stem-family structure are probably overstated. But I suspect that the problems with the MOMSIM figures are less extreme.

MOMSIM and SOCSIM share the Whopper Assumption that the characteristics of members of the same kin group are uncorrelated. For reasons explained above, this assumption almost inevitably leads to overestimates of the proportion of the population that could reside in stem families.

However, MOMSIM avoids other problems integral to the SOCSIM model that may tend to exaggerate the potential frequency of stem living arrangements. First, in MOMSIM fertility is handled by data on children ever born instead of by age-specific rates. As I argue in appendix C, the use of age-specific rates will lead to overstatement of the frequency of persons with one or more descendant kin of any specific type.

Second, MOMSIM avoids overstatement of stem living arrangements that derive from unrealistically low marriage rates. In the last chapter, I pointed out that under the SOCSIM rules the only way to create a new household is to marry. Because SOCSIM is based on a small closed population, marriage rates in the model may be unrealistically low. These two factors may lead to an unrealistically low frequency of nonstem households. MOMSIM, by constrast, is an open model based on individual-level measurement, so these problems simply do not arise.

I have great misgivings about the use of hypothetical rules in any

14. In the case of a marriage between two eldest children, Rule Systems 2 and 3 operate analogously to Rule System 1. See note 13.

microsimulation. If we could estimate detailed propensities for all periods, hypothetical rules would be unnecessary; we could at least approximately describe residential preferences empirically. Given the limitations of the data, this strategy is impossible. Under these circumstances, the use of hypothetical rules may be justified. But we should bear in mind that the rules are partly the investigator's own creation. The utility of residence rules is greatest if we recognize the limitations of the method and treat our results with appropriate skepticism.

Conclusion

To recapitulate, MOMSIM generates detailed estimates of the availability of kin under a given set of demographic conditions. This is accomplished by assigning demographic characteristics to simulated individuals to create hypothetical kin groups. The procedures for assignment of characteristics involve a variety of assumptions, some of which probably result in substantial errors. The most problematic assumption is the Whopper Assumption, which leads to exaggeration of the availability of living kin for coresidence. Additional assumptions, together with a detailed description of the MOMSIM model, appear in appendix C.

I have also described two analytic strategies to make use of the data generated by MOMSIM. The first strategy makes use of standard residential propensities calculated from the U.S. census in 1900. Use of standard propensities enables us to estimate what the residence patterns of a given population would be like if the population made residence decisions similar to those of the U.S. population in 1900, but experienced different demographic conditions. The second strategy makes use of hypothetical rules to estimate the maximum possible frequency of stem families, given a set of demographic parameters.

For those who have survived until now, the rest is easy sailing. The reader may judge if the results of the model, presented in the next chapter, justify its Byzantine methodology.

6   Simulation Results

Very well! We settles it by the slide rule.
Howland Owl, in Walt Kelly, Pogo (1949)

Toad, with no one to check his statements, or to criticize in an
unfriendly spirit, rather let himself go. Indeed, much that he related
belonged more properly to the category of what-might-have-
happened . . . These are always the best and the raciest of adventures;
and why should they not be truly ours, as much as the somewhat
inadequate things that really come off?
Kenneth Grahame, The Wind in the Willows (1908)

What follows should be viewed as informed speculation. I will present
detailed tables that lend a misleading air of clinical accuracy. These tables
are the product of a kind of historical and demographic experiment.
Simulation enables us to explore the implications of a set of assumptions,
but it does not reveal historical fact. Nevertheless, it can be instructive to
unravel the implications of one's assumptions and, like Mr. Toad, to
relate what-might-have-happened.

The potential effects of demographic conditions on extended-family
structure prove to be considerably more complicated than scholars have
previously supposed. The great strength of the standard-propensities
approach described in the last chapter lies in its ability to uncover these
complex demographic mechanisms. But the present chapter is more
concerned with historical issues than with theoretical ones. To avoid
losing the historical argument in a welter of demographic detail, my more
general analysis of the effects of demographic conditions on extended-
family structure has been relegated to appendix D. There, I look at the
ways in which each category of demographic behavior—births, marriages, and deaths—interacts with family structure.

This chapter explores the implications of the demographic transition
for the frequency and characteristics of extended families. Compared to
their forebears in the mid-eighteenth century, the English and Americans
of the late-nineteenth century lived longer, had fewer children, and
married earlier. The timing and magnitude of these changes differed on
the two sides of the Atlantic.[1] But if the demographic paths of England

---

1. Between the mid-eighteenth century and the late-nineteenth century, the overall
direction of demographic change in America was roughly similar to that in England. But this

and America were different, their destination was the same: by 1900, the basic demographic characteristics of the two countries were strikingly similar.[2]

general statement obscures the complexity of the situation; in particular, the timing and magnitude of demographic changes were different. Age at marriage was apparently somewhat lower in the United States by 1900 than it had been in the eighteenth century, but it is unclear just when this change occurred. Yasuba (1961: 112–15) argues that age at marriage *increased* during the nineteenth century in America. However, he infers this from data on the overall percentage of married women in the population and fails to account for changes in the proportion marrying, widowhood, and remarriage. Wells (1971: 275) suggests that marriage age among women was on the rise throughout the eighteenth century, and Osterud and Fulton's (1976) data for Sturbridge show a dramatic increase in female marriage age between the mid-eighteenth century and 1820–1839. The longest time series available is D. S. Smith's (1973a: 55) data for Hingham, Massachusetts, which show considerable fluctuation in marriage age during the eighteenth century, a slight decline at the outset of the nineteenth century, and remarkable stability from then until 1880. National data show an additional drop at the end of the century. In England, by contrast, age at marriage declined in the latter half of the eighteenth century and the first half of the nineteenth; after 1871, the trend reversed. See Great Britain, General Register Office (1841–1900), Wrigley and Schofield (1983). But if England preceded America in the decline of marriage age, the opposite is the case for the decline of fertility and mortality. The trends in these variables are shown in note 2.

2. By the turn of the century, demographic conditions in the two countries had converged. The approximate crude birth and death rates in each country between 1800 and 1900 are:

	Births		Deaths	
Year	U.S.	England	U.S.	England
1800	52	38	22	26
1850	42	36	21	23
1900	29	29	17	17

These estimates are based on a variety of sources: Coale and Zelnik (1963: 21, 34), McClelland and Zeckhauser (1982): 109, 156–58), Glass (1951: 85), Mitchell and Deane (1962), Wrigley and Schofield (1981: 529), Thompson and Whelpton (1933: 263), Yasuba (1961: 99). In cases where the leading authorities disagreed, I averaged their estimates. Compare Great Britain, General Register Office (1851, 1898), U.S. Bureau of the Census (1975), Linder and Grove (1947), Preston, Keyfitz, and Schoen (1972), Grabill, Kiser, and Whelpton (1958), Tranter (1973), Vinovskis (1981). Data in Coale and Zelnik (1963: 34, 40) indicate that fertility patterns in the United States and England were extremely close thoughout the period 1860–1900.

The United States and England were also quite close with respect to marriage age in 1900. The median age at marriage was 25.9 for men in the United States, compared with 25.4 in England and Wales. Female marriages age showed a more substantial difference; the median was 21.9 in the United States and 24.6 in England and Wales. As far as the availability of kin is concerned, the female difference would be partly counterbalanced by the male difference; overall, the analysis in appendix D suggests that the difference in

I have constructed four hypothetical populations to illustrate the consequences of demographic change. The first of these is designed to mimic the demographic experience of England and America in 1900. Since demographic conditions were nearly alike in the last half of the nineteenth century, a single model can serve as a reasonable proxy for both countries. The second population reflects the demography of England around 1725. This date clearly precedes the increase in the frequency of extended families.[3] The other two populations represent demographic extremes; they are somewhat exaggerated characterizations of demographic conditions in developing countries and in the late-twentieth-century industrial world. As we shall see, these last two populations provide a revealing perspective from which to view the historical simulations.

I have not attempted to model the demographic experience of the American colonies for several reasons. For one thing, we lack reliable demographic statistics for colonial America as a whole.[4] Moreover, as pointed out in chapter 1, data on family structure for the American colonies are exceedingly scarce. The point of this exercise is to help us

---

marriage age between the United States and England in 1900 would not make more than a 1 to 2 percent difference in the frequency of extended families. But even this difference is probably exaggerated. Both the American and English figures are based on period rather than cohort data; as noted, American marriage ages were declining at the end of the century, whereas English marriage ages were going up; thus, if we had retrospective data on marriage in 1900, we might find that the median was actually lower in England. The marriage data appear in U.S. Bureau of the Census (1975) and Great Britian, General Register Office (1898).

3. Some historians may question the use of a simple before-and-after scheme for the analysis of the extended family. Given the present state of knowledge about changes in family structure, however, a more subtle analysis is not warranted. In recent years we have learned a great deal about the chronology of demographic change in eighteenth- and nineteenth-century England, but we have no such firm grasp of the specific timing of changes in family structure. Although there is solid evidence that the frequency of extended families was much lower in seventeenth- and early-eighteenth-century England than in England or America in the late-nineteenth century, we cannot presently go much beyond this simple dichotomy. The simplicity of my analysis therefore reflects the evidence.

My turn-of-the-century model is intended to represent both England and America, but it was actually based on American data. The American data in this period are far superior to the English; my method calls for a large, individual-level data set that provides information on marriage duration and cumulative fertility. The U.S. 1900 Public Use Sample meets these requirements; no comparable data are available for England in this period.

4. The American colonial data are scattered, and there were dramatic regional variations between New England and the Chesapeake, and between the frontier and longer-settled regions. Since we lack reliable general estimates for the colonial period, broad statements are necessarily partly guesswork. The principal sources for American colonial demography are cited in notes 1 and 6.

understand the historical interaction of demography and family structure; it wouldn't make sense to focus on an area in which we know little about either one.

The fact that we cannot accurately model the demography of the family in colonial America may be no great loss. The early-eighteenth-century population of the American colonies is not the ideal antecedent of the United States at the end of the nineteenth century. For the most part, the turn-of-the-century population was not descended from the colonists of 200 years before, either literally or culturally.[5] Moreover, the demographic behavior of early Americans was peculiar by the standards of the time.[6] And we should bear in mind that the American colonists at the beginning of the eighteenth century were exceptional in a variety of other respects as well. They differed from those who remained in Britain in their social origins, sex ratio, religion, education, politics, and property. Their numbers were small, and their position at the edge of the wilderness was extraordinary and temporary.[7] If their living arrangements resembled those of the English population, this would be testimony to the resilience of residential behavior under extreme structural conditions. But because of the unusual circumstances of the American colonists in the first half of the eighteenth century, they may be inappropriate as a benchmark for comparison with the American population of 1900; the

5. Some historians would argue that colonial America in 1700—especially Puritan New England—is indeed the most appropriate cultural antecedent of America in 1900. The Puritans clearly had influence beyond their insignificant numbers.

6. The seventeenth-century American colonies differed markedly from their counterparts in the old country in their age at marriage, fertility, and mortality. Although these differences diminished somewhat by the eighteenth century, even then the colonists lived longer, married earlier, and had many more children than English people did. In eighteenth-century New England—the region for which the best statistics are available—life expectancy at age 20–29 ranged from 33 to 40 in the various localities that have been studied, which is 4 or 5 years higher than in England. The disparity in fertility is even greater; estimates of gross reproduction rate for New England run about 2.9 to 3.2 children, as against just over 2 in England. The mean age at marriage in the New England localities during the first half of the eighteenth century was about 26 for men and 24 for women. These figures are reasonably similar to the English pattern, but still a bit younger. On the whole, as suggested by B. Laslett (1973), one would expect that demographic constraints on extended-family structure were less severe in colonial America than in early modern England. On American colonial demographic patterns see Greven (1970: 177–78, 183, 193–96, 200–1, 206, 208), Lockridge (1970: 66, 93–94), Demos (1965, 1970), Norton (1971), Walsh and Menard (1974), Potter (1965), D. S. Smith (1972, 1973a), Nugent (1981: 46, 49, 57), Jones (1918), Higgs and Stettler (1970), Farber (1972), D. B. Smith (1978), Vinovskis (1971, 1972). A useful overview of this literature appears in McCusker and Menard (1985). For English comparisons, see Wrigley and Schofield (1983: 250, 255, 529).

7. The unbalanced sex ratio might have especially important consequences for family structure; on this topic, see Moller (1945) and Menard (1973).

preindustrial English population probably suits this purpose at least as well.

Enough of rationalization: let us turn to the results. I first present findings based on the standard-propensities technique. This phase of the analysis estimates the effects of demographic change on the frequency and characteristics of extended families, assuming constant preferences. I then turn to hypothetical rules to look at the potential frequency of stem families under each set of demographic conditions.

The Standard Propensities Results

This section describes the specific kinds of family structure that would be found in populations that shared the standard residential propensities of 1900 but had different demographic conditions. Holding residential propensities constant, the simulation results indicate what proportion of the population would have resided in extended families under four types of demographic regimes—those of the United States and England in 1900, preindustrial England, mid-twentieth-century industrial societies, and contemporary developing countries. This information helps us assess the extent to which demographic factors can account for the rise of the extended family in the nineteenth century and its decline in the twentieth.

The demographic parameters employed to represent the United States and England in 1900 and England during the first half of the eighteenth century appear in table 6.1. The 1900 population is labeled "STD," since it is the basis of the standard propensities; the preindustrial population is labeled "PRE." Except for mortality, the parameters shown for the STD population were calculated from the 1900 Public Use Sample of the U.S. federal census; mortality was based on the 1900–1902 U.S. life table.[8] The PRE parameters conform as closely as feasible to the best available empirical data for the period; in particular, I approximate English demographic behavior for the first half of the eighteenth century estimated in Wrigley and Schofield's *Population History*.[9] Compared to the 1900 standard

8. This is the "Glover" life table; U.S. Bureau of the Census (1921). The demographic parameters conform remarkably closely to figures given in U.S. Bureau of the Census (1975). Bear in mind that the mean age of mothers over 49 at the birth of their children is not equivalent to mean generation length; some mothers die before they have an opportunity to bear children at later ages. Therefore, the figures shown are somewhat higher than mean generation length would be.

9. Wrigley and Schofield (1983). The PRE run makes little use of the adjustment technique described in appendix C. Instead of adjusting age at marriage, spouse intervals, and percent never married, I employed a distribution for marital status by age based on the files of the

Table 6.1. Basic Demographic Parameters for Simulation Runs: Preindustrial Run and
Standard Population

Name of Run	PRE	STD
Median female age at marriage	25.2	22.2
Median male age at marriage	26.1	25.0
Mean age interval between spouses	2.1	4.0
Mean age at childbirth for mothers who survive to age 45	34.7	31.3
Percent of women never married at 40	14.1	8.6
Female expectation of life at birth	34.8	48.3
Male expectation of life at birth	32.5	44.7
Total fertility rate	4.62	3.79

population, the PRE model assumes late marriage, a high proportion
never marrying, and high mortality and fertility.

Table 6.2 outlines the family structure that results under preindustrial
demographic conditions if we apply the residential propensities of the
1900 standard population. The STD run—which reflects the actual demographic conditions of 1900—is also shown. The top row of the table
indicates the percentage of persons who would have resided in extended
families in a population that shared the demographic conditions shown in
table 6.1 and the residential propensities calculated for 1900.

The figures in table 6.2 indicate that the demographic conditions of
England before 1750 profoundly discouraged extended-family structure.
Overall, if there were no differences in residential propensities, only
about 13 percent of the eighteenth-century population would have resided in extended families, compared with about 21 percent in 1900.

Results from the PRE and STD are consistent with the hypothesis that there
was no change in residential propensities over a century and a half.
According to this reasoning, the rise of the extended family in the
nineteenth century was entirely a consequence of demographic change.

When I first got these results, I was surprised. Wachter, Hammel, and
Laslett, on the basis of results of the SOCSIM model, had concluded that
demographic factors have only slight consequences for family structure.

Cambridge Group in P. Laslett (1977a). The total fertility rate required little adjustment,
since the PRE model used MOMSIM's stable fertility option and therefore incorporates higher
fertility automatically; see appendix C. Mortality was based on regional model life tables. A
slightly adjusted version of the Level 7 Model West life table from Coale and Demeny
(1983) was employed.

Table 6.2. Preindustrial and Standard Simulation Runs: Measures of Family Structure, Assuming 1900 Standard Propensities

Name of Run	PRE	STD
Percent of individuals residing in:		
Extended families	12.8	21.0
Vertically extended families	5.3	11.9
Horizontally extended families	8.4	11.1
Percent of individuals residing with kin, by kin's relation to head:		
Siblings	3.7	4.8
Siblings-in-law	2.8	3.6
Nephews/Nieces	2.6	3.4
Uncles/Aunts	0.5	0.5
Parents	2.7	4.2
Parents-in-law	1.8	2.9
Grandchildren/Children-in-law	1.2	5.0
Percent of individuals residing with kin, by kin's sex and marital status:		
Males		
Single	3.4	8.0
Married	0.8	1.7
Widowed	1.5	1.9
Females		
Single	6.7	8.3
Married	1.0	1.9
Widowed	2.9	5.3
Percent of individuals residing with kin, by kin's age group:		
0–9	1.7	4.6
10–19	2.1	4.5
20–29	2.6	3.8
30–39	2.6	2.1
40–49	1.7	2.3
50–59	1.0	1.8
60–69	1.9	2.9
70+	2.9	4.7

In spite of the problems with socsim outlined in chapter 4, I was initially persuaded of the general thesis that demography really doesn't matter much. That conclusion fit my own prejudices; I wanted to believe that the rise of the extended family in the nineteenth century was not merely an artifact of changing demography, but actually reflected significant cultural change.

Bear in mind that the results in table 6.2 do not actually prove that residential preferences remained constant between the first half of the eighteenth century and the close of the nineteenth century. In fact, there may have been radical changes in residential propensities that tended to cancel out. Under these circumstances, by pure coincidence the empirically observed frequency of extended families might still be similar to the frequency produced by the model when we assume constant propensities (see appendix D).

Clues to whether residential propensities actually changed may be gleaned from the more detailed breakdowns near the top of table 6.2. The second and third rows of table 6.2 provide an indication of specific *types* of extended families that would occur under each demographic regime. There are two main classifications: vertical extension is defined here as residence with parents, parents-in-law, children-in-law, or grandchildren; horizontally extended families contain other types of extended kin. Preindustrial demographic conditions would discourage both vertical and horizontal extension, but the effect is especially marked for vertically extended families. The low frequency of vertically extended families in the PRE run is a consequence of both late marriage and early death (see the infamous appendix D).

If residential propensities actually did not change during the late eighteenth and nineteenth centuries, we would expect to find that horizontally extended relationships were substantially more common than vertically extended relationships in the real preindustrial population, just as in the PRE hypothetical population. The preindustrial data are unfortunately ambiguous; they do not show a general predominance of horizontal extension before 1750, but this finding may stem from measurement problems.[10] Although it cannot yet be proven, however, I suspect that

10. According to Wall (1983b: 500), 51 percent of extended kin were parents, parents-in-law, children-in-law, or grandchildren in the period 1650–1749. This figure, however, refers to the percentage of relatives who were vertically extended, not the percentage of people residing with vertically extended kin. If vertically extended kin occurred in combination more frequently than horizontally extended kin, 51 percent vertically extended kin might translate into a considerably smaller percentage of vertically extended living arrangements. P. Laslett's (1972a: 81, 84) data suggests that 58 percent of extended households contained three generations, but this figure is based on his "standard 100 communities," which includes some nineteenth-century localities. Moreover, there is no way to tell the relative percentage of horizontally extended families; some households contain both vertically and horizontally extended kin.

The direction of change in the relative frequency of vertically and horizontally extended kin does appear to be consistent with a hypothesis of standard propensities. Wall's (1983b: 500) data indicate an increase in the proportion of kin who were vertically extended, from 51 percent in 1650–1749 to 62 percent in 1750–1820 and 59 percent in 1851. But these figures probably overstate the degree of change, because of bias resulting from changing headship patterns. More specifically, over time it became more common for first-generation kin to be

residential propensities were not actually constant. Overall, it is most plausible that the propensity to reside with vertically extended kin was higher in the preindustrial period than it was in 1900, and the propensity to reside with horizontally extended kin was correspondingly lower.[11]

I also ran the simulation model using demographic conditions that approximate those of mid-twentieth-century Western industrial societies. This run—called MOD—assumes low fertility, low mortality, and moderate age at marriage. The specific parameters are given in table 6.3; the results appear in table 6.4.

If we again assume standard propensities, the overall percentage of the population residing in extended families under the MOD conditions would be almost the same as in the standard 1900 population, despite marked differences in demographic conditions. The high life expectancy of the twentieth-century developed world favors the formation of extended families, but this effect is almost canceled out by low fertility (see appen-

---

listed as the heads of households containing three-generation families. Thus, there was a decline in the relative frequency of parents and an increase in the relative frequency of grandchildren. At any given point, grandchildren tend to be more numerous than parents, since they tend to occur in combination. Accordingly, these figures may exaggerate the extent of change. It is precisely this problem of variable-headship patterns that led me to adopt constant criteria for family headship in my own work; see appendix A.

11. In particular, I suspect that the main changes were a decline in the propensity to reside with married parents and an increase in the propensity to reside with single siblings. There are several reasons to believe this. First, the findings of the stem-rules model (table 6.7) are inconsistent with the hypothesis that the propensities to reside with married kin were as low for the preindustrial period as in the 1900 standard population. In 1900, vertical extension usually meant residence with a widowed parent (see appendix D). This cannot have been the case in the preindustrial period, because there wouldn't have been enough widowed parents to account for the observed frequency of stem families (see discussion of the stem-rules results below). This implies that propensities to reside with married parents decreased by the end of the nineteenth century. Second, if the propensities to reside with married persons went down, then other propensities—for residing with widowed and single kin—must have gone up, because the overall propensities did not change much. If some propensities declined, others must have risen to compensate. Third, if there were any changes in propensities, the most plausible direction is the one that I indicate. In 1900, the propensities for residing with married extended kin were exceedingly low; it seems unlikely that they could have been lower still in the early eighteenth century. On the other hand, the propensities for some types of single kin were extremely high in 1900 and I doubt that they could have been much higher in the eighteenth century. Thus, there is greater possibility for changes in the direction I suggest than in the opposite direction and such change is also suggested by the analysis with stem rules. At a less purely quantitative level, I am also responding to literary evidence from Berkner (1972b) and others on the form of extended families in the preindustrial period.

Table 6.3. Basic Demographic Parameters for Simulation Runs:
          Mid-Twentieth-Century Run and Standard Population

Name of Run	MOD	STD
Median female age at marriage	22.2	22.2
Median male age at marriage	24.3	25.0
Mean age interval between spouses	2.5	4.0
Mean age at childbirth for mothers who survive to age 45	29.6	31.3
Percent of women never married at 40	7.5	8.6
Female expectation of life at birth	76.7	48.3
Male expectation of life at birth	73.4	44.7
Total fertility rate	2.51	3.79

dix D). Although there is little change in the aggregate frequency of extended families, the MOD demographic conditions do encourage a shift from horizontal to vertical extension.

The PRE, STD, and MOD runs of MOMSIM reflect, at least in rough outline, the sequence of demographic change in the West over the past two centuries. Tables 6.2 and 6.4 therefore allow some cautious generalizations about the effects of demographic shifts on extended-family structure over the long term. Overall, demographic change has relaxed constraints on the formation of extended families. At the same time, we can be confident that there has been a significant shift toward conditions favoring the formation of vertically, rather than horizontally, extended families.

As I noted in chapter 1, the frequency of extended families actually *declined* substantially in twentieth-century England and America. If residential propensities had remained constant, the frequency of extended families would have *increased* during the twentieth century. These findings demonstrate that residential preferences have not, in fact, remained constant since 1900. This result underlines the fact that demographic factors, although critical, are not the sole source of change in extended-family structure. Demographic factors were much more important as an influence on extended-family structure *before* 1900 than afterwards.

The other run using standard propensities—called DEV—is not intended to describe a real population, but it is heuristically useful. Although this run is not strictly related to the main questions addressed in this work, it illustrates the potential impact of demographic factors on extended-family structure. This run incorporates early marriage, a high proportion marrying, high fertility, and high mortality—in general, a somewhat

Table 6.4. Mid-Twentieth-Century and Standard Simulation Runs: Measures of Family Structure, Assuming 1900 Standard Propensities

Name of Run	MOD	STD
Percent of individuals residing in:		
Extended families	22.2	21.0
Vertically extended families	15.3	11.9
Horizontally extended families	9.3	11.1
Percent of individuals residing with kin, by kin's relation to head:		
Siblings	4.0	4.8
Siblings-in-law	3.0	3.6
Nephews/Nieces	2.8	3.4
Uncles/Aunts	0.6	0.5
Parents	4.7	4.2
Parents-in-law	3.3	2.9
Grandchildren/Children-in-law	7.5	5.0
Percent of individuals residing with kin, by kin's sex and marital status:		
Males		
Single	7.7	8.0
Married	2.6	1.7
Widowed	1.8	1.9
Females		
Single	9.2	8.3
Married	3.0	1.9
Widowed	4.1	5.3
Percent of individuals residing with kin, by kin's age group:		
0–9	5.3	4.6
10–19	4.3	4.5
20–29	3.6	3.8
30–39	2.3	2.1
40–49	2.1	2.3
50–59	1.2	1.8
60–69	3.1	2.9
70+	6.4	4.7

exaggerated picture of demographic conditions in contemporary developing societies.[12] Table 6.5 shows the demographic assumptions of the DEV run and table 6.6 indicates the family structure that would result from these assumptions together with the 1900 standard propensities.

12. The DEV run has especially exaggerated mortality; mortality was assumed to be higher than ordinarily exists in Third World countries today. I adopted this practice because the DEV run is partly designed to test Levy's thesis that the high mortality characteristic of premodern societies would preclude a high frequency of stem families. See Levy et al. (1965) and my discussion in chapter 4.

Table 6.5. Basic Demographic Parameters for Simulation Runs: Exaggerated Third
World Run and Standard Population

Name of Run	DEV	STD
Median female age at marriage	18.6	22.2
Median male age at marriage	21.3	25.0
Mean age interval between spouses	3.7	4.0
Mean age at childbirth for mothers who survive to age 45	27.7	31.3
Percent of women never married at 40	0.4	8.6
Female expectation of life at birth	22.9	48.3
Male expectation of life at birth	21.9	44.7
Total fertility rate	8.00	3.79

Under the DEV, or exaggerated Third World, demographic assumptions, the aggregate frequency of residence with extended kin resulting from standard propensities is low—almost as low as for the PRE run. But quite different mechanisms underlie this superficial similarity. In the DEV run, early marriage encourages vertical extension and discourages horizontal extension; high fertility favors all sorts of extended families, but especially horizontally extended ones; and high mortality constrains residence with all types of kin (see appendix D). These effects counteract one another, so, under the DEV conditions, the frequency of vertical extension is almost equal to the frequency of horizontal extension.

The results of the standard propensities runs warrant several conclusions. We can be virtually certain that the rise of the extended family in the nineteenth century was encouraged by changing demographic conditions. In fact, the results of MOMSIM are consistent with the interpretation that demographic change was the sole cause of the increasing frequency of extended families. We should not, however, conclude that residential propensities did not change.[13]

In the West, the eighteenth-and nineteenth-century trends—increas-

13. The use of standard propensities for analyzing the effects of demography on extended-family structure has limitations. The method should be viewed as no more than a means of weighting the availability of different kinds of kin in a plausible way. In appendix D, I have stressed the underlying structure of the 1900 standard propensities and the specific mechanisms by which the availability of kin can dictate family structure. As long as we bear in mind the patterns of standard propensities and the limitations of the aggregate statistics produced by the technique, standard propensities are a useful device for assessing the implications of the simulation results. We should remember, however, that propensities are not always constant; in fact, residential propensities are to some extent a function of demographic conditions. The pattern of propensities prevailing in the United States in 1900 might not reveal a great deal about the effects of demography on family structure in populations that have markedly different residential preferences.

Table 6.6. Exaggerated Third World and Standard Simulation Runs: Measures of
Family Structure, Assuming 1900 Standard Propensities

Name of Run	DEV	STD
Percent of individuals residing in:		
Extended families	13.3	21.0
Vertically extended families	7.2	11.9
Horizontally extended families	7.4	11.1
Percent of individuals residing with kin, by kin's relation to head:		
Siblings	2.8	4.8
Siblings-in-law	2.3	3.6
Nephews/Nieces	2.8	3.4
Uncles/Aunts	0.2	0.5
Parents	3.5	4.2
Parents-in-law	2.1	2.9
Grandchildren/Children-in-law	1.9	5.0
Percent of individuals residing with kin, by kin's sex and marital status:		
Males		
Single	4.2	8.0
Married	1.2	1.7
Widowed	1.2	1.9
Females		
Single	4.1	8.3
Married	1.2	1.9
Widowed	5.5	5.3
Percent of individuals residing with kin, by kin's age group:		
0–9	3.0	4.6
10–19	3.2	4.5
20–29	2.7	3.8
30–39	1.2	2.1
40–49	1.9	2.3
50–59	2.6	1.8
60–69	1.7	2.9
70+	0.8	4.7

ing potential for extended families and especially for horizontal extension—continued into the twentieth century, albeit at a more moderate
rate. After the turn of the century, fertility, mortality, and marriage age
fell further, which relaxed constraints on the formation of extended
families and especially encouraged vertical extension. Yet despite these
more favorable conditions, the frequency of extended families actually
fell after 1900. In the contemporary developing world, on the other hand,
prevailing demographic conditions encourage family structure that bears

some resemblance to the living arrangements of preindustrial England; however, different mechanisms produce these similar results.

Hypothetical Rules and Stem-Family Structure

Debates among historians and sociologists about the preindustrial family have placed great emphasis on the constraints and choices relating to stem living arrangements in the eighteenth century. Was the low frequency of stem families the result of residential preferences, as Laslett suggests, or was it principally a function of demographic constraints, as Berkner argues? The use of hypothetical rules with simulation can provide a tentative answer to this question.

If we can describe a particular family structure exactly, MOMSIM can tell us the maximum percentage of a population that could have adopted that living arrangement. This can be achieved through the use of hypothetical rules. As described in the last chapter, hypothetical rules are used here to estimate the percentage of persons who could have resided in stem families under a given set of demographic conditions. Stem families are here defined as those families that include a parent, their ever-married child, and either a child-in-law or a grandchild.[14]

To test the potential for forming stem families under various demographic conditions, I ran the model with three different systems of rules. Rule System 1 specifies that the eldest currently living married son remains in his parents' household after marriage; if no sons exist, the eldest daughter remains; and everyone else leaves the household upon marriage or upon reaching age 21, whichever comes first. Rule System 2 differs from Rule System 1 only in that there is no preference for sons over daughters in the former. Rule System 3 is the same as Rule System 2, except that unmarried children and grandchildren remain in their parental family for their entire lives, instead of leaving at 21. Rule System 3 can be viewed as a means of estimating a maximum plausible frequency of stem families.

Under the STD demographic conditions (which represent the United States and England in 1900), a maximum of 36.3 percent of the population could have resided in stem families if Rule System 1 had been followed. The comparable figure for the preindustrial period was substantially lower, reaching only 21.6 percent.

Although the stem-rules technique is very different from the standard-

---

14. This definition is not quite equivalent to the definition of stem families adopted by Wachter, Hammel, and Laslett (1978), but it is very close; in their terms it is MLN plus XLN.

propensities approach, these results have similar implications for the rise of the extended family. Changing demographic conditions between the eighteenth and nineteenth centuries could have led to a dramatic increase in stem-type living arrangements, if everything else had remained constant.

This conclusion also holds for the results obtained using the other sets of stem-family-formation rules. The results of combining the PRE demographic conditions with each system of hypothetical rules are shown in table 6.7. The first row shows the percentage of the population that had the *potential* to reside in stem families under each rule system. Note that the figures are fairly low for all three rule systems. Thus, under preindustrial demographic conditions, a relatively small fraction of the population could have adopted stem-family structure.

The second row of table 6.7 shows the mean size of stem families under each set of rules. The third row of the table gives some rough estimates of the percentage of the population that actually resided in stem families in preindustrial England. We know the approximate percentage of stem *households* in preindustrial England, but we do not know—simply because no tabulations have been published—the proportion of *individuals* residing in stem families.

To convert the observed percentage of stem households in preindustrial England into an estimate of the percentage of persons residing in stem families, we need to employ data from a variety of sources and to make several rather shaky assumptions. The figures in the third row of table 6.7 should therefore be viewed as very rough approximations, and I suspect that they err on the low side. Even so, these individual-level estimates are considerably higher than the percentage of stem *households* in preindustrial England; this is because stem families tended to be considerably larger than nuclear families.[15]

15. To calculate these statistics, we need first to know the mean number of persons per household residing as lodgers, servants, and other nonfamily members. I am assuming that such individuals did not reside with their own stem subfamily; a few may actually have done so, but I am seeking a conservative estimate. Wall's data (1983b: 499) indicate that 0.87 persons per household were boarders or lodgers during 1650–1749 in England. The assumption that servants and lodgers did not reside in their own stem subfamilies is plausible because these were often temporary household statuses, disproportionately consisting of young single people. See Hajnal (1982) and R. M. Smith (1981). Second, we need to know the size of stem families. Again, the empirical figures have not been tabulated and published, but for the purposes of evaluating the results of MOMSIM it is appropriate to use the mean size of stem families taken from table 6.7. Third, we need to know the mean size of nonstem families. This is also unknown, but I have assumed that the figure for nonstem families is equal to the empirically observed mean size of all families after we subtract

Table 6.7. Measures of Stem-Family Structure, Assuming Stem Hypothetical Rules and PRE Demographic Conditions

Rule System	1	2	3
Maximum percentage of population in stem families	21.6	22.1	29.0
Mean size of stem families	5.65	5.81	6.76
Estimated percentage of preindustrial English population residing in stem families[a]	16.1	16.4	18.6
Estimated propensity to reside in stem families in preindustrial England[a]	75.6	74.4	64.2

[a]See note 15.

The estimated propensity to reside in stem families under the PRE demographic conditions is listed in the final row of table 6.7. These are estimates of the percentage of those people who could have resided in stem families who "actually" did so, calculated by dividing the third row of table 6.7 by the first row of the same table. These estimated propensities are crude, but, like the figures in the third row (the estimated

servants, lodgers, grandchildren, children-in-law, and parents of the head. According to Wall (1983b: 497–500), mean household size in 1650–1749 was 4.44. Of these household members, an average of 0.26 were attached lodgers, and 0.61 were servants. The total number of extended relatives per household was 0.16, of whom 51 percent were parents, parents-in-law, children-in-law, and grandchildren. If we subtract all these categories of household members, mean family size of nonvertically extended families would be 3.49. This, too, is conservative; even without the presence of extended kin, stem families would actually tend to be larger than the nonstem families. Stem families, after all, cannot consist of solitaries.

Once we have made these assumptions, the formula for calculating the percentage of persons in stem families is

$$\frac{\text{number in stems}}{\text{total population}} = \frac{\text{PHS} \times \text{MSS}}{(\text{MLS} \times 100) + (\text{MSN} \times \text{PHN}) + (\text{PHS} \times \text{MSS})}$$

where PHS is the percentage of households of the stem type. For these calculations, I used the figure from the Cambridge Group's sixty-two communities, which is 13.2 percent. This figure appears in Laslett's contribution to Wachter, Hammel, and Laslett (1978). MSS is the mean size of stem families. This is taken from my microsimulation model. MLS is the mean number of servant and lodgers per household. This is assumed to be 0.87. MSN is the mean size of nonstem families (household members minus servants and lodgers). This is assumed to be 3.49. PHN is the percentage of households that are nonstem (100 minus PHS).

The numerator of the equation, PHS × MSS, is the number of persons residing in stem families per 100 households. MLS × 100 is the number of lodgers and servants per 100 households; MSN × PHN is the number of persons in nonstem families per 100 households. Thus, the denominator adds up to the total population per 100 households. Note that if MLS and MSN are overestimates, as suggested above, the overall result is biased downward.

percentage of persons in stem families), these propensities are probably a little on the low side.

The estimated propensities to reside in stem families suggest a marked preference for stem-family structure in preindustrial England. They imply that somewhere around two-thirds to three-quarters of the people who *could* have resided in stem families *actually* did so. These results are striking. They imply even greater conformity to stem-family organization than the leading advocates of the stem-family hypothesis have claimed.[16]

Anyone who has undertaken demographic microsimulation—and even the alert general reader—must be aware that there are innumerable ways for errors to creep into such an exercise. Furthermore, as I have repeatedly stressed, we should not place too much confidence in results obtained by using hypothetical rules. It may therefore be premature to assert that Berkner is right and Laslett is wrong. But keep in mind that the assumptions of demographic models—especially the two special cases of the Whopper Assumption described in the last chapter—should lead to an overestimate of the availability of kin for residence in stem families. If anything, then, the preference for stem families was probably even greater than suggested in table 6.7.

The standard propensities results presented earlier surprised me; the results of the stem-family runs were a shock. As one who was weaned on Peter Laslett's *The World We Have Lost*, I wholeheartedly believed that the preindustrial English preferred to live in nuclear families. Moreover, my results seemed to contradict the results of the socsim model described in chapter 4.

On closer examination, it turns out that the results of the stem-family runs from momsim are remarkably close to the socsim results. The main set of socsim rules—the "primoreal" rules—are very roughly comparable to my Rule System 3. Under primoreal rules, the socsim model produces between 27.7 percent and 34.4 percent stem families, assuming demog-

---

16. Berkner (1972b), for example, argues that stem-family organization predominated only among the landholding class, since it served principally as an institution for the transmission of property. Servants and lodgers were not ordinarily landholders; thus, the proportion of the population "at risk" of adopting stem-family structure would be no more than 80 percent, since, according to Wall (1983b: 499), 20 percent were servants and lodgers. Furthermore, many families had no property, so the proportion of persons in families that held land was far lower. See Wall (1983b: 499), Goody, Thirsk, and Thompson (1976), and Thirsk (1967).

raphic parameters closest to my own.[17] Under Rule System 3, my model predicts that 29 percent of the population could reside in stem families. Even allowing for the fact that I am measuring at the level of individuals and SOCSIM measures at the household level, the difference between the models in the frequency of stem-family structure is trivial. As noted in chapter 5 and appendix C, the SOCSIM model incorporates several features that might be expected to exaggerate the frequency of stem families. Given the radical differences in the structure of our models, the close similarity of results is remarkable.

The difference in the results produced by MOMSIM and those produced by SOCSIM is primarily one of presentation and interpretation. As I pointed out in chapter 4, the SOCSIM results are consistent with the hypothesis that most people who could have resided in stem families actually did so. Laslett's argument that people preferred nuclear living arrangements hinges largely on his observation that the maximum possible percentage of stem households did not exist in preindustrial England.[18] My own simulation results also suggest that not everyone who could have resided in stem families did so. But that is to be expected, and it certainly does not demonstrate a preference for nuclear families. Few social behaviors are completely universal; we should not ask whether *everyone* opted for stem families, but rather whether such residence decisions predominated. Our best evidence suggests that they did.

The second table dealing with hypothetical rules—table 6.8—shows the maximum possible percentage of persons who could reside in stem families under Rule System 1 and the MOD and DEV demographic parameters.

17. SOCSIM's primoreal rules incorporate a preference for male heirs, whereas my Rule System 3 does not. As comparison of Rule System 1 and 2 illustrates, however, such a preference has little impact on the outcome of the model. More important, the primoreal rule system is the only one of theirs based on the age of the second generation and all three of my rule systems are based on that criterion. At the same time, Rule System 3 is the only one of mine that does not incorporate a provision for unmarried children to leave their parental household and none of the SOCSIM rules incorporate such a provision. Thus, the closest comparison is between Rule System 3 and the primoreal rules.

Wachter and Hammel did not do any runs that attempted to mimic preindustrial demographic conditions closely and this makes comparison difficult. But although they don't have any combinations of demographic parameters directly comparable to those given in Wrigley and Schofield (1983), their runs R2, R3, R5, and R6 bracket my parameters. The percentage of stem families (by my definition, which is MLN plus XLN in their terms) produced by SOCSIM for these runs is 34.4 percent, 30 percent, 32 percent, and 27.7 percent (Wachter, Hammel, and Laslett 1978: 45), compared with 29 percent for my Rule System 3.

18. See chapter 4.

Table 6.8. Measures of Stem-Family Structure, Assuming Stem Hypothetical Rules:
Combination Demographic Models

	MOD	DEV	STD
Maximum percentage of population in stem families			
under Rule System 1	47.9	40.2	36.3
Mean size of stem families	5.38	6.80	6.26

These figures indicate that the small potential for stem families in the preindustrial West is an anomaly.

Under MOD demographic conditions, almost half of the population could reside in stem families—more than twice the proportion who could do so under the PRE conditions. Yet the empirically observed frequency of families with stem structure was somewhat lower in the mid-twentieth century than in the mid-eighteenth century.[19] One conclusion therefore seems inescapable: there must have been a tremendous decline in the propensity to reside in stem families during the past 200 years.

The results of the DEV run are equally striking: 40 percent of a population with such demographic characteristics—high mortality, early marriage, and high fertility—could reside in a stem family under Rule System 1. This is substantially higher than the comparable figure for the United States in 1900, largely because of earlier marriage age.

The reader may recall that, under standard propensities, the DEV conditions produced a small overall frequency of extended families. The stem rules suggest a very different conclusion. We should bear in mind that MOMSIM's results depend entirely on what we choose to measure.

The high frequency of potential stem living arrangements under the DEV parameters weakens Levy's contention that high mortality precludes widespread adoption of three-generation families in less-developed countries.[20] In fact, the early marriage and high fertility associated with such populations exert countervailing pressures to high mortality. In-

19. Exactly comparable figures are not presently available, but see Dahlin (1980) and D. S. Smith (1984).

20. As shown in table 6.6, the DEV conditions do limit extension if one assumes standard propensities from 1900. The stem rules, however, provide a measure of the *maximum* frequency of a type of three-generation family. Since Levy focused on the capacity for forming three-generation families, the stem rules may be more appropriate than the standard propensities as a device for testing his hypothesis that high mortality would prevent extended-family structure (Levy, 1965). Bear in mind that the mortality regime postulated by the DEV run is more extreme than is ordinarily found in contemporary Third World populations.

deed, the frequency of stem families could be almost as high in developing nations as in Western industrial countries.

By itself, then, high mortality is insufficient to preclude a high frequency of stem families; it takes a combination of high mortality with late marriage to produce a major constraint on stem-family structure. Such a combination of demographic characteristics is rare; in fact, preindustrial northwestern Europe may be unique in this respect. In eastern and southern Europe, where a higher frequency of stem families has been found, people married earlier, in some places much earlier.[21] The DEV results therefore suggest that geographical differences in the frequency of stem families across preindustrial Europe may have been a function of demographic factors.

Conclusion

The results of MOMSIM have important implications for the history of the family. The demographic conditions prevailing at the end of the nineteenth century were highly favorable to the formation of extended families. By contrast, the frequency of available extended kin was substantially lower in preindustrial England. At the very least, demographic change may be viewed as a necessary condition for the rise of the extended family in the nineteenth century.

On the issue of stem families we should be more cautious. Nevertheless, my results suggest a strong preference for stem-family structure in England before the nineteenth century. In fact, the simulation results imply that the stem family was, in Levy's terms, the "ideal" type of family in preindustrial England.[22]

Overall, this research demonstrates that the supply of kin is highly sensitive to variation in demographic conditions. Thus, all studies of family structure—whether concerned with historical change, the life course, or differentials between or within populations—should carefully consider the potential effects of demographic factors.

The effects of these factors are not always obvious. Different demographic variables may cancel one another out; their effects may be additive; or they may not interact at all. I have only alluded to these theoretical issues in this chapter; readers who wish to understand more

21. Hajnal (1965). In parts of Russia where the frequency of complex households was very high, age at marriage was extremely low—as low as a median of 15 for women and 16 for men; see Mitterauer and Sieder (1982: 37). On marriage age and the differences in family structure between northwestern Europe and southern and eastern Europe, see note 5 in chapter 4.

22. Levy (1965).

about the interaction of demography and kinship and about MOMSIM should consult appendix D.

One more substantive issue remains. In chapter 3, I stressed the dramatic class differences in the frequency of extended families in nineteenth-century England and America. There were also important class differences in demographic conditions. It is therefore worth investigating whether demographic factors can explain the class patterns of family structure. The answer is no. However, demography had interesting consequences for the *characteristics* of extended families in different economic strata.

It would be anticlimactic to present results on this topic here. Those who would like to find out what lies at the intersection of demography and economics should turn to appendix E. But read the next chapter—the conclusion—first.

7 Conclusion

> He fell asleep murmuring "Sanity is not statistical," with the feeling
> that this remark contained in it a profound wisdom.
>
> George Orwell, *1984* (1949)

> When we asked Pooh what the opposite of an Introduction was, he
> said "The what of a what?" which didn't help us as much as we had
> hoped, but luckily Owl kept his head and told us that the opposite of
> an Introduction, my dear Pooh, was a Contradiction; and, as he is
> very good at long words, I am sure that's what it is.
>
> Why we are having a Contradiction is because last week . . . I
> happened to say very quickly, "What about nine times a hundred and
> seven?" And when we had done that one, we had one about cows
> going through a gate at two a minute, and there are three hundred in
> the field, so how many are left after an hour and a half? We find these
> very exciting, and when we have been excited quite enough we curl
> up and go to sleep. And Pooh, sitting wakeful a little longer on his
> chair by our pillow, thinks Grand Thoughts to himself about Noth-
> ing, until he, too, closes his eyes and nods his head.
>
> A. A. Milne, *The House at Pooh Corner* (1928)

We have done many sums and have counted a great many things, and it
has all been very exciting. But now it is time for the Contradiction.

By inventing imaginary people and having them jump through hoops, I
have determined that demographic changes could account for the rise of
the extended family in the nineteenth century. This of course assumes
that everything else was constant. In fact, virtually nothing else was
constant. And so, demography may not be the most important thing,
after all.

Some historians have argued that the stem-family system predominated in the preindustrial West because it provided a means of conserving
agricultural inheritance and of ensuring a steady supply of labor on the
family farm.[1] My demographic analysis lends support to this stem-family
hypothesis, since it suggests that there was a marked preference for
residence in stem families in eighteenth-century England.

Let us assume that the stem-family hypothesis is correct. This would
imply that the main motives for living in extended families were tied to

---

1. Berkner (1972a) and see chapter 4.

the preindustrial system of agriculture. Thus, one would expect that the general shift of employment away from agriculture and toward wage labor in the nineteenth century would have led to a decline in the propensity to reside in extended families.

The simulation results suggest that no such general decline in the propensity to reside in extended families took place. This means, given our assumptions, that there must have been some new motive for living in extended families in the nineteenth century. In other words, as the agricultural incentives for extended living arrangements gradually declined, some new incentive must have come into play.

Such a new incentive has been proposed by historians of the Victorian family. Unlike the stem family—which served as a means of conserving property—the nineteenth-century extended family has been viewed as a means of coping with a lack of property. According to this interpretation, material hardship engendered by wage labor and industrial conditions led to a new interdependence among extended kin. Huddling within an extended family was a tactic for survival.[2]

I hope that my economic analysis in chapter 3 has laid this hardship thesis to rest. Extended families were far more common among the bourgeoisie than they were among the industrial working class. Furthermore, there is no evidence that extended living arrangements were often a strategy for mutual assistance in the face of poverty or "critical life situations."

The opposite hypothesis is more plausible. Extended families were something of a luxury in the nineteenth century. With a rise in the standard of living, perhaps more people could afford to support dependent kin. As the old economic incentives for extended families declined, the economic constraints on extended families may also have diminished. With these two processes occurring simultaneously, there might be no apparent change in residential preferences.

Rising incomes may have been a condition for the rise of the extended family. But they do not tell the whole story. In the twentieth century incomes have continued to rise, while the propensity to reside in extended families has declined precipitously. Explanation in terms of rising incomes assumes that people had an underlying desire to live in extended families. Such a desire, as the twentieth-century experience demonstrates, is far from universal. But the Victorians seem to have had a special predisposition for extended living arrangements.

We need not assume that family structure was merely a marionette to

2. This literature is discussed in chapter 2.

the puppeteers of economics and demography. Economic and demographic changes created conditions that made extended families possible. Still, the Victorians did not reside with their extended kin merely because it was possible for them to do so; they also had to *choose* extended-family structure.

We must look for sources of explanation beyond demography and economics. To understand the rise of the extended family, we should, in particular, study the peculiar context of Victorian norms and values. We should ask if there were aspects of Victorian *culture* that especially favored the formation of extended families.[3]

If we ignored nonquantitative evidence, we could entertain the view that no cultural change occurred until the twentieth century; my demographic and economic analyses are completely consistent with the hypothesis that people had always wanted to live with extended kin, but before the nineteenth century economic and demographic constraints prevented them from doing so.

But the thesis that attitudes toward kin and toward the family remained constant is ahistorical. Contemporary rhetoric demonstrates that the Victorians held views about the family very different from those of their forebears in the eighteenth century. The sheer volume of intensely emo-

---

3. When we leave the tidy quantifiable worlds of economics and demography and enter the world of ideas and beliefs, it is easy to lose our way. We can no longer neatly divide society into narrow statistical boxes. But most aspects of human interaction cannot be easily counted, and if we look only at numbers we may miss the main show.

A painstaking and judicious reading of contemporary sources is generally thought to entitle historians to make generalizations on the nature of social change that, by their very nature, cannot be proven. I have undertaken no such careful study of literary evidence from the Victorian era. At the close of my work, however, I ask that the reader indulge me in a few speculations, though my principal guide must be the work of the historians who have gone before.

Though my failure to explore thoroughly the qualitative sources on the family was due largely to lack of time, there were other considerations as well, aptly summarized by Margaret Atwood: "But you don't find out, exactly, and things get pickier and pickier, and more and more stale, and it all collapses in a welter of commas and shredded footnotes. And after a while it's like anything else: you've got stuck in it and you can't get out, and you wonder how you got there in the first place . . . And besides that, everything's been done already, fished out, and you yourself wallowing around in the dregs at the bottom of the barrel, one of those ninth year graduate students, poor bastards, scribbling through manuscripts for new material or slaving away on the definitive edition of Ruskin's dinner-invitations and theatre-stubs" (Atwood 1976: 99–100).

This is not to say that quantitative research does not have problems of its own. There is always the problem of funding. The comments of Maurice Maltravers apply to my own case: "My immediate difficulty is that the university has denied me further use of the computer . . . Without it, I cannot complete the Ultimate Machine" (Lafferty 1970: 238).

tional outpourings on the topic testifies to the Victorian preoccupation with the family.[4] A selection from the writing of Walter T. Griffin, published in 1886, will serve to communicate the flavor of this literature:

> If you desired to gather up all tender memories, all lights and shadows of the heart, all banquetings and reunions, all filial, fraternal, paternal, conjugal affections, and had just four letters with which to spell out that height and depth and length and breadth and magnitude of and eternity of meaning, you would write it out with these four capital letters: H-O-M-E. Here is a world where no storms intrude—a haven of safety against the tempests of life—a little world of joy and love, of innocence and tranquility . . . All are linked to each other by the most intimate and endearing ties; husband to wife, wife to husband; parents to children, children to parents; brothers and sisters to sisters and brothers: a power like that of electricity seems to run through the family group.[5]

Griffin continues in this breathless vein for another 600 pages. This almost desperate glorification of home and family was not confined to the innumerable advice books of the period; the same sentiments permeate fiction, diaries, correspondence, sermons, biographies, and even histories.

But there were a few skeptical voices. At the outset of this volume, I quoted Samuel Butler's critique of the extended family. Now that we have examined the operation of structural factors in some depth, the comments of this astute observer of the Victorian scene bear repetition. "I believe that more unhappiness comes from this source than any other—I mean from the attempt to prolong the family connection unduly and to make people hang together artificially who would never naturally do so. The mischief among the lower classes is not so great, but among the middle and upper classes it is killing a large number daily. And the old people do not really like it so much better than the young."[6]

The advice books of the late nineteenth century typically described the home as a refuge from the "anxieties of the outer world," wherein harmony prevailed and innocence was protected.[7] For many, as Butler's

4. Of course, outpourings on *every* topic increased with rising incomes and higher literacy. I am asserting that a higher *proportion* of published works dealt with the family in the nineteenth century than in the preceding century.

5. Griffin (1886: 24).

6. Butler (1912: 33). See also Butler (1903).

7. A wide variety of historians have explored this pervasive theme in Victorian culture. The classic treatments are Houghton (1957: 86, 341–50, 391–93), and Banks and Banks

comment suggests, the home may have more closely resembled a prison.[8] Yet bourgeois respectability required that needy close relatives be maintained, even if they were an economic liability. Griffin is explicit about this: "The injunction to provide for one's household, binds all members of the family . . . the head of the family, overlooking this duty, is worse than an infidel; the other members, disclaiming the obligation, are not free from sin. Never enjoy luxury or wealth and leave a deserving parent, brother, or sister in want or discomfort. If in affluence, be ashamed to allow even a distant relation to live on the charity of strangers."[9] The sentimentalization of childhood, the idealization of the mother-child relationship, and the rise of romantic love all contributed to the sense of obligation between close relations.[10] Open conflict was tantamount to a denial of some of the most cherished bourgeois Victorian values.

The Victorian glorification of home and family has sometimes been seen as an idealization of intense affective relationships between members of the nuclear group. Thus, some historians have explicitly linked this rhetoric to a rise in the ideal of the *nuclear* family. But we should bear in mind that extended kin were generally either the nuclear kin of childhood—such as parents and siblings—or the dependents of nuclear kin—such as grandchildren. The stereotypical image of the Victorian home did not exclude such relations; the advice books are full of admonitions regarding the "duties of brothers and sisters" and the "obligations" of married children to their elderly parents.[11] And the coresident spinster sister and widowed mother are stock figures of the bourgeois Victorian novel.[12]

Walter Houghton has placed great stress on the home as a source of stability and security for the Victorians, a "shelter *from* the anxieties of

(1964: 58–59, 65–66, 74, 108–9). See also Ryan (1976: 33–56), Wohl (1978), Banks (1981), Lockhead (1964), Young (1964: 150–53), Burton (1971), Frankle (1969), Davidoff (1976). On domestic privacy, see Sennett (1970).

8. Mintz (1983) and Freeman and Klaus (1984); see also Anderson (1984). There can be little doubt that the Victorian home was actually rather oppressive. As far as the extended family is concerned, the real significance of Victorian attitudes to home and family is that they reinforced the bonds of obligation between close relatives.

9. Griffin (1886: 535).

10. The importance of these three ideals has been stressed by the "sentimental" school of family historians; see especially Shorter (1976), Stone (1977a), Aries (1962), Flandrin (1979), Trumbach (1978). A useful discussion of this genre of social history appears in Anderson (1980). See also Degler (1980) and Lebsock (1984) on companionate marriage, and Buckley (1951) and Houghton (1957) on the idea of romantic love.

11. See, for example, Hague (1855), Robins (1896), Griffin (1886), James (1832).

12. Showalter (1977), Auerbach (1978, 1982), Mintz (1983).

modern life . . . a shelter *for* those moral and spiritual values which the commercial spirit and the critical spirit were threatening to destroy."[13] The outer world was deemed dangerous and the family was seen as a "walled garden" protecting childlike innocence and virtue. These walls not only kept the outer world out; they also kept close relations in.

We need not look far to find plausible sources of fear and insecurity that drove the Victorians to seek refuge in family life. The increased pace of urbanization, occupational and geographic mobility, and the acceleration of economic and social change created unprecedented turmoil and a sense of uncertainty about the future. Of course, life had always been uncertain, and the most important sources of risk—dearth and disease— were actually declining in the nineteenth century. What was new was the sense that individuals had control over their own fate and were responsible for whatever befell them.[14]

The rhetoric of Samuel Smiles, stressing individual will and personal responsibility, had some basis in fact: Victorians, especially bourgeois Victorians, were personally responsible for decisions about their own occupation, marriage, place of residence, and religion to a greater extent than any previous generations.[15] No longer were these critical decisions primarily controlled by parents, community, and church. In an age of improvement, expectations of success in all spheres of life were high. Those who did not meet those expectations—a group that probably comprised the bulk of the population—were told that they had only themselves to blame. The ideology of free will carried with it the burden

13. Houghton (1957: 343).

14. The theme of disorder in the nineteenth century and the consequent role stress and anxiety have been stressed by Smith-Rosenberg (1971, 1972, 1978, 1985). Thompson (1977: 501) and Medick and Sabean (1984: 22) argue that emotional attachment is actually promoted by mutual economic dependence. I suppose that this would provide a means of reconciling the interpretations of Michael Anderson and Edward Shorter. One cringes at the thought.

15. This is not to say that Victorians actually had meaningful control over their lives. For most, the limits of behavior were severely circumscribed by economic constraints. As external sources of control diminished, internal ones increased; guilt replaced coercion. The themes of declining control by parents, community, and church have been explored by many historians; see Ryan (1976), Stone (1977a), Flandrin (1979), Trumbach (1978), Aries (1962), Shorter (1976). These authors and others differ on the timing of these changes, on whether they began among the upper or the lower classes, and on their fundamental causes. A few historians argue that external controls actually increased; see Lasch (1977), Zaretsky (1976), and Foucault (1980). Perhaps, as Marcuse put it, "Freedom is a *Form of Domination.*" Thus, the growth of personal responsibility may be seen as a form of social control (Marcuse 1970: 2). On the other hand, according to Joplin (1970), "Freedom's just another word for nothing left to lose."

of guilt and self-doubt; the psychological stresses of that burden created insecurity. In this setting, sentiment operated as a secular religion.[16] Unable to cope, many people retreated into the home, the family, and intense affective relationships.

The romantic glorification of home and family is only one of many possible responses to psychological insecurity. Nevertheless, it held a peculiar attraction for the Victorians. As Houghton argues, they idealized their childhood—the period of their lives during which they had been free from the need to make critical decisions.[17] "The home of childhood,—what hallowed associations cluster around it," wrote one contemporary. "The very *name* excites emotions which no language can describe."[18] As adults, the Victorians sought solace from insecurity by clinging to the only environment in which they had ever felt secure. Only in their home and family could they hope to find refuge from "the anxieties of modern life."[19] And so the Victorians often continued to reside with parents or siblings long after they had grown.

There is no need to assume that the worship of the "Household Gods" was actually effective in alleviating insecurity; the point is simply that many Victorians thought it was. Indeed, it is perfectly plausible that living in an extended family often aggravated feelings of insecurity.

I suspect, in fact, that the rise of the extended family in the nineteenth century served no effective social purpose. Social theorists often assume that norms, behavior, and social institutions must serve a useful purpose; otherwise they would not exist. It is conceivable that taking in extended relations did meet some functional need, but we have no a priori reason to assume this was so. Unless extended-family structure was adopted in the late nineteenth century because it offered real solutions to social

16. Ruskin's definition of home as I have noted before is revealing on this score: "This is the true nature of home—it is the place of peace; the shelter, not only from all injury, but from all terror, doubt, and division. In so far as it is not this, it is not home; so far as the anxieties of the outer life penetrate into it, and the inconsistently-minded, unknown, unloved, or hostile society of the outer world is allowed by either husband or wife to cross over the threshold, it ceases to be home; it is then only a part of that outer world which you have roofed over, and lighted fire in. But so far as it is a sacred place, a vestal temple, a temple of the hearth watched over by Household Gods, before whose faces none may come but those whom they can receive with love,—so far as it is this, and roof and fire are types only of a nobler shade and light . . . so far it vindicates the name, and fulfills the praise, of Home" (Ruskin 1865: 99, section 68). In addition to Houghton's (1957: 343–44) comments on this passage, see Brooks (1978).

17. Houghton (1957: 343–44).

18. Griffin (1886: 24).

19. Houghton (1957: 343–44).

needs, any functional consequences of extended-family structure would have been purely fortuitous.

If the Victorian family did serve a useful social purpose, that purpose is not an obvious one. The structural factors that apparently encouraged extended-family structure in the nineteenth century—such as increased wealth and reduced mortality—did not create a *need* for the extended family; they only created the *possibility* for a high frequency of extended families.[20]

We should beware of the temptation to analyze society exclusively in functional terms. Such an approach reduces the study of society to an exegesis on the workings of a marvelous machine. It hampers analysis of society's flaws and internal contradictions and blinds us to "the play of the contingent and the unforeseen."[21]

The rise of the extended family in the nineteenth century was not an inevitable adaptation to the needs of industrialization or modernization. It is more appropriately viewed as a historical accident, the outcome of a confluence of demographic, economic, and psychological conditions. The separation of these three factors according to disciplinary boundaries is somewhat artificial; they are, in fact, intertwined aspects of a larger historical process.[22] Neither economics, nor demography, nor psychology should be viewed as the fundamental cause of the prolonged connections of the Victorian family; each of these conditions was necessary and none was sufficient.

20. If I am correct in arguing that the Victorian idealization of the family created a sense of obligation toward kin, then even in the psychological sphere the *reasons* for extended-family structure may have been unrelated to any *purpose* the extended family may have served. Under these circumstances, a functional analysis of the extended family cannot help us to understand why extended families were so common among the Victorians.

21. According to the functionalist paradigm, every part of the machine has a role to play in the fulfillment of that goal. The language of social theory has a built-in bias toward functionalist interpretations. We speak of social structure, the social system, social organization, the social order. This view of society has deep historical roots; it is not the creation of twentieth-century sociology. In Western society, the hierarchical organization of both secular and religious life has been consistently justified and rationalized in functionalist terms.

I am sympathetic with the plight of Herbert Albert Laurens Fisher (1936: vii): "One intellectual excitement has, however, been denied me. Men wiser and more learned than I have discerned in history a plot, a rhythm, a predetermined pattern. These harmonies are concealed from me. I can see . . . only one safe rule for the historian: that he should recognize in the development of human destinies the play of the contingent and unforeseen."

22. For example, increasing life expectancy is, of course, closely related to rising incomes. In the argument presented above, psychological change is also interconnected with

economic change; however, this relationship remains speculative and perhaps unresolvable. Moreover, it would oversimplify to suggest that economic change *caused* psychological change.

Causal analysis is a funny business. For any event to occur, there are innumerable necessary conditions. Historians are in the habit of picking out one or several conditions for an event and labeling them as causes, which presumably assigns them great importance. To rank as causes, conditions must have some chronological proximity to the event in question, but the most recent conditions are usually relegated to secondary status and designated "immediate" causes, to distinguish them from the more important "root" or "fundamental" causes. The latter types of causes may not be cultural ones, except in cases where an invading hoard is involved. When one has no opinion about which of several conditions is most interesting, the solution is to label all of them on an equal footing; this is called "multicausal explanation." No one seems to have resolved the problem of what to do when several important conditions—ones that are likely candidates for being termed causes—are all conditions of one another. The comments of Zonker Harris are relevant in this context: "Most problems, like answers, have finite resolutions. The basis for these resolutions contain many of the ambiguities which conditional man daily struggles with. Accordingly, most problematic solutions are fallible. Mercifully, all else fails; conversely, hope lies in a myriad of polemics" (Trudeau 1973: 13–14).

Appendixes
Bibliography
Index

Appendix A
Notes on the
Measurement of Historical
Family Structure

> Poirot's gaze took on an admiring quality. "You have been of a marvelous promptness," he observed. "How exactly did you go to work, if I may ask?"
> "Certainly," said the inspector. "To begin with—method. That's what I always say—method!"
>
> Agatha Christie, *The Murder of Roger Ackroyd* (1926)

> God save us from what they call households.
>
> Emily Dickinson, *Collected Poems* (1960)

The data presented in chapter 1 relates, for the most part, to the percentage of extended households in various communities. Throughout the remainder of this volume I present figures based on a subtly but significantly different measurement strategy. First, I focus on extended *families* rather than extended *households*. Second, I classify relationships among family members in a way that is independent of headship specified by census enumerators. Finally, and most important, I adopt individual rather than household-level measurement; in other words, I assess the percentage of the population residing in extended families rather than the percentage of households that were extended. This appendix lays out my somewhat unorthodox approach and explains the intuitive and statistical rationales for my measurement strategy.

Family Extension versus Household Extension

My research focuses on the extent to which individuals resided with their extended relatives. It is not a study of *household* structure; instead, I am concerned with *family* structure.[1] A family is defined as any group of

1. I have avoided, for the most part, adopting any standard family-classification schemes, such as the one described by P. Laslett (1972a). This is partly because I am skeptical of the utility of any general classification system. Virtually every new question that we ask about household structure requires a new system of classification. No single system of classifica-

related persons who reside in the same household. By this definition, many families can reside in the same household. Boarders, lodgers, and servants not related by blood or marriage do not belong to the same family as the head of household. Instead, such persons constitute separate families. Under my definition, there are no constraints on the size or structure of families; they often consist of single individuals. Where direct information about family relationships was not available for the servants and lodgers, it was inferred on the basis of surname, age, sex, and marital status.

A hypothetical example may clarify these points. Imagine a household listing drawn from a census manuscript that contains the following individuals: household head, wife, son, mother of household head, a male lodger unrelated to the household head, the lodger's wife, and an unrelated female servant. This household contains three families. The first family is that of the household head together with his wife, child, and mother. This family is an extended family; the mother of the household head is the extended relative present. The second family consists of the married lodgers; the third family consists of the solitary servant. Neither the second nor the third family present in this household is classified as an extended family.

As this example indicates, my analysis ignores coresidence of individuals who are not related to one another. Household structure is a separate topic—albeit a related one. Since this is an investigation of the reasons why individuals frequently resided with their own extended kin in the late nineteenth century, boarders, lodgers, and servants are important only because they constitute separate families that did not often contain extended kin.

Household Headship and Family Structure

The relation-to-head variable that appears on many census forms provides us with the information necessary to measure two distinct phe-

---

tion is useful for all analytical problems; it is best to develop classification schemes suited to the problem at hand, through a process of experimentation.

For this reason I doubt the wisdom of incorporating a family-type classification into the data at the time of coding, since whatever scheme one adopts will probably have to be altered many times in any case. To allow for this versatility, classification should be carried out by machine. It has recently been argued that classification should be done by hand because it requires the "judgment" of the historian; see B. Laslett (1982: 3–10). Any system of classification, however, if it is not arbitrary, must be governed by a clearly specified set of rules, and if the rules are specific enough they can be followed by a machine.

One very simple scheme that seems to have relatively broad application is the vertical-horizontal dichotomy described in chapters 4 and 6 and applied most extensively in appendix E.

nomena: household headship patterns and biological relationships. Both of these are important aspects of household structure, but they should not be confused. Patterns of household headship are useful indicators of authority and dependence, and they can frequently lend insight into processes of family formation and dissolution. I employ headship for this purpose in appendix E. The pattern of biological relationships, however, is more fundamental; if we wish to understand the family life cycle, the family economy, or internal family dynamics, it is essential that we understand how all individuals in the household are biologically related to one another.

To extract biological relationships from the information given in the census, we must ensure that the analysis is based on a consistent reference point. The fact that census manuscripts describe family relationships from the point of view of the household head has sometimes dictated the classification system adopted by historians, especially when household structure is classified by machine instead of by hand. For example, a household consisting of a head, wife, son, and daughter is ordinarily classified as a nuclear household, while a household containing a father, mother, head, and sister is usually classified as an extended household, even though the two are biologically identical.

To compare household structure over time or between groups, we should adopt a standard reference person for assessing kinship and not rely on the census taker's choice of household head. This practice insures that contrasting headship patterns will not be misinterpreted as differences in the biological pattern of family structure.[2]

For this study, I employed standard criteria to determine the "head" of each group of coresident kin. In general, the family head is defined as the eldest adult male member of the largest nuclear group within any group of coresident kin. If no adult (over age 20) males are present, the family head is the eldest female member of the largest nuclear group. This definition is sexist, in that there is a preference for male reference persons over female reference persons.

I opted for a sexist definition because it minimizes the number of transformations of the census listings; under my definition, family headship is frequently the same as household headship as listed in the census. When the household consists of a single nuclear family, no transformation of headship is ordinarily needed. A new reference person must be assigned for about a quarter of extended families, and households with several families always require new family heads. A computer program was used to convert from relation-to-household-head to rela-

2. See note 10, chapter 6.

tion-to-family-head. Because my system maximizes the number of nu-clear-family members, these criteria tend to minimize the frequency of extended kin.

The Unit of Measurement

Quantitative historical research on family structure has almost univer-sally adopted the household as the basic unit of measurement. I have adopted a different approach, relying entirely on individual-level measurement. There are sound intuitive, statistical, and analytical advantages to measurement by individuals, but most of these advantages have been overlooked by historians of the family.

Several historians have pointed out that if we wish to describe the residential experience of a population, we should measure household structure in terms of the individual rather than the household.[3] Thus, for example, instead of measuring the percentage of households that are extended, we might measure the percentage of individuals who live in extended households. In short, measurement of household structure by individuals makes intuitive sense if we are interested in analyzing the experience of people rather than the experience of households.

But individual-level measurement has a sound statistical rationale as well. Percentages and rates—such as percentages of extended households or general fertility rates—are basically fractions. The numerator consists of the cases that exhibit the characteristic we are trying to measure. The denominator should consist of those cases that could conceivably exhibit that characteristic; in demographic terms, the denominator is the "population at risk." Thus, we measure fertility relative to the population capable of giving birth (usually approximated as the population of women of childbearing age), and we measure the vote received by a political candidate relative to the voting population instead of relative to the population as a whole.

To the extent that our denominators include individuals who cannot possess the given characteristic, our statistics are blurred. Especially if we are comparing groups, the inclusion of irrelevant cases in the denomina-tor can lead to misleading conclusions. Consider, for example, the com-

3. A variety of historians have noted the differences between individual-level and household-level measurement, but the disadvantages of household-level measurement have not been fully explored, and historians almost universally continue to employ house-hold-level measures. For discussions of the issue, see Watkins (1980), D. S. Smith (1979b: 84–86), Berkner (1977a: 159–63). Historians exploring the life-course approach have been forced to adopt individual-level measurement and have noted some of the advantages of doing so; see Elder (1975, 1978a, 1978b), Kertzer (1984), De Vos and Ruggles (1986), Vinovskis (1978). An early approach to the problem was suggested by Halpern (1972).

parison of the socialist vote in two countries, one with universal suffrage and one with highly restricted suffrage. If we measured the percentage of the entire population that voted socialist rather than the percentage of the voting population that voted socialist, our figures would reflect the extent of suffrage more than the extent of support for socialism.

Just as the total population is a poor denominator for the measurement of voting data, so too is the total number of households in a population a poor denominator for the measurement of household structure. Suppose we wish to measure the incidence of extended-household structure in a population of fixed size. The usual method is to divide the number of households containing extended relatives by the total number of households. The implicit assumption is that all households in the population have the potential to be extended. This is usually false. Extended households tend to be larger than nonextended households, both because they cannot consist of "solitaries" and because they must include kin outside of the nuclear family. As the number of extended households increases, the total number of households tends to decline, if all else is held constant.

This pattern is illustrated by table A.1. We have three hypothetical populations of the same size, and we assume that under all circumstances

Table A.1. Measures of Extended Family Structure for Hypothetical Populations, Assuming Constant Family Size

	Population "A"	Population "B"	Population "C"
Assumed characteristics			
a. Size of population	200	200	200
b. Mean size of extended households	5	5	5
c. Mean size of nonextended households	3	3	3
d. Number of extended households	4	19	40
e. Total number of households $(((a - bd)/c) + d)$	64	54	40
f. Population living in extended households $(b \times d)$	20	95	200
g. Maximum possible number of extended households (a/b)	40	40	40
Measures of extended household structure			
Percent of households extended (d/e)	6.3	35.2	100.0
Percent of potentially extended households actually extended (d/g)	10.0	47.5	100.0
Percent of population living in extended households (f/a)	10.0	47.5	100.0

extended households will have a mean of five members, whereas nonextended households will have a mean of three. Population "C" assumes that all households are extended; since extended household size is five, and there are 200 people in the population, population "C" has forty extended households. Population "A" assumes four extended households, and population "B" assumes nineteen.

The larger the number of extended households, the smaller will be the total number of households. Given that the size of all three populations is 200, and the average size of extended households in each population is five, we know that the maximum number of households that could be extended in each population is forty. In other words, the number of households "at risk" of being extended is forty in all three populations, even though the total number of households varies substantially between populations.

If we measure household structure relative to the population of households at risk of being extended, then 10 percent of the households in population "A" that could be extended were extended, whereas in population "B" the figure is 48 percent. According to the conventional measure, which uses the total number of households as the denominator, the percentages of extended household are considerably smaller, 6 percent and 35 percent respectively.

In most populations, the total number of households is higher than the potential number of extended households. If we use the total number of households as our denominator, we will accordingly underestimate the true prevalence of extended households.

If we instead adopt the individual as our unit of measurement, we avoid underestimating the prevalence of extended households. The bottom row of table A.1 shows the percentage of individuals in each hypothetical population living in extended households. In population "A," 10 percent of the population live in extended households, whereas in population "B," 48 percent live in extended households. Note that we get the same results when we measure household structure relative to the individual as we do when the household is the unit of measurement and we restrict ourselves to the population of households that are potentially extended. This is because all *individuals* in the population are "at risk" of residing in an extended household.

In table A.1, we assumed that the mean size of extended households and the mean size of nonextended households were fixed. This assumption, of course, is unrealistic; the size distribution of households can vary greatly between populations.

The potential effects of such variation are illustrated in table A.2.

Table A.2. Measures of Extended Family Structure for Hypothetical Populations, Assuming Variable Family Size

	Population "D"	Population "E"	Population "F"
Assumed characteristics			
a. Size of population	200	200	200
b. Mean size of extended households	6	5	4
c. Mean size of nonextended households	2	3	4
d. Number of extended households	12	10	9
e. Total number of households			
$(((a - bd)/c) + d)$	76	60	50
f. Population living in			
extended households $(b \times d)$	72	50	36
g. Maximum possible number of			
extended households (a/b)	33	40	50
Measures of extended household structure			
Percent of households			
extended (d/e)	15.8	16.7	18.0
Percent of potentially extended			
households actually extended (d/g)	36.0	25.0	18.0
Percent of population living in			
extended households (f/a)	36.0	25.0	18.0

Again, we have three populations of identical size, but this time the mean size of extended and nonextended households varies between populations. Population "D," with the largest mean size of extended households and the lowest mean size of nonextended households, has the highest number of extended households and the greatest percentage of the population living in extended households. Paradoxically, when we look at the conventional measure—the percentage of households extended— we see that population "D" has the lowest percentage of extended households. At the other extreme, population "F," with the smallest mean size of extended households and the largest mean size of nonextended households, has the lowest number of extended households and the lowest percentage of the population living in them, but it contains the highest percentage of extended households.

Suppose that populations "D," "E," and "F" represented three successive time periods. By choosing the wrong unit of measurement—the household—we would not only underestimate the magnitude of change, but we would also mistake the direction of change. In real historical populations, the degree of error is smaller, but it is often crucial.

Choosing the correct denominator is not merely a statistical fine point;

it is absolutely critical when we measure percentages or rates of any kind. In the political example cited above, choosing the wrong denominator can result in percentages that correspond to the extent of suffrage more than to the extent of support for socialism. In the case of household structure, choosing the total number of households as the denominator can lead to statistics that are largely dictated by the distribution of household sizes between household types. Because historians have consistently used an inappropriate measure of household structure, their conclusions concerning long-term change in household structure may be badly mistaken.

Ultimately, we must ask ourselves what we are trying to measure. When we analyze household structure, we are usually concerned with residence decisions. To measure this, we need two numbers: a numerator that is sensitive to residence decisions, in order to indicate behavior, and a denominator that is completely unaffected by residence decisions, so that we will have a basis for evaluating the size of the numerator.

The conventional numerator—the number of households of a particular type—is quite sensitive to residence decisions, so it is not an intrinsically bad measure. On the other hand, the conventional denominator—the total number of households—is also influenced by residence decisions. We cannot effectively use the denominator (number of households) to evaluate the numerator (number of extended households), because numerator and denominator are inextricably intertwined. To make matters even more confusing, the relationship between numerator and denominator is neither consistent nor predictable. Our results are obscured by the fact that both numerator and denominator are affected, to differing degrees, by residence decisions, the very thing that we are trying to measure.

This statistical morass can be avoided by using the individual as the unit of measurement of household structure, because the total number of individuals in a population is independent of their residence decisions, and thus independent of household size and household type.

The confounding effects of household size on the potential number of households of a given type present no problem if we abandon the household as our unit of measurement. As table A.1 indicates, adopting the individual as the unit of measurement yields the same results as adopting the household as the unit of measurement and limiting the denominator to those households that could have a given structure.

Moreover, if we are interested in residence decisions, the individual is intuitively a more appropriate unit of measurement than is the household. It is, after all, not the household as a unit that makes residence decisions, but rather the group of individuals living in the household or potentially living in the household.[4]

For many reasons, then, the total population of individuals is an appropriate denominator for the measurement of household structure. I have therefore chosen to measure family structure in terms of the percentage of the population residing in families of a given type.

The individual is not, however, the only unit of measurement appropriate for the study of household structure. The best unit of measurement depends on the particular problem under study. In some cases, we may want to limit ourselves to individuals of a particular age or sex, or, as Berkner has suggested, adopt "marital units" as the unit of measurement.[5] Whatever unit of measurement we choose, it is important to make sure that the denominators are unaffected by household size, household structure, or residence decisions.

The Effects of Intervening Variables

The recent emphasis on the family life course has focused attention on the fact that household structure varies dramatically with age. Nevertheless, many historians and sociologists continue to neglect differences in age structure when they compare household structure between groups or over time.[6] Reliance on the household as the unit of measurement of household structure tends to perpetuate this practice, because it is virtually impossible to account for differences in age structure as long as individuals remain grouped together in households. Indeed, we cannot even classify households by age in any straightforward manner because each household contains a variety of individuals of different ages. If we adopt the individual as the unit of measurement, however, it is easy to account for variation in age structure.

Differences in age structure may affect household structure for a variety of reasons. Some of the variation in household structure is a consequence of demographic constraints on the availability of kin. A method of correction for these factors is described in chapter 5 and appendix C. Other differences in household structure between age

---

4. It is, of course, true that in nuclear families residence decisions may be made collectively or all power may rest with the family head. When it comes to extended families with adult extended kin, however, mutual consent for coresidence is probably necessary. These issues are discussed in chapters 2 and 3.

5. Berkner (1977a).

6. This is in sharp contrast to demographers, who have shifted away from age-dependent measures like crude birthrates, unless faced with very limited data, and have increasingly adopted age-independent measures like the total fertility rate. See Hajnal (1947b).

groups may depend on norms or economic constraints. For example, the elderly may reside with their adult children more frequently than do the middle-aged, because the former are more likely to be economically dependent. If a population has a high proportion of elderly people, the overall percentage of the population living with their adult children might also be relatively high, even if at each age the percentage of people living with adult children was relatively low.

One way of controlling for differences in age structure when comparing household structure between groups, provided we measure by individuals, is simply to break down all household statistics into narrow age groups. Suppose, for example, we were comparing the household structure of immigrants with that of the native born. If the immigrants tended to be younger than the native born, and young people were less likely than old people to reside in extended households, then a lower overall percentage of immigrants might live in extended households simply because of age differences. By disaggregating the population into narrow age groups, we could control for age, and isolate any difference between the immigrants and the native born at specific ages.[7]

There are times, however, when we are interested in what the overall differences in household structure between two groups would be if the two groups had an identical age distribution. If we measure household structure at the individual level, a variety of statistical techniques may be applied to control for age. For example, one may employ direct standardization, a demographic technique used to control for differential age structure when comparing birth, death, and marriage rates.[8] Alternatively, regression techniques may be used, as they are in appendix D.

Age is not the only variable that is straightforward at the level of the individual but intractable at the level of the household; other examples are sex and marital status. What I have said about age applies equally to any characteristic that describes an individual rather than a group. In short, if one wishes to control for variation in individual-level variables,

7. Even if there are no *overall* differences in household structure between two groups, it is usually a good idea to break down all household-structure statistics by age, since differences in the age pattern of household structure are frequently analytically revealing. To carry our example further, even if the immigrants and the native born were equally likely to reside in extended households, there might be significant differences in the age pattern of extended-household structure between the two groups; such differences could lend insight into contrasting processes of extended-family formation.

8. A description of direct standardization appears in Shryock and Siegel (1973: 289–91, 419–21).

then one must use the individual instead of the household as the basic unit of measurement.

There are also, of course, variables that can be assessed only by looking at the entire family. Family structure itself is one of these; another example is family income. There are still other variables that must be measured at an even higher level of aggregation, such as city size. All of these can be incorporated into an analysis at the level of the individual, since the individual is the lowest possible level of aggregation. One can attach a particular city size or family income to every individual record, but one cannot associate a particular marital status with every city or every family. Thus, measurement by individuals allows one to incorporate the greatest possible range of variables into a single analysis.

The arguments given in this appendix do not provide the only rationale for measurement by individuals; as I indicate in chapters 2 and 5 and appendix C, individual-level measurement offers distinct theoretical advantages and allows more accurate demographic modeling than is possible with household-level measurement.

The methodological discussion presented above is sufficient for understanding chapter 3; only the simplest statistics are employed there. But the heart of this volume is my analysis of the demography of the extended family, and that topic requires much more sophisticated techniques. Accordingly, chapters 4 and 5 and appendix C also deal with issues of measurement.

Appendix B
Data and Setting

The next point to be considered was the mode of bringing together the lover and the raven, and the first branch of this consideration was the *locale* . . . It has always seemed to me that a close *circumspection of space* is absolutely necessary to the effect of insulated incident: it has the force of a frame to a picture.

Edgar Allen Poe, Poems of Edgar Allen Poe (1882)

"Got something for you, we have," said Clarence. "Information. That's what you're after, isn't it."

"It depends," said Tuppence. "What kind of information?"

"Oh, not information about nowadays. All long ago."

"Historical information," said one of the girls, who appeared to be the intellectual chief of the group. "Most interesting if you're doing research into the past."

"I see," said Tuppence, concealing the fact that she did not see. "What's this place here?"

Agatha Christie, Postern of Fate (1973)

Social historians have a tendency to focus on the local and the specific. The community study is a valuable tool; there is much to be learned by looking at particular times in particular places.

The rise of the extended family was not, however, a local phenomenon; as I have stressed, it apparently occurred both in England and America. Despite my use of local data, therefore, this is not a community study. The data for this research were not chosen because of any special characteristics of locality. Instead, I employed the best data sets available to me.

Altogether, I used seven data sets, which provide information about some 300,000 individuals. Four of these pertained to Erie County, New York, in 1855, 1880, 1900, and 1915. These data were gathered and converted to machine-readable form under the direction of Michael Katz, Lawrence Glasco, and Mark Stern. Taken together, the Erie County samples constitute the longest time series of data available for any nineteenth-century locality. Even more important for a study of extended-family structure, the 1855 New York state census provides the earliest American evidence on relationship to head of household.[1]

Two data files drawn from the 1871 manuscript census of two textile towns in Lancashire, England, were also employed. These towns were selected to reflect the range of variation that existed in the Lancashire textile districts during this period.

The data from Erie County and Lancashire provided the basis for my analysis of the economics of the extended family. The Erie County samples allowed study of chronological change; the Lancashire data allowed comparison of the English and American experience.

Despite the advantages of the Erie County and Lancashire samples, they were not sufficient for my analysis of the *demography* of extended-family structure. For this phase of the research, I turned to the 1900 Public Use Sample, which is larger and incorporates more demographic information than the other data files.

The community study allows the social historian to link local conditions to local behavior. Comparative analysis allows the opposite strategy: if there was similar behavior in places with markedly different conditions, we can rule out particular local conditions as the reason for the behavior.

To take advantage of this strategy, one must know something about local conditions. I have therefore provided a thumbnail sketch of conditions in each community that I studied.

During the second half of the nineteenth century, Buffalo was a boomtown. As the western terminus of the Erie Canal, its population and economic growth were tied to the fate of the waterway. The city grew from 75,000 inhabitants in 1855 to 200,000 in 1880 and to 450,000 by 1915. Much of Buffalo's growth was fueled by European immigration, especially from Germany and Poland.

The economic history of the city reflected the successive periods of America's industrial and technological development. In the mid-nineteenth century, the city was primarily a commercial center, its economy based on the shipment of goods from the Great Lakes to the Erie Canal. Throughout the nineteenth century, Buffalo's manufacturing sector was based on the raw materials flowing into the city from the West—

1. The 1855 census is especially useful because it includes two other unusual variables—value of dwelling and years resident locally.

The data set consists of a 100 percent sample of Buffalo in 1855, which was originally converted to machine-readable form by Lawrence Glasco (1973); a 20 percent sample of the rest of Erie County in 1855; and samples ranging from 7 percent to 10 percent for Erie County as a whole in 1880, 1900, and 1915. With the exception of the Glasco sample, all of these data were prepared under the direction of Mark Stern and Michael B. Katz.

lumber, grain, and livestock. This trade encouraged diverse industrial development, including furniture making, milling, brewing, butchering, and tanning. Proximity to Pennsylvania coal and Minnesota iron transformed the city into a center for steel and automobile production after the turn of the century.[2]

The sample also includes Buffalo's rural hinterland. For 1855, the population census of Erie County was linked to the agricultural census, in order to obtain data on the characteristics of farms. With its grain- and dairy-based economy, Erie County remained one of New York's major agricultural regions until after World War II.

The Lancashire sample derives from two textile towns, Turton-near-Bolton and Salford. Turton and Salford contrast markedly with each other and with Erie County. Unlike Erie County, which had a diverse industrial base and ethnic composition, these English localities were relatively homogeneous. Both towns were dominated by the textile industry, which by 1871 was suffering from the effects of foreign competition. The population of Turton was almost entirely English born, whereas about 20 percent of the Salford population consisted of immigrants, mostly from Ireland.

Turton-near-Bolton was widely viewed as a model mill town. The town's economy was dominated by the Ashworth family spinning mills, and about half the workers lived in cottages built and rented by the Ashworth family. According to William Dodd, a factory cripple and a sharp critic of the factory system, these were "good substantial stone buildings, roomy, well drained, and well lighted, having one door in front and another in the back."[3] The workers were unusually prosperous; even during the depression years of the 1840s, travelers remarked on the material comforts the operatives enjoyed.[4] There is also evidence of remarkably high standards of health, sanitation, and literacy.[5] But the

2. Considerable secondary research on the social and economic characteristics of Buffalo in this period has been carried out. See, for example, Stern (1979), Katz, Doucet, and Stern (1982), Glasco (1973, 1978), Yans-McLaughlin (1977), Shelton (1976), Allen (1896). Some useful contemporary sources include Barry and Elmes (1924), Carpenter (1927), Buffalo Board of Health (1855), Poole (1905), Buffalo Chamber of Commerce (1911–1914).

3. Dodd (1842). There were two types of cottages, some with two rooms and others with four. The average house contained 5.6 people, including 2.75 mill workers. *Hansard* (1844: 1146). The best source on the Ashworth family and conditions in Turton generally is Boyson (1970). See also Calman (1875).

4. Faucher (1844: 111), W. C. Taylor (1842: 150), Boyson (1970: 124), Dodd (1842: 89), Ashworth (1842: 74–81).

5. On health conditions, see Razzell and Wainwright (1973: 187), Faucher (1844: 114), Taylor (1842: 150). On literacy, see *Parliamentary Papers* (1833: XX, 884), Senior (1837:

benefits of Turton did not come without cost; Ashworth exercised a strict paternalistic superintendence over his workers. Drinking or keeping improper company could result in dismissal, and the homes of workers were inspected frequently for cleanliness and "habits of life."[6]

Conditions in Salford were very different; Engels described the city as "the classic slum."[7] Housing conditions were among the worst in England, and the sanitation system was virtually nonexistent.[8] Mortality was devastating; in 1871, over half the children died within their first years.[9] The levels of poverty, crime, and illiteracy in Salford were notorious.[10] Yet there was another aspect to Salford: its outlying boroughs of Broughton, Pendleton, and Pendlebury were by the 1870s becoming fashionable suburban retreats for manufacturers, bankers, merchants, and professionals.[11]

47). The political opinions of the Turton workers were apparently fairly far to the left; see Faucher (1844: 114) and *Parliamentary Papers* (1860: XXII, 465–66).

6. Ashworth (1844), Faucher (1844: 113), *Parliamentary Papers* (1834: XX, 760, 762). Engels, speaking of visits to Ashworth's mills and others like them wrote that "you see an easy patriarchal relation, you see the life of the overlookers, you see what the bourgeoisie promises the workers if they become its slaves, mentally and morally" (1958: 186). One aspect of Ashworth's paternalism that may have had an effect on family structure was his active discouragement of mothers from working (*Parliamentary Papers* 1860: XII, 475). Boyson, the historian of the Ashworth family, suggests that "it was possibly in Ashworth's interests for the wives to stay at home and raise large families, and as always he had little difficulty in developing a moral tone where his interests were concerned" (Boyson 1970: 106). Whether or not it was in his interests, Ashworth did actively recruit his workers' children (*Parliamentary Papers* 1866: XXIV, 99). Although there is considerable testimony that Ashworth's paternalism led to job security, in at least one instance he fired a middle-aged worker and refused to take responsibility (*Hansard* 1844: 1146). It should also be noted that much of the evidence cited here derives from an earlier period than the census sample. By 1871 the town was in decline, although conditions were still better than in other parts of the region. See Whittle (1885: 354) and French (1859: 48).

7. Engles describes Salford at some length (1958: 61–63).

8. Roberts (1971: 13–16, 76), Greenall (1974: 35–58).

9. Throughout the seventies, annual mortality was worse in Salford than in Liverpool or Manchester. "Look at the death toll!" exclaimed a contemporary critic. "Is it not disgraceful to a community . . . that forty-eight per cent, or close to one-half of the children born in Salford perish within the first five years of life!" This was written in 1880; in 1871, the figure was 52.2 percent (*Tenth Annual Report on the Health of Salford with Statistical Abstracts for the Decennium* 1880: introduction).

10. On literacy, see Neal (1851), Roberts (1971: 68–69, 129–32), Manchester Statistical Society (1836). On crime, see Neal (1851) and the letter to the editor of the *Salford Weekly News* of 31 March 1877. On poverty, see Farnie (unpublished, Salford Central Library), Chadwick (1860: 1–36).

11. To obtain an adequate number of bourgeois families, these boroughs were oversampled.

The samples from Erie County and Lancashire form the basis for my analysis of the effects of economic factors on extended-family structure. For this aspect of the research it was advantageous to use local data. Because the material conditions and economic organization of Erie County, Turton, and Salford were strikingly different, comparison of these localities can suggest the extent to which economic factors at the community level dictate residential decisions. Furthermore, one is forced to use local data to study family structure before 1900, because national samples are not yet available for either England or America.

But the heart of my research concerns not economics but rather demography. In this phase of the study, I turn to national data. Information about demographic conditions is more readily available at the national level than for localities. Moreover, my research strategy for demographic analysis—described in chapter 5—requires a large sample of the census.

Accordingly, much of the research employs the 1900 Public Use Sample of the U.S. federal census.[12] This data set—which provides data on over 100,000 persons—is probably the largest and highest quality historical census sample available in machine-readable form. It incorporates several variables essential for my demographic analysis that are not available on earlier censuses: children ever born, children surviving, and duration of marriage.

Despite the dramatic contrast in local conditions among Turton, Salford, and Erie County, similar patterns of family structure were found in all three communities. The overall frequency of extended living arrangements differed only slightly between these localities. Twenty-two percent of the Erie County sample in 1880 resided with extended relatives, compared with 21 percent in Turton and 23 percent in Salford. Because there were virtually no significant differences in family structure between Turton and Salford, the two files were combined to produce the tabulations used in this study.

Evidence from the national sample reinforces the conclusions suggested by the local data sources. In broad outline, patterns of family structure in Lancashire and in Erie County were replicated at the national level in 1900.

This overall similarity is a result of strikingly similar decisions on the part of individuals; the propensity for individuals to reside with relatives of specific types—classified according to relationship, age, sex, and marital status—was closely parallel in the three communities and the national

12. This is described in Graham (1980).

sample.[13] Furthermore, differentials in family structure by class, geographic mobility, and life course followed the same general patterns in Lancashire, Erie County, and the United States as a whole.

Such similarities in family living arrangements suggest that the patterns I describe were not simply a response to local conditions or even national ones. Accordingly, I have stressed demographic and economic explanations for the high frequency of extended families in the nineteenth century that might apply to both England and America; my conclusions, I believe, are equally generalizable.

13. For a description of residential propensities, see chapters 5 and 6.

Appendix C
MOMSIM
An Individual-Level Model
of Demography and Kinship

"Can you handle involuted matrix, Maimonides-conditioned, third-aspect numbers in the Cauchy sequence with simultaneous non-temporal involvement of the Fieschi manifold?"

"Maurice, I can do it and fry up a bunch of eggs to go with it at the same time."

R. A. Lafferty, *Nine Hundred Grandmothers* (1970)

For several reasons, I have not been able to compose the notes for this part of my narrative into any regular or connected shape. I give the notes disjointed as I find them, or have now drawn them up from memory. . . . Whenever it could answer my purpose to transplant them from the natural or chronological order, I have not scrupled to do so. Sometimes I speak in the present, sometimes in the past tense. . . . Much has been omitted. I could not, without effort, constrain myself to the task of either recalling, or constructing into a regular narrative, the whole burthen of horrors which lies upon my brain.

Thomas De Quincey, *Confessions of an English Opium Eater* (1822)

There are some respects in which designing a demographic microsimulation is similar to eating opium. Both are highly addictive, both induce euphoria, and both lead to despair and frustration. Further, I suspect that one can never really recover from either experience.

Were I to recount in full my descent from a mere analytic dabbler to a full-blown Monte Carlo modeler, the story would be longer than De Quincy's *Confessions*. I have consequently limited my tale to a description of my model as it stands. This may make it difficult for the reader to understand the rationale behind some of the peculiarities of my approach; my method evolved in a long and tortuous process of experimentation. The final product represents my attempt to maximize four competing virtues: accuracy, efficiency, versatility, and simplicity. In this effort, a fifth virtue—intuitive accessibility—has perhaps fallen by the wayside.

But the model is not really difficult to understand; it is simply difficult to explain. The problem is that in order to understand any one aspect of the model, one really needs to know about all the other aspects; thus, no matter in what order the model is explained, there will always be some confusion at the beginning. But the patient reader will be rewarded with comprehension.

General Characteristics of the Model

The model described in this appendix is called momsim. My model differs in intent from the models of the family described in chapter 4 in three crucial respects. First, it is not a model of household structure; instead, it is a model of kinship. Second, kinship is assessed at the level of the individual, rather than at the level of the household or family. Finally, hypothetical rules are not employed as an integral part of the model.

Momsim also differs radically from previous microsimulation models in terms of its organization. Other demographic microsimulations begin with a population that has known characteristics and then age that population month by month or year by year. In each time interval, every individual is exposed to a certain risk of death, marriage, and childbearing. It is thus necessary to keep track of the entire population at all times.

The purpose of momsim is simply to generate groups of related individuals who exhibit the demographic behavior of an observed population. Historical sources such as the manuscript census provide information only about those who resided together; by contrast, momsim is designed to reveal the characteristics of all relatives, regardless of their living arrangements. There is no need for this model to age the entire population simultaneously. Instead, the model successively ages each separate group of related people.

Each family group begins with a female ancestor, who is born as many as 160 years before the "present." The ancestor marries and has children in accordance with observed probabilities and each of her children in turn is exposed to risks of marriage, childbirth, and death. In this fashion, the model generates groups of related individuals. When each group is complete, all characteristics—including the timing of all events—are tabulated or written on tape for later analysis and the process begins again with a new ancestor. The procedure is repeated until an adequate sample of families has been generated.

The approach of treating each family group successively rather than aging all families concurrently offers a variety of advantages. First, it is logistically simpler to handle families one at a time. Moreover, this approach allows one to generate large samples even when the storage capacity of the computer is small. This is important because microsimulation incorporates a random element; for each simulated individual, the likelihood of marrying, giving birth, or dying is based on empirical distributions, but the actual allocation of these events is determined randomly. This can lead to significant random error unless the simulation model is capable of generating a large number of cases.[1] If one ages the entire population simultaneously, it is often difficult to generate enough cases to reduce random error to a negligible level, since the number of cases that can conveniently be handled simultaneously is limited by the storage capacity of the computer.[2] Since MOMSIM generates cases successively, the number of cases is unrestricted by storage, so random error can be largely eliminated.

The successive treatment of families also allows greater flexibility. Under the usual system, events must be allocated in strict chronological order. One cannot, for example, assign a woman's age at death before assigning her age at the birth of her children; within the model, time proceeds uniformly, and childbirth "happens" before death. But the MOMSIM model does not have to obey strict chronological rules. Life-course events are allocated in whatever order yields the greatest efficiency and accuracy. Because of the limitations of the available historical data and because of certain design considerations of the computer program, a strict chronological sequence of allocation would compromise the efficiency, accuracy, and convenience of the model. The reasons for this will become clear presently.

A major goal in the design of the model was simplicity. Complex models based on extremely fine subgroups of the population that mimic a wide variety of behaviors are fine for contemporary social-science research, in which one can rely on sample surveys, Social Security data, and a variety of other sources.[3] Historians, however, are limited in their work

1. As Wachter and Hammel point out, this can also be an advantage if one is interested in analyzing variability between small populations. However, this could exaggerate variability; it is possible that demographic processes are less stochastic than this kind of model assumes and there exist interrelationships between demographic variables—at the level of individuals, kin groups, and communities—that are not accounted for in the model and that tend to counteract extreme situations. See my discussion of the "Whopper Assumption" in chapter 5. The Whopper Assumption refers to the fact that members of kin groups tend to share similar demographic characteristics. As Goldie Hawn put it, "If your parents didn't have any children, you probably won't either" (Thomlinson 1975: 97).

2. There are ways around this; one can, for example, write the characteristics of each individual on disk or tape between each iteration. However, this slows processing and increases costs.

3. I am thinking of models like DYNASIM, described by Guy Orcutt (1961) and Orcutt et al. (1976).

primarily to census manuscripts and a few sparse vital statistics. We are forced, therefore, either to keep our models simple or to invent information on behavior.

The simulation approach described here has several features that help keep it simple. First, as noted above, hypothetical rules are not employed as part of the demographic framework.[4] Second, this method is restricted to demographic variables, narrowly defined; there is no attempt to incorporate variables such as race, geographic mobility, and class. To assess the effects of demography on family structure for subgroups of the population, one must run the model separately for each subgroup. This feature is shared by most other demographic simulations.[5] Third, the model is "open," in the sense that marriage partners do not have to be located within the simulated population, but are instead created as they are needed. In this sense, the simulated population may be viewed as a sample of a larger population.[6]

MOMSIM is kept simple one additional way: it does not attempt to model change over long periods of time. Simulations ordinarily have this capability, since one of their chief virtues is that one may continue the allocation of demographic events or other behaviors generation after generation and thus project the population into the future. This model, however, is designed exclusively as a tool for evaluating period data on family structure, so there is no need for long-range projection.

4. My own use of hypothetical rules is external to the demographic framework of the model; as in the analytic models discussed in chapter 4, they simply determine what is measured. See the discussion in chapter 5.

5. The narrow demographic variables—fertility, mortality, and nuptiality—are, of course, largely dictated by social behavior. For example, mortality is influenced by social and economic conditions, and fertility is heavily affected by marital patterns and social constraints. Whatever the sources of demographic behavior, the consequences are direct and inescapable: nobody lives with relatives who do not exist. Other variables, such as migration and race, are fundamentally different. Migration and race influence the range of living relations only because migrants, nonmigrants, blacks, and whites all have different patterns of births and deaths. To the extent that we wish to analyze the effects of demographic factors for these subgroups, we must carry out the analysis for each group separately.

The model can be run separately for any subgroup of the population that is relatively stable in terms of membership. This would include, for example, race, ethnicity, and birthplace. Occupational class and education are appropriate as long as the categories are broadly defined and occupational and educational mobility are not too rapid (or the demographic characteristics of the highly mobile within a given rank do not differ too greatly from those who are not mobile). An application of the model for analysis of class differences is described in appendix E. The reasons why this kind of analysis is inappropriate for assessing migration are pointed out in note 1 of chapter 5.

6. The distinctions between closed and open models are discussed in Sheps (1969) and Horvitz et al. (1969).

Of course, the chief application of MOMSIM is to analyze historical change. In order to do this, one must repeatedly run the simulation using demographic data for different periods; this approach is utilized in chapter 6. Moreover, even though MOMSIM is designed to yield accurate results at only one moment in time, time is a crucial variable; to determine the characteristics of a population at a given time, it is necessary to model events that occurred as far back as 160 years earlier. MOMSIM then halts the process at a single year, and this is the only year in which the complete set of kin relationships will appear. It is in this sense that MOMSIM is static; although time is a factor in the model, MOMSIM is not intended to model processes of change and it is not, in its present form, useful for that purpose.

Input Data and Allocation Procedures

Microsimulation works by assigning vital events to members of a hypothetical population. These events are assigned according to predetermined tables of probabilities. This section describes the probability tables employed by MOMSIM and the means by which characteristics are allocated. The way these procedures fit into the overall structure of the model and how they are used to create a hypothetical population of kin groups is discussed in the following sections. If you get confused, that is understandable, but if you bear with me it may all become clear in the end.

MOMSIM is based on demographic probabilities that are calculated directly from a sample of the manuscript census. The model was developed and tested using probabilities from the Public Use Sample of the U.S. census for 1900.[7] I chose to use this sample because it is large enough to calculate detailed demographic probabilities and because it is the earliest sample to provide information on cumulative fertility and marriage duration.

Using such micro-level data—rather than already aggregated demographic data such as age-specific fertility rates—has several advantages. The probability distributions can be much more detailed than is usual for simulations; the distributions can be tailored to the specific requirements of the model; a greater number of variables can be incorporated than is customary; and empirically based interrelationships between demographic variables can be integrated into the model. The following is a list of the basic input tables for MOMSIM.

7. This sample, which was converted to machine-readable form under the direction of Samuel Preston at the University of Washington, is available from the Inter-University Consortium for Political and Social Research, Ann Arbor, Michigan. It is described in Graham (1980); also see appendix B.

1. Percent ever married, by age and sex.
2. Distribution of age intervals between spouses, by current age, age at marriage, and sex.
3. Distribution of number of children ever born, by duration of marriage and age of mother.
4. Distribution of intervals between marriage and birth of infants.
5. Distribution of age at death, by sex.
6. Percent of ever-widowed persons currently widowed, by age and sex.

The first input table is simply the proportion of individuals of each age and sex who have ever married. This can be easily calculated from a census or from vital statistics. MOMSIM employs these data on marital status to assign age at first marriage.

The procedure for assigning first marriage age is straightforward. Table C.1 provides an example; it is part of the cumulative probability distribution of the proportion ever married by age and sex for the United States in 1900. Suppose we wish to assign a marriage age to a woman. First, the model generates a random number between 0 and 1—let us say, 0.5932. Note that in table C.1, 55.44 percent of the female population had married by age 23, and 67.34 percent had married by age 24. Since 59.32 falls between these two values, we know that this woman married be-

Table C.1. Proportion of Population Ever Married, by Age and Sex, United States, 1900

Age	Males	Females	Age	Males	Females
14	0.0048	0.0092	31	0.7285	0.8632
15	0.0058	0.0119	32	0.7289	0.8399
16	0.0057	0.0426	33	0.7532	0.8926
17	0.0125	0.1111	34	0.7765	0.8778
18	0.0233	0.1748	35	0.7510	0.8694
19	0.0386	0.2838	36	0.7876	0.9006
20	0.0910	0.3706	37	0.8151	0.9112
21	0.1539	0.4376	38	0.8338	0.9097
22	0.2178	0.5299	39	0.8258	0.9147
23	0.2759	0.5544	40	0.8266	0.9028
24	0.3609	0.6734	41	0.8697	0.9449
25	0.4149	0.6921	42	0.8612	0.9450
26	0.5125	0.7435	43	0.8812	0.9302
27	0.5701	0.7820	44	0.8948	0.9527
28	0.5804	0.7965	45	0.8738	0.9425
29	0.6527	0.8149	46	0.9024	0.9444
30	0.6709	0.8034			

tween exact age 23 and exact age 24. To calculate the woman's exact age at marriage, MOMSIM assumes that within individual years marriages are distributed evenly and interpolates.[8]

Most microsimulations handle the allocation of age at marriage through the use of age-specific marriage rates. For each age that an unmarried individual is alive a separate random number is generated. This random number is compared to the proportion of unmarried persons at that age who marry within the age interval. If the random number is less than the probability, the person marries. Since age is usually expressed in months, hundreds of random numbers may have to be generated in order for a single marriage to take place. The MOMSIM approach yields exactly the same distribution of marriage ages but requires only one random number for each marriage. This is one of the reasons why MOMSIM is comparatively inexpensive to run.

If a person marries, he or she needs a spouse, and MOMSIM creates one. Since MOMSIM is an open model, we assume that a partner exists for each married person, but we must decide the spouse's age. This is the function of the second probability distribution. The age interval between husbands and wives varies with their ages at marriage, so the age-interval table is broken into eight categories of marriage age. Since marriage ages are different for men and women, separate tables are also provided for each sex. For each category of age at marriage and each sex, the table indicates the proportion of marriages within any given interval, with the intervals ranging from −15 to +30. Negative intervals indicate that the wife is older than the husband.

8. Thus, to calculate the exact age at marriage, we interpolate using the following formula:

$$n + \frac{R - P_n}{P_{n+1} - P_n}$$

where n is age last birthday before marriage, R is the random number, P_n is the proportion married at age n, and P_{n+1} is the proportion married at age $n + 1$. In my example, the exact age at marriage is therefore 23.326. As table C.1 indicates, women tended to marry significantly younger than men did in 1900. Professor William H. Walling, a contemporary observer, deplored this fact: "It is inconceivable with what stupid and ridiculous vanity lecherous old men are wont to seek for young wives . . . In these monstrous alliances . . . married life will become odious to the unhappy victim, and criminal hopes will arise in her heart, the chains which bind her will seem too cumbersome to wear, and she will secretly long for the death of her superannuated husband. In fact, the amours of old men are ridiculous and hideous . . . Such are the terrible penalties reserved for the improvident and foolish pride of those dissolute old men who expend their last breath of life in the quest of perfidious pleasures . . . Alas! for the old dotard who dares to drink of this enchanted cup!" (Walling 1904: 81–83).

These probability distributions are arranged cumulatively, with a range from 0 to 1. Because the table is cumulative, we can adopt exactly the same assignment procedure for age intervals between spouses as was employed for first marriage age. After the model selects the appropriate part of the table, based on the woman's marriage age, it generates a random number between 0 and 1. The point in the cumulative probability distribution of age intervals that corresponds to the random number is assigned as the age interval between husband and wife. Once again, when the exact age interval is needed, we assume an even distribution within specific years and interpolate. The spouse's age is then calculated by subtraction.

The assignment of fertility in MOMSIM is more complex. The analysis of fertility has been a special focus of demographic microsimulation models in the past, so there is a substantial literature on techniques for simulating births.[9] The approach followed in MOMSIM, however, differs greatly from that ordinarily used in fertility models. Typically, demographic micro-simulations handle fertility through the use of age-specific rates, in a manner analogous to the usual allocation of marriage age described above. That is, most microsimulations generate a separate random number for every time interval that each woman is eligible to conceive. If the probability of conception is greater than the random number, a conception is assigned to the woman. This approach can be greatly elaborated for studying a wide range of determinants of fertility, such as fetal mortality, prolonged breastfeeding, contraceptive use, and sexual abstinence.

An early version of MOMSIM employed age-specific fertility rates for the allocation of births to women, but I abandoned this strategy when I found that it yielded a highly unrealistic *distribution* of children ever born to women. The technique proved to be accurate for estimating the mean children ever born at each age, but the standard deviation of children ever born was much too small. Some women have many children and some have few; a random number generator simply does not introduce enough variation among women. Thus, the conventional approach substantially underestimates the proportion of women with no children ever born or no children surviving.

This error creates no great problem for demographic models that are specifically oriented to the study of fertility, since such models are primarily concerned with aggregate measures of fertility, such as the Gross Reproduction Rate. For models designed to reveal the availability of kin,

9. See, for example, Santow (1978), Jaquard and Leridon (1974).

however, the use of age-specific rates in the allocation of fertility produces unacceptable inaccuracy. We are not primarily concerned with the
mean number of available kin of a given type; rather, we are interested in
the percentage of persons who had *any* kin of a given type available for
coresidence. The frequency distribution of the number of kin available is
therefore just as important as the central tendency.

The allocation of births according to age-specific rates not only overestimates the proportion of women with any children ever born, it also
overestimates the proportion of individuals with any descendants or
horizontally extended kin of a given type. This is because the distribution
of kin among individuals is in large measure determined by the distribution of children among mothers.

The authors of the socsim microsimulation model also apparently
recognized that the allocation of fertility through the use of age-specific
rates yields too-uniform fertility behavior. To compensate for this, they
introduced additional variability. Each woman in the simulated population was assigned a "low," "medium," or "high" fertility-adjustment
factor at birth, and this adjustment was used to modify the risk of bearing
children throughout that woman's reproductive span. Although it is
better than nothing, this approach is not ideal.[10]

Although it would be possible to create a more sophisticated adjustment technique than that employed by socsim, a much simpler approach
is available. The current version of momsim does not employ age-specific
rates to assign births. Instead, each woman is assigned a total number of
children ever born on the basis of empirically determined probability
distributions.[11] This guarantees that the distribution of children ever born
in the simulated population will correspond closely to that in a real

10. Wachter, Hammel, and Laslett (1978). The socsim approach to the variability of
fecundity is necessarily oversimplified; presumably, the actual variation is continuous.
Dividing women into three categories—low, medium, and high—is unlikely to yield a
distribution of children ever born that closely parallels that of a real population. Furthermore, the authors of socsim apparently had no means of estimating realistic fecundity
adjustments for their population, so the values they employed were probably rather
arbitrary. One cannot tell for sure, but I suspect that socsim underestimates the variability
of fecundity and this would lead to overestimation of the availability of kin. For an
alternate—and more sophisticated—means of controlling the variability of fertility, see
Crafts and Ireland (1975); see also Jacquard and Leridon (1974).

11. This variable is included in U.S. censuses since 1900. In census and survey data from
some contemporary Third World nations, children-ever-born data are frequently biased
downward for older women. Methods for detecting such biases are discussed in Shyrock and
Siegel (1973). Such biases are not apparent in the U.S. census data.

population, so that no adjustments to the variability of fertility are needed.

The use of the distribution of children ever born rather than age-specific rates to allocate fertility is appropriate because MOMSIM is not concerned with the determinants of fertility but rather with its consequences; a given level of fertility is simply assumed. However, because this is a model of the availability of kin, it is crucial that the variability of fertility between mothers is realistic, and the children-ever-born approach ensures this.

Several factors influence the number of children born to a woman, including her current age and her age at marriage, death, widowhood, menarche, and menopause. MOMSIM takes these factors into account by classifying each woman according to two criteria: her maximum age at childbirth and the duration of her childbearing period. The maximum age of a woman at childbirth is defined by her current age, her age at death, or her age at menopause (presumed to be 49), whichever is youngest. For currently widowed women, the maximum age at childbirth cannot be greater than the woman's age at the death of her husband. The duration of childbearing is defined as the interval between marriage or menarche (presumed to be 13), whichever occurs last, and the maximum age at childbirth. The means of dealing with births that occur prior to marriage is described below.

MOMSIM employs separate distributions of number of children ever born for each combination of fifteen maximum ages at childbirth and thirty-eight durations of childbearing. Just like the probability distributions governing first marriages and age intervals between spouses, the children-ever-born distributions are arranged cumulatively, from zero children up to twenty-five. Once again, these tables are calculated from the census.

To assign the number of children ever born to a simulated woman, the model first selects the appropriate distribution on the basis of maximum age at childbirth and duration of childbearing. Then the model generates a random number and assigns the corresponding number of children. The assignment procedure works in the same way as those described above for first marriages and age intervals between spouses, except that no interpolation is necessary because children do not come in fractions.

It is not enough simply to assign the number of children ever born to each woman in the simulated population; one must also determine *when* those children were born. The possible range of a woman's ages at childbirth is defined by her duration of childbearing and her maximum age at childbirth. Within these absolute constraints, births tend to be concentrated toward the younger end of the reproductive span.

In order to assign the exact age of mothers at the birth of their children, MOMSIM employs the distribution of intervals between marriage and the birth of children. Census data do not include the ages of all children ever born, but they do provide ages for children still resident in the household. To minimize error resulting from child mortality and departures from home, the data were restricted to children under age 2.

Once again, the table on intervals between marriage and childbirth is arranged as a cumulative probability distribution, with a range of zero to thirty-five years between marriage and childbirth. The assignment of intervals between marriage and childbirth is carried out separately for each child, according to the same procedures followed when allocating other characteristics. The probability distribution is restricted to the acceptable reproductive span appropriate for each woman. Again, this is defined by the duration of the woman's childbearing period and her maximum age at childbirth. Once we know the interval between marriage and childbirth, the mother's age at the birth of each child and the current age of each child can be obtained through subtraction.

One disadvantage of this approach is that it does not necessarily produce a realistic distribution of intervals between successive children. After experimenting extensively with techniques for allocating intervals between successive children on the basis of observed distributions, I decided that the logistical difficulties introduced by such refinements outweigh the potential improvements in accuracy. Nevertheless, as a compromise I incorporated provisions for specifying a minimum interval between successive children. The runs included in this work specified a minimum interval of nine months (0.75 years).

An advantage of the children-ever-born approach is that it allows us to account for historical change in fertility. Fertility was falling in the late nineteenth century. Thus, older women in 1900 had greater age-specific fertility than did women in younger cohorts. The procedure I have described will yield results that reflect changes in fertility between successive cohorts: the assignment of fertility is based on the woman's maximum age at childbirth, which in turn is constrained by her current age. Because the probability tables are based on retrospective data, they capture changes in fertility occurring during the past generation.

This is all very well if one is analyzing a population for which one has detailed retrospective data on completed fertility for women of all ages, but that situation is relatively unusual. In most cases, if one lacks evidence to the contrary, one will want to assume that fertility is stable across time.

Assigning stable fertility rates requires one additional wrinkle in the fertility procedure. MOMSIM incorporates an optional feature for assuming stable fertility. When this optional feature is invoked, all women are treated as if their maximum age at childbirth was 49, regardless of their current age or age at death. They are then assigned children according to the method outlined above. If their current age or age at death is less than 49, the odds are that they will be assigned too many children. Thus, we must remove the extra children; this is done by eliminating any children born after the woman's current age or age at death. The effect of this optional feature is to give all women in the population the same age-specific fertility experience as the 49-year-olds.[12]

MOMSIM handles illegitimacy by pretending that it does not exist. Within the model, the designation "ever married" means either that a woman has married *or* that she has given birth. Similarly, the relationship "husband" means either husband *or* father of the woman's illegitimate children. This simplification was made primarily for logistical reasons. However, this practice also conforms to a principle adopted throughout: the model is concerned with *biological* relationships rather than social ones.

The procedure for handling illegitimacy is carried out in the preparation of the input tables. In the table indicating marital status, single women with children ever born are reclassified as ever married. The modification of the probability table on children ever born is slightly more complex. If a woman has had children but is listed as single, then a value for her duration of marriage is imputed by means of a "hot deck" procedure, on the basis of her age group and number of children ever born.[13] In the other tables, single women are omitted.

Within the model, then, marriage does not mean that a ceremony has

12. To evaluate the period data for 1900 on residence patterns, it was necessary to account for fertility differentials between cohorts. The standard propensities employed in chapters 5 and 6 and appendix D were therefore calculated using cohort-specific retrospective data on children ever born. With the exception of the STD model in chapter 6, however, all of the other runs presented in this book were based on the stable-fertility version of the fertility procedure. Mortality change also occurred in the nineteenth century, but the current implementation of MOMSIM does not account for cohort differences in mortality.

13. That is, for such women the model assigns the marriage duration of the previous woman in the data file who was in the same age group and who had the same number of children ever born. The details of the method and its rationale are discussed in note 5, chapter 3.

taken place, but rather that a woman is eligible to bear children. As long as this definition is also adopted at the stage of analysis (e.g., in the calculation of propensities, discussed in chapter 5), then this unorthodox definition does not create any real problems. However, since nonmarital fertility does not exist in MOMSIM, the model cannot be used to study the relationship of illegitimacy to residence patterns. This is probably no great loss, since the historical census data on the living arrangements of unwed mothers is doubtless rather unreliable.

Similarly, MOMSIM ignores divorce. Because the proportion of divorced people was negligible before the twentieth century, and this research is primarily concerned with eighteenth- and nineteenth-century family structure, I have pretended that divorce was nonexistent. To extend the model for analysis of contemporary populations, it will be necessary to modify MOMSIM to take account of divorce.

Remarriage is a more important matter. Under a high-mortality regime, a large proportion of persons who survive to old age experience the death of a spouse. Many of these people remarry. In order for MOMSIM to accurately estimate the proportion of kin of specific types who were currently married or currently widowed, it is necessary to incorporate provisions for remarriage.

Unfortunately, remarriage is one of the most elusive demographic behaviors to measure with available historical data.[14] The census tells us the proportion of persons of each age who are currently married or currently widowed, but we cannot directly measure the proportion who were once widowed but have since remarried.

The solution to this problem was provided by the microsimulation. It is a simple matter for the model to generate the proportion of a population of each age and sex who are ever widowed; this is simply a function of marriage age, age intervals between spouses, and mortality. At the same time, we can empirically measure the proportion of persons of each age and sex who are *currently* widowed. This information is contained in the sixth input table. By combining information on ever-widowed and currently widowed women, we can calculate the distribution of probabilities that an ever-widowed person of a given age and sex has remarried.

This probability distribution provides the basis for MOMSIM's remarriage routine. As soon as the characteristics of a married couple have been assigned, the model determines if one of the spouses is currently dead.[15] If so, the table providing the probabilities of remarriage is con-

14. But see Dupaquier et al. (1981) and Wrigley and Schofield (1983).
15. The remarriage routine is only necessary if *exactly* one spouse is dead; if both are dead, no new spouse need be assigned.

sulted, and a random number is generated. If the random number is less than or equal to the probability of remarriage, then a new spouse is created. Since we know that the new spouse must be alive, his or her age at death is constrained accordingly.

The MOMSIM remarriage routine may seem a bit roundabout, but it works quite well. As one would expect, the proportion of the simulated population of each age and sex who are currently widowed is essentially identical to the empirically observed proportion in the census population.

The final probability table is used to assign age at death. This is the only assignment that cannot be based on a census; instead, we must use a life table. MOMSIM uses the proportion of persons of each sex who have died by each exact age.[16]

As before, a single random number is generated for each individual in the population. Death occurs at the point in the cumulative probability distribution that corresponds to the random number. Calculation of the exact age at death requires interpolation. I should note that when we are assigning the death of a spouse, we must constrain the result to ensure that death occurs after marriage.

Strategy for Assigning Characteristics

The assignment procedures outlined above allow us to "create" married couples and provide them with their basic characteristics: age at marriage, age interval between husband and wife, number of children, age at the birth of each child, and age at death. Figure C.1 is a simplified flowchart of the subroutine used to assign the characteristics of each couple.

Current age is the first characteristic assigned. As mentioned earlier, MOMSIM "freezes" the simulated population at one moment, and the full set of characteristics will only be complete at that moment. Thus, each simulated individual has a current age, which is his or her age at the moment the population is frozen. For the eldest generation, these ages are systematically (rather than randomly) assigned to yield a significant number of individuals of each type at each current age. The mechanism for current-age assignment and the use of current age in the tabulation procedures is described below. For now, suffice it to note that knowledge of current age is essential for assignment of remarriage and fertility.

Gender is assigned next. Just over half of all infants—50.7 percent—

---

16. In terms of the life table, this is:

$$1.0 - \frac{l_x}{100,000}$$

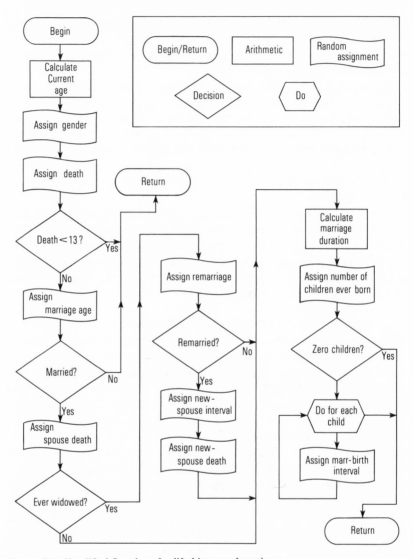

Figure C.1. Simplified flowchart for life-history subroutine

are assigned to be males, and the rest are females. Like all other assign-ments, gender at birth is determined randomly.

As will become apparent, other characteristics are not assigned in the order in which they actually occur. In particular, death is assigned after gender but before marriage or childbearing. It is efficient to assign death before these other characteristics, because if a person dies in infancy it is unnecessary to assign a spouse or children. But there is also a more compelling rationale. The number of children ever born and the interval between marriage and childbirth are partly determined by the duration of marriage and we cannot calculate marriage duration without knowing age at death.

After age at death is assigned, the model checks to see if the person died before age 13; if so, he or she will never marry and the life history is complete. If the individual survives to age 13, MOMSIM assigns an age at marriage. Some individuals never marry, and these cases are also complete. Otherwise the model checks to see if marriage occurred before death and before the individual's current age.

Those who do not marry before they die and before their current age are complete; for the others, a spouse must be created. MOMSIM therefore assigns the age interval between husband and wife, and the spouse's age at death. The age at death of the spouse is constrained; it cannot be less than his or her age at marriage, since we already know that the marriage took place. Next, the model determines whether or not either of the marriage partners has died. If so, either husband or wife is ever widowed and the model must call the remarriage routine to determine if a new spouse must be assigned. If it turns out that a remarriage has taken place, then the new spouse's characteristics must be assigned. The age at death of the new spouse is constrained even further than that of the first spouse; he or she must be "currently" alive.

Once the model has taken care of marriage and death of the individual and his or her spouse, it is ready to assign children. First, the duration of the childbearing period and the maximum age at childbirth are calculated as described above. Then the number of children ever born is assigned. Finally, the model assigns the interval between marriage and childbirth for each child. As noted, this information is sufficient to calculate the mother's age at the birth of each child. In between each assignment of the interval between marriage and childbirth, any previously assigned children are sorted by age. This step is necessary in order to set a minimum age interval between successive children.

When all characteristics have been assigned, MOMSIM stores them and proceeds to the next individual. This is all that is necessary to assign life histories to individuals.

I will describe the overall structure of the model and the means by which MOMSIM calculates kin relations in a moment. First, however, I will go over the main assumptions that are implicit in the procedure for assigning the life history of individuals.

Assumptions in Assignment of Individual Characteristics

MOMSIM's most extreme assumption is probably the Whopper Assumption described in chapter 5. But there are other assumptions as well. Like all demographic models, MOMSIM is based on assumptions about the interrelationships between the characteristics assigned to each individual. Each individual has a maximum of six main characteristics: age at death, age at marriage, number of children, age at birth of each child, age interval between self and spouse, and remarriage. The assumptions for each characteristic are as follows:

1. Age at death is assumed to be unaffected by any of the other variables. Of course, age at death is not *unrelated* to the other variables; early death, for example, can preclude marriage and childbearing. Nevertheless, in the model, mortality does not *depend* on anything else.

We lack sufficient data to test the relationship between age at death and the five other characteristics in most real historical populations. We can be fairly certain, however, that age at death was actually influenced by other demographic factors. For example, since childbearing entails certain health risks, female mortality should probably depend to some extent on parity.[17] Furthermore, if Ann Landers is to be believed, the unmarried state is highly unhealthy, so single persons should experience higher mortality.[18] But we have little historical evidence that relates mortality to the other variables considered here; in practice, the best we can do is cross our fingers and hope that the interrelationships don't make much difference.

2. The model assumes that age at marriage is unaffected by any of the other variables except death, which can prevent marriage from taking place. This assumption is probably reasonably justified. In the real world, marriage age can be affected by premarital pregnancy, but given the definition of marriage employed within MOMSIM (see above), this problem does not arise here.

3. Age intervals between spouses are assumed to depend on none of the other characteristics except age at marriage. In the United States in 1900, there were no significant relationships between number of children ever born or ages of mothers at the birth of their children and age intervals between spouses, once age at marriage and birth cohort were

17. Shorter (1982), Imhof (1981), F. N. Smith (1979).
18. Landers (1975).

controlled. Thus, to the extent that it can be tested, this assumption seems warranted.

4. The number of children ever born is assumed to depend on the maximum age at childbirth and the duration of the childbearing period. Recall that the maximum age at childbirth is defined as current age, age at menopause, age at death, or, for widows, age at spouse's death, whichever is lowest. The duration of the childbearing period is the interval between menarche or marriage—whichever occurs last—and the maximum age of childbirth. Thus, the number of children ever born is influenced to some extent by *all* of the other five characteristics.

This fact does not mean that all possible interrelationships between children ever born and the other characteristics are thereby taken into account. For one thing, age intervals between spouses are assumed to be irrelevant unless the husband is dead and the mother has not remarried. This is unrealistic, since male secondary sterility probably increases with age.[19] Fortunately, however, in 1900 this relationship was of minor importance. Further refinement of the fertility-assignment procedure may not be feasible, because the size of the input table for this variable—over 10,000 cells—is already pushing the limits of practicality.

5. MOMSIM also assumes that the age of mothers at the births of their children is dependent only on age at marriage and maximum age of childbirth. As pointed out in my discussion of the assignment procedure for this variable, the age of a mother at the birth of a child should also depend on the mother's age at the birth of her *other* children. Except for the introduction of a minimum interval between successive children, the model does not take the distribution of intervals between children into account.

The model further assumes that the distribution of intervals between mothers and children does not vary with marriage age, except to the extent that marriage age dictates the duration of the childbearing period. This assumption is probably untrue. Early marriages, for example, may take place because the woman is already pregnant, so the interval between marriage and childbirth may be shorter for those who marry exceptionally young.

Although neither of these problems is insignificant, they are logistically difficult or impossible to correct.

6. Finally, the model assumes that the probability of remarriage is unaffected by anything except for age and ever-widowed marital status.

19. Mineau and Trussell (1982).

Though untestable with available data, this is probably also untrue. In particular, I suspect that the probability of remarriage is influenced by age at becoming widowed and duration of widowhood. I have recently modified MOMSIM, and the new version incorporates a much more complex remarriage routine that partly takes care of these problems. The new remarriage strategy is sensitive to age of widowhood and it allows multiple remarriages. The refinement had little effect on kin frequencies produced by the model.[20] While this is encouraging, we lack sufficient historical evidence on remarriage to ever rid ourselves of implausible assumptions.

In sum, the assignment of life histories to individuals involves a number of assumptions that are probably or demonstrably wrong. This does not mean that the model will necessarily yield biased estimates of kinship. None of the assumptions yields biased estimates for the value of any particular characteristic; the problems are limited to the potential for unrealistic *combinations* of characteristics. This may have trivial importance for the aggregate frequencies of available kin.

Accuracy of the Life-History Allocations

The accuracy of the model—at least as far as the assignment of life-history characteristics is concerned—can be tested. The 1900 U.S. census provides a unique variable on the number of children surviving for each woman. The MOMSIM model can produce the same figure, but it does so in a very roundabout way. To determine the number of children surviving for any simulated woman, the model must go through ten steps:

1. Assign age at death.
2. Assign age at marriage.
3. Assign spouse's age.
4. Assign spouse's age at death.
5. If the spouse is dead, assign remarriage and assign new spouse's age at death if necessary.
6. Calculate duration of the childbearing period.
7. On the basis of childbearing duration, assign children ever born.
8. Assign age interval between marriage and birth of each child.
9. Calculate each child's current age.
10. Assign mortality to each child.

20. A version of the model employing the new remarriage routine was employed in Devos and Ruggles (1986).

Thus, in order to estimate the number of children surviving for each woman, all of the major features of the procedure for allocating life histories must be utilized. Any substantial error in the assignment of life-history characteristics would lead to errors in the frequency of surviving children.

As figure C.2 shows, MOMSIM provides good estimates of the mean number of children surviving. Some error can be expected in the estimates for those age groups in which only a small number of women had children. Despite such fluctuations, the greatest error in the mean number of children surviving is only a few tenths of a child, and the average error is under a tenth of a child.

For the analysis of family structure, the percentage of women with one or more surviving children is a more critical measure than the mean number of surviving children. Moreover, as noted earlier, the distribution of kin is more difficult to estimate than the mean number of kin. Figure C.3 shows the percentage of women who have any children in both the real population and the simulated population. On average, the simulated population falls within two and a half percentage points of the real population. It's not perfect, but this is a greater degree of accuracy than historians usually expect.[21]

The evidence on children surviving in 1900 suggests that the assumptions involved in assigning characteristics to individuals do not substantially compromise the accuracy of the model.

Organization of the Model

Let us next consider the *overall* structure of MOMSIM. It is not enough to create a population of simulated individuals. To estimate the availability of kin, MOMSIM must also keep track of the interrelationships *between* individuals.

---

21. The errors may stem from disproportionately high mortality in families with many children, particularly since early infant mortality increases the risk of conception by interrupting lactation. See Knodel (1968). This would be a special case of the Whopper Assumption; see discussion in chapter 5.

Note that the simulation tends to overstate the frequency of surviving children at ages over 45, by a little under a tenth of a child on average. This error probably results from my use of a period life table in an era of declining mortality for children. Internal evidence in the 1900 census suggests that one would expect errors of roughly this magnitude (some 3 percent) among children over 15; see Preston and Haines (1984) and D. S. Smith (1983). I am indebted to Daniel Scott Smith for pointing out this problem.

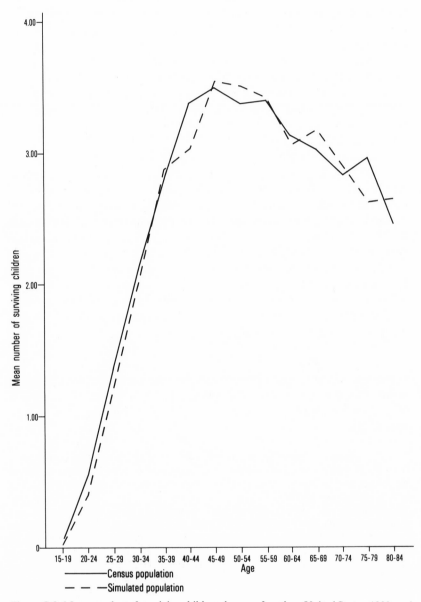

Figure C.2. Mean number of surviving children, by age of mother: United States, 1900, and simulated population

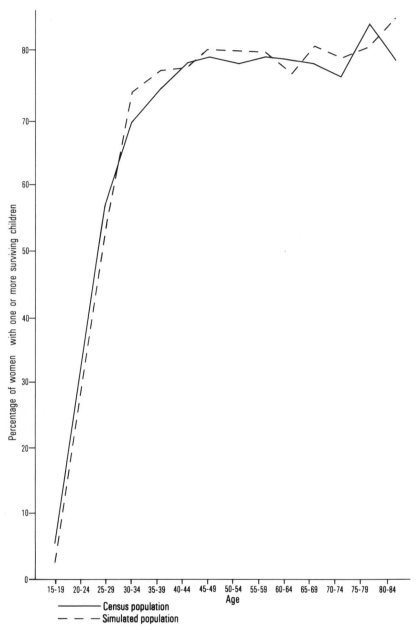

Figure C.3. Percentage of women with one or more surviving children, by age of mother: United States, 1900, and simulated population

MOMSIM works by generating *groups* of kin. Each kin group begins with a single female ancestor, who is given a current age at the outset. This current age falls within the range of 13 to 160; a significant number of ancestors are systematically assigned to each current age. No ancestors are assigned ages less than 13 because persons under 13 are assumed to have no descendants. After assignment of her current age, each of the female ancestors is assigned a life history. This entails, as outlined above, the creation of a spouse and children if necessary. The current age of an ancestor may exceed her age at death; indeed, at the older ages—say, over 110—*all* ancestors are dead. They are still necessary for the analysis of kinship, however, if they have living descendants.

After the life history of an ancestor has been assigned, MOMSIM assigns the life history of each of her children. Once again, this may involve the creation of a spouse and children—or, from the point of view of the ancestor, a child-in-law and grandchildren. Finally, the model assigns life-history characteristics to the third generation, the grandchildren of the original ancestor.

These three generations of relatives provide sufficient basis for estimating the frequency of all major types of kin. The timing of events in all three generations of the kin group are stored in terms of the female ancestor's age at occurrence. This makes it convenient to determine if any given individual is "currently" dead or alive and "currently" married or widowed.

A complete kin group might look something like figure C.4. The characteristics of this kin group appear in table C.2. Each individual in figure C.4 is identified with a letter that corresponds to the identifying letters in table C.2. The female ancestor in this example has been assigned a current age of 60. She has a living spouse, aged 64, two living married children, and one living widowed child. Her fourth child, identified by the letter E, died at the age of 5, when her mother was age 32. The ancestor also has two living children-in-law and six living grandchildren. All of these kin can, of course, be classified by their age, sex, and marital status.

To assess the frequency of kin other than spouses, children, children-in-law, and grandchildren, we must look at the availability of kin from the perspective of members of the kin group *other than* the female ancestor. The second generation—the living sons and daughters of the ancestor, identified by D, F, and G—allows us to assess the frequency of parents, siblings, siblings-in-law (sibling's spouse), and nephews and nieces. Person D, for example, has one living married nephew, identified by O, and two living unmarried nieces, identified by M and N. D also has a living

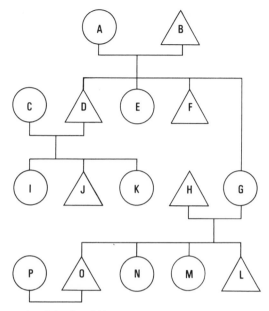

Figure C.4. Example of simulated kin group

widowed brother, a living married sister, and a living brother-in-law, identified by F, G, and H, respectively.

The third generation is used to estimate the frequencies of aunts, uncles, grandparents, and cousins. Let us consider things from the perspective of the individual identified by K. She has a widowed uncle, F, a married uncle, H, and a married aunt, G. In addition, she has two living grandparents, A and B, and three cousins, M, N, and O.

Only two important kin types remain: parents-in-law and the other sort of sibling-in-law, spouse's sibling. These can be measured from the perspective of the children-in-law of the ancestor, who are identified in figure C.4 by C and H. Each has two spouse's siblings and two parents-in-law. We should bear in mind that children-in-law of the ancestor have necessarily married; they are not created by the model unless they are needed as spouses for the second generation. Therefore, any statistics on the availability of kin from the perspective of children-in-law must be deflated to account for all of the never-married people who have never had the opportunity to become children-in-law. This presents no real problem, since we know the proportion of persons at each age who have never married, and we know that such persons cannot have any parents-in-law or spouse's siblings.

Table C.2. Characteristics for a Hypothetical Kin Group

	I.D. in Figure C.4						
	A	B	C	D	E	F	G
Relation to female ancestor	self	husband	daughter-in-law	son	daughter	son	daughter
Current age	60	64	34	35	33	30	28
Marital status	married	married	married	married	single	widowed	married
Age at marriage	24	28	25	26	999	25	14
Age at death	85	60	72	50	5	75	62
Number of children	4	4	3	3	0	0	4
Mother's age at birth	—	—	—	25	27	30	32

By the same token, such an adjustment must be carried out for any measurements taken from the perspective of a male ancestor. Since each kin group begins with a female ancestor, and male ancestors are only created as they are needed to marry first-generation females, never-married male ancestors do not exist. Because of the definition of marriage within MOMSIM, however, we know that never-married persons can have no descendants.[22]

In order to make meaningful estimates of the availability of kin under a given set of demographic conditions, MOMSIM must generate many kin groups. In practice, I have found it necessary to create about 10,000 kin groups to ensure reliable results. The number of individuals thus created depends on the demographic assumptions, but it generally exceeds 100,000.

The specific approach to tabulating results depends on the particular method of analysis that is to be employed. Alternative analytic approaches are discussed in chapter 6. MOMSIM automatically creates a general-purpose tabulation—hereafter referred to as the "main table"—that can provide the basis for a variety of analytic strategies. The main table shows the proportion of individuals of each age, sex, and marital status who have surviving kin of each type, age, sex, and marital status. This table consists of 60,000 cells. Although many of these cells are always empty (5-year-olds, for example, never have grandchildren), the table is far too complex to analyze directly. Nevertheless, the main table provides a useful means of storing the aggregated results of MOMSIM.

22. Except in the case of adultery. MOMSIM doesn't recognize the existence of such improprieties.

			I.D. in Figure C.4					
H	I	J	K	L	M	N	O	P
son-in-law	grand-daughter	grand-son	grand-daughter	grand-son	grand-daughter	grand-daughter	grand-son	grand-daughter-in-law
30	9	5	2	11	9	8	14	16
married	single	single	single	single	single	single	married	married
16	999	999	999	999	999	999	14	16
38	35	58	77	1	58	90	77	17
4	0	0	0	0	0	0	0	0
—	25	29	32	17	19	20	14	—

MOMSIM is unusual in that it creates only three generations. Typically, demographic microsimulation models are designed so that they can continue to generate successive generations indefinitely. I chose to limit the model to three generations because that is a sufficient number to calculate frequencies of all the significant types of kin. Furthermore, it is logistically simpler to store information about the interrelationships between kin when the number of generations is kept small.

The Piggyback Projection Model

Because MOMSIM does not project the population over a substantial period, it does not produce a stable age distribution. Within specific generations, in fact, the age distribution produced by the model will be highly unrealistic. For this reason, *all* aggregate statistics on the availability of kin produced by MOMSIM must be standardized by a realistic age distribution.

The age structure of a population is actually a substantial determinant of the availability of kin. It is therefore crucial that the results of the model are standardized according to a reasonable age distribution. When MOMSIM is employed to estimate the availability of kin for a real population and the age distribution of that population is known, we can simply standardize the results of the simulation by the observed age distribution. But, the most useful application of MOMSIM is to estimate the availability of kin for hypothetical populations in which the age distribution is not known. In such cases, it is necessary to calculate an age distribution that corresponds to the demographic conditions employed in any specific run of the model.

MOMSIM incorporates a "piggyback" projection model to calculate a realistic age distribution. The model is essentially a macrosimulation of the type described in chapter 4. The piggyback model is based on age-specific rates of fertility, mortality, and nuptiality which are tabulated when MOMSIM assigns life histories to individuals. These rates are assumed to be stable. After the main MOMSIM model—the microsimulation—has completed its task, the population projection model goes to work. Instead of generating hypothetical individuals, the projection model generates hypothetical *groups*. Each group represents the population of a given age, sex, and marital status.

Within the projection model, time proceeds by single years. In each year, the members of each group are exposed to the appropriate risks of death, marriage, or bearing children. The proportion dying are removed from each group; the proportion of unmarried persons marrying are shifted into the married group of the same age and sex; and the number of married women in each age group who give birth are counted. At the end of each year, the entire population is shifted into the next older age group, and all of the newborn infants are placed in the youngest age group. In this fashion, the model projects the population for several centuries. When the age distribution of the model has stabilized, it is converted into percentage terms so that it can be used to standardize the results of the microsimulation model.[23]

The MOMSIM Adjustment Technique

An additional potential source of error in the model must be pointed out. MOMSIM incorporates a shortcut technique for adjusting the demographic probability distributions that underlie the model, and this technique may result in unrealistic demographic assumptions.

As I have explained, the main purpose of my model is to generate data about the availability of kin under a variety of different demographic conditions. The most straightforward means of postulating alternative demographic behaviors is simply to plug alternate demographic rates into the model. For example, to understand the effects of mortality on family structure, I have employed mortality distributions based on several different model life tables. But substitution of alternate demographic probabilities is not always possible.

23. Further details about procedures for population projection can be found in Keyfitz (1968) and Pressat (1972). This discussion may seem belabored to some; even so, I have perhaps failed to meet the criterion of Adlai Stevenson: "Think not because 'tis understood / By men of sense, 'tis therefore good / Make it so clear and simply planned / no blockhead can misunderstand" (Stevenson 1965: 72).

For some of the demographic variables employed by MOMSIM—such as children ever born, age intervals between spouses, and intervals between marriage and childbirth—alternative distributions are not readily available. MOMSIM therefore incorporates a procedure for *adjusting* the demographic characteristics of the U.S. population in 1900 to create alternative populations.

The adjustment technique can be used for any of the demographic variables employed in MOMSIM. I will explain the method by reference to the mortality distribution. Since alternative mortality can be postulated either by substituting distributions taken from model life tables or through the use of the adjustment technique, mortality is a convenient variable for comparing results obtained through the two approaches.

As explained before, MOMSIM assigns age at death by generating a random number between zero and one. The point in the cumulative probability distribution of age at death that corresponds to the random number is the age at death assigned. The larger the random number, the later the age at death.

Suppose we wish to create an alternative population with a higher life expectancy than the standard population. The adjustment technique works by randomly selecting a portion of the simulated population and generating a *second* random number to assign their age at death. The range of the second random number is constrained so that it is necessarily larger than the first. By using the second random number, the model assigns a higher age at death than it otherwise would have given. By controlling the proportion of the population selected for adjustment, one can control the overall degree of adjustment.

The intuitive explanation of this method is more accessible. A portion of the population is blessed with a second lease on life. Instead of dying when ordained by the random-number generator, these persons are given another chance. From that time onward, however, they must suffer the same age-specific risk of death as everyone else. When such individuals die for the second time, the effect is permanent.

MOMSIM can use the same technique to adjust life expectancy downward. In this case, however, the model generates a *lower* random number to determine age at death the second time around.

The mortality distributions that result from the adjustment technique are not quite the same as one would expect in a real population, but the method works surprisingly well, especially when the degree of adjustment is moderate. The differences between the age-specific death rates derived from adjustment and those taken from a model life table with the same life expectancy at birth are small enough to have little appreciable effect on kinship patterns. When we alter average life expectancy by as much as twenty years, the use of adjustment as opposed to substitution of life tables yields estimates of the availability of specific types of kin that never differ by more than 5 percent.

The adjustment technique can be used to alter any of the demographic probability distributions employed by MOMSIM. When the method is used to adjust the distribution of age at first marriage, the errors are even smaller than they are for the mortality adjustment. But even though the adjustment technique works well for marriage and death, there is no guarantee that it is equally appropriate for other variables.[24] The results obtained through adjustment of rates should therefore be treated with caution. Further details on the distributions obtained through adjustment appear in appendix D.

Conclusion

And so ends the saga of MOMSIM. Readers who have made it through this appendix truly deserve applause. But you don't have to stop now; if you enjoyed this discussion, you'll just love appendix D.

It should be clear by now that I have not resolved the problems of the demography of kinship. The assumptions of demographic models—especially the Whopper Assumption discussed in chapter 5—lead to fairly drastic oversimplifications and doubtless result in substantial overestimates of the availability of kin for coresidence in extended families. We cannot rid ourselves of these assumptions in the absence of highly detailed information on the characteristics of kin groups as a whole, and if such information were available, there wouldn't be any point to constructing a model. This is sad, but true.

24. An additional test could be carried out for fertility. MOMSIM calculates age-specific fertility rates for use in the piggyback projection model, even though the *basis* for the model's fertility routine consists of distributions of the number of children ever born. The data on age-specific fertility could be compared with Coale and Trussell's (1974) standard-age pattern of fertility. I have not applied this test systematically, but age-specific fertility rates produced by adjustment seem reasonable to the casual eye. To borrow a phrase from Eldridge Cleaver, "It was a gamble on an equation constructed in delirium, and it was right" (Cleaver 1968: 143).

Appendix D
The Effects of Demography on Extended-Family Structure

What [historical demographers] like best is writing papers—long papers, on small subjects, with no conclusions.

Colin McEvedy and Richard Jones,
Atlas of World Population History (1978)

"To be quite candid, Jeeves, I have frequently noticed before now a tendency of disposition on your part to become—what's the word?"

"I could not say, sir."

"Eloquent? No, it's not eloquent. Elusive? No, it's not elusive. It's on the tip of my tongue. Begins with an 'e' and means being a jolly sight too clever."

"Elaborate, sir?"

"That is the exact word I was after. Too elaborate, Jeeves—that is what you are frequently prone to become. Your methods are not simple, not straightforward. You cloud the issue with a lot of fancy stuff that is not of the essence."

P. G. Wodehouse, *Right Ho, Jeeves* (1934)

This appendix explores the specific mechanisms by which demographic factors can affect extended-family structure. Such analysis is significant from the perspective of demographic theory, and it may hold interest for related disciplines, such as anthropology. Moreover, this detailed look at the demography of the extended family is important for historians because it reveals the reasons behind the findings presented in chapter 6.

In the discussion that follows, I isolate the ways in which each demographic factor—fertility, mortality, and nuptiality—could constrain or augment specific kinds of extended living arrangements. To accomplish this, I analyze the consequences of varying each variable over a wide range while holding all other variables constant.

Both of my analytic strategies—the standard propensities method and the hypothetical stem-family rules—are employed in turn in this appendix. Because I describe the interaction of demography and family structure in considerable detail, some readers may find the complexity of the following sections rather daunting. Although the discussion is highly detailed, however, nothing presented here should be conceptually difficult for those who have made it through chapters 5 and 6 and appendix C.

There are limitations to the approaches adopted here. In particular, my implicit assumption that propensities would remain constant while demographic parameters changed is unwarranted. As we will see, residential propensities are partially *dependent* on demographic conditions. Moreover, it is unrealistic to assume that most demographic parameters would remain constant while one aspect of the system changed. I have isolated specific demographic variables in order to analyze their individual effects more clearly. Only by making these counterfactual assumptions can we distinguish the operation of each demographic factor.

Before turning to the analysis based on standard residential propensities, I shall present the 1900 residential propensities themselves. To take full advantage of the standard-propensities approach, it is necessary first to understand the patterns of residential propensities in the standard population.

The 1900 Standard Propensities

The detailed residential propensities for the United States in 1900 are of intrinsic interest: they constitute a revealing description of residence decisions at the turn of the century. But my presentation of these statistics also serves documentary purposes. As the dedicated reader will recall, the residential propensities from 1900 are used as a standard yardstick to indicate how changing demographic conditions would have altered family structure, had residence decisions remained constant. Accordingly, these standard residential propensities serve as a framework for much that follows.

Let me briefly recapitulate the method for calculating the standard residential propensities. Momsim first generates frequencies of available extended kin of specific types under demographic conditions that closely parallel those of the U.S. population in 1900. The frequency of *actual coresidence* with specific kin types is then calculated directly from the census. By dividing the figures on residence with kin by the figures on the availability of kin, we calculate residential propensities. In brief, residential propensities are the proportions of individuals with living kin of a given type who actually resided with such kin.

The 1900 residential propensities for the most important kin types are shown in table D.1. To reiterate, the residential propensities indicate what percentage of the entire population who could have resided with each type of extended kin actually did so. I have omitted the minor kin types—such as aunts, uncles, and cousins—because the propensities to reside with such relatives are uniformly low and thus have little impact on family structure.

As has been my practice throughout this work, these measurements were taken at the individual level. Bear in mind, however, that extended kin are classified by their type of relationship to the family head. The sibling category, for example, does not refer to the brothers and sisters of everyone in the population; rather, it refers to siblings of family heads. Of course, the extended kin of the family head are usually also extended kin of other family members. Only the *classification* of kin types is based on the head of family; calculation of propensities is based on the experience of all family members.[1]

Several patterns in table D.1 deserve mention. Most important, the propensities to reside with married kin are uniformly low compared with the propensities to reside with single and widowed kin. Typically, the propensity to reside with unattached kin is tenfold or more the propensity to reside with married kin of the same type, age, and sex; the proportion of adult "unattached individuals" in the population is clearly an important influence on family extension. In addition, the residential propensities tend to be higher for female kin than for male kin, and the head's own relatives are more likely to coreside than are the kin of the head's spouse. Age of kin is also related to residential propensities. For siblings, siblings-in-law, parents, and parents-in-law, the highest propensities tend to cluster in the oldest age groups. High propensities also occur, however, for parents and parents-in-law who are unusually young.

The frequency of residence with kin is the product of both the availability of kin and the propensity to reside with kin. In the sections that follow, the propensities to reside with kin are assumed to be constant (identical to the U.S. population in 1900), whereas the availability of kin is allowed to vary. This resort to standard propensities helps us to understand the ways in which demographic conditions can influence family structure.

---

1. The "head" referred to here is the family head, not the household head; under my definition, the two are not always the same. For the definition, see appendix A.

Note that the principal demographic characteristics of the 1900 population on which the standard propensities are based—life expectancy, marriage age, and total fertility—are neither exceptionally high nor exceptionally low. The U.S. population actually had rather middling demographic behavior, compared to the broad range of historical and contemporary populations for which data are available. This is convenient, since one need not then adjust the characteristics too greatly to mimic a wide variety of demographic conditions.

Table D.1. Residential Propensities for Major Kin Groups in 1900 (Percentages of Those Persons Who Could Have Resided with a Given Type of Extended Kin Who Actually Did So[a])

| | Siblings of Head | | | | | |
| | Brothers | | | Sisters | | |
Age of Siblings	Single	Married	Widowed	Single	Married	Widowed
0–9	6.1	(0.0)	(0.0)	4.7	(0.0)	(0.0)
10–19	5.6	(0.0)	(0.0)	5.0	0.0	(0.0)
20–29	6.4	0.8	(8.6)	8.0	0.5	(10.0)
30–39	4.8	**0.2**	(2.7)	11.1	**0.2**	2.8
40–49	4.8	**0.2**	2.6	22.8	**0.2**	1.5
50–59	4.8	0.1	1.9	10.8	0.2	1.5
60–69	8.3	0.0	3.3	(33.7)	0.1	0.8
70+	(13.8)	0.0	1.9	(65.7)	0.0	2.3

| | Siblings-in-Law of Head | | | | | |
| | Brothers-in-Law | | | Sisters-in-Law | | |
Age of Siblings-in-Law	Single	Married	Widowed	Single	Married	Widowed
0–9	0.8	(0.0)	(0.0)	(1.2)	(0.0)	(0.0)
10–19	2.2	(0.0)	(0.0)	3.9	1.3	(2.8)
20–29	3.2	0.8	(0.0)	4.5	0.9	2.1
30–39	2.2	**0.4**	6.8	7.3	**0.2**	0.7
40–49	1.8	**0.2**	2.2	16.4	**0.1**	1.8
50–59	4.4	0.2	(1.6)	(10.8)	0.1	1.6
60–69	(6.5)	0.3	(2.9)	(26.8)	0.1	0.7
70+	(27.3)	(0.8)	(1.9)	(29.4)	(0.1)	(5.0)

| | Parents of Head | | | | | |
| | Fathers | | | Mothers | | |
Age of Parents	Single	Married	Widowed	Single	Married	Widowed
40–49	—	1.5	(12.8)	—	2.6	(28.4)
50–59	—	1.1	(3.4)	—	1.8	17.3
60–69	—	1.8	8.6	—	3.4	14.4
70+	—	3.2	17.3	—	3.2	20.4

Table D.1. (*continued*)

| Age of Parents-in-Law | Parents-in-Law of Head | | | | | |
| | Fathers-in-Law | | | Mothers-in-Law | | |
	Single	Married	Widowed	Single	Married	Widowed
40–49	—	0.5	(10.9)	—	1.2	(11.6)
50–59	—	0.6	4.6	—	0.7	8.8
60–69	—	0.8	7.0	—	1.6	12.2
70+	—	2.7	13.0	—	2.5	16.1

| Age of Grandchildren | Grandchildren of Head | | | | | |
| | Grandsons | | | Granddaughters | | |
	Single	Married	Widowed	Single	Married	Widowed
0–9	24.2	(0.0)	(0.0)	24.1	(0.0)	(9.6)
10–19	19.0	(6.9)	(0.0)	19.1	(2.4)	(11.1)
20–29	12.1	2.6	(0.0)	(13.0)	1.4	(11.1)
30–39	(11.6)	(0.0)	(1.5)	(11.0)	(0.0)	(0.0)

| Age of Nephews/Nieces | Nephews/Nieces of Head | | | | | |
| | Nephews | | | Nieces | | |
	Single	Married	Widowed	Single	Married	Widowed
0–9	**0.6**	(0.0)	(0.0)	**0.6**	(0.0)	(0.0)
10–19	**0.9**	0.0	(0.0)	**0.9**	0.0	(0.0)
20–29	**0.5**	**0.0**	(0.0)	**0.6**	**0.0**	0.0
30–39	0.3	**0.0**	0.0	0.4	**0.0**	0.1
40–49	0.2	**0.0**	0.0	1.5	**0.0**	0.1

[a]Categories of relatives for which the availability of kin is under 1 percent are shown in parentheses; for these kin types, coresidence will tend to be low even if propensities are high. By contrast, categories of relatives for which the availability of kin reaches 20 percent—which are more likely to have important effects on family structure—appear in boldface type.

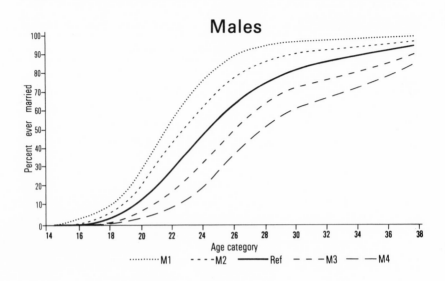

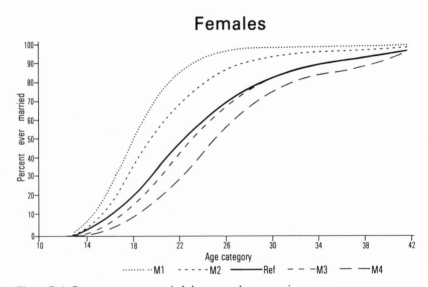

Figure D.1. Percentage ever married, by age and sex: marriage runs

Marital Patterns and Standard Propensities

Age at marriage is probably the most significant demographic influence on extended-family structure. To test the effect of this variable, I derived four alternative distributions of age at first marriage using the adjustment technique described in appendix C. These distributions, M1 through M4, are illustrated in figure D.1. The four adjusted distributions are not necessarily typical of the nuptial patterns of real populations, but they satisfactorily illustrate the general effects of marriage age on family structure.

The main characteristics for each run appear in table D.2. In each case, the consequences of varying age at marriage are evaluated by comparison to a reference population, which is labeled REF. The reference population is essentially similar to the U.S. population in 1900, which is the STD population of chapter 6. But unlike the STD model, the REF model is based on the assumption of stable fertility. As described in appendix C, MOMSIM's stable-fertility option assumes that all women in the population share the age-specific fertility rates experienced by women who have reached the end of their childbearing years. Since fertility was declining in the United States in the late nineteenth century and the stable-fertility option in MOMSIM bases fertility on the experience of older women, the total fertility rate of the REF population is considerably higher than that of the STD population.

Median female age at marriage varies from 18.1 years for model M1 to 25.2 years for model M4; the mean age of mothers at the birth of their children varies proportionately. To isolate the influence of marriage age, it was necessary to hold the other demographic characteristics constant.

Table D.2. Basic Demographic Parameters of Marriage Runs

	M1	M2	REF	M3	M4
Median age at first marriage					
Females	18.1	19.3	22.2	23.2	25.2
Males	21.4	22.9	25.0	26.7	29.5
Mean age at childbirth for					
mothers who survive to age 45	27.6	29.0	30.7	32.0	34.3
Life expectancy at birth					
Females	48.0	48.1	48.4	48.5	48.0
Males	45.2	45.5	46.0	44.8	45.0
Total fertility rate	4.90	4.85	4.93	4.97	4.88

Neither mortality nor fertility were allowed to vary, save for the effect of random fluctuation introduced by the Monte Carlo technique.[2]

Table D.3 shows the kinds of families that would result from each set of conditions if propensities remained constant. The top row of this table shows the median female age at marriage; these figures are the same as those appearing in table D.2. The second row indicates the percentage of individuals that would have resided in extended families if marriage age alone were altered. Observe that if we hold the other factors constant, the proportion of extended families rises with increasing age at marriage. As we will see, this relationship is primarily a result of the fact that late marriage increases the relative availability of unattached kin—that is, single and widowed kin.

The second and third rows of table D.3 provide more detail about specific types of extended families. As noted in the text, vertical extension is defined here as residence with parents, parents-in-law, children-in-law, or grandchildren; horizontally extended families contain other types of extended kin. Changing marriage age has opposite effects on vertical and horizontal extension. As marriage age goes up, the frequency of vertically extended families declines, whereas the frequency of horizontally extended families increases.

In addition to these general classifications, table D.3 shows the proportion of individuals who would reside with extended kin of each type, age, sex, and marital status if marriage age changed and propensities remained constant. In general, late marriage discourages residence with parents, parents-in-law, and grandchildren; it encourages residence with siblings, siblings-in-law, and single women. Furthermore, later marriage would lead to a lower frequency of residence with young kin and to a higher frequency of residence with older sons.

The underlying sources of these patterns may not be immediately apparent. To explicate the mechanism, I have provided, in tables D.4 and D.5, detailed breakdowns of the availability of two specific kin types for each run of the model. For the other demographic factors—mortality and fertility—I shall not go into such detail; the analysis of marriage age serves to illustrate the specific interactions between demography and extended-family structure.

As explained in chapters 5 and 6, under the standard-propensities

2. Life expectancy was not altered; the same probabilities were employed as for the REF model. A small degree of adjustment was necessary to avoid variation in fertility. As explained in appendix C, fertility in MOMSIM is partly determined by age at marriage. I therefore adjusted fertility downward for models M1 and M2 and upward for models M3 and M4 in order to counteract the influence of marriage age on the duration of childbearing.

Table D.3. Marriage Runs: Measures of Family Structure, Assuming 1900 Standard
Propensities

	M1	M2	REF	M3	M4
Median female age at first marriage	18.1	19.3	22.2	23.2	25.2
Percent of individuals residing in:					
Extended families	18.4	19.7	20.3	21.6	23.2
Vertically extended families	12.9	11.8	11.0	9.3	8.9
Horizontally extended families	7.5	9.8	11.2	14.0	16.0
Percent of individuals residing with kin, by kin's relation to head:					
Siblings	2.6	3.9	4.8	6.9	7.9
Siblings-in-law	2.2	3.2	3.7	4.6	5.7
Nephews/Nieces	3.2	3.4	3.4	3.3	3.4
Uncles/Aunts	0.4	0.6	0.6	0.9	1.0
Parents	5.1	4.4	4.2	4.1	4.2
Parents-in-law	3.1	2.8	2.7	2.6	3.1
Grandchildren/Children-in-law	5.1	4.9	4.4	3.0	2.1
Percent of individuals residing with kin, by kin's sex and marital status:					
Males					
Single	6.1	7.1	7.4	7.3	7.5
Married	2.2	1.9	1.7	1.4	1.3
Widowed	1.8	1.6	1.5	1.5	1.7
Females					
Single	5.2	7.1	8.5	10.6	12.3
Married	2.5	2.3	1.7	1.7	1.5
Widowed	6.2	5.3	5.3	5.0	5.4
Percent of individuals residing with kin, by kin's age group:					
0–9	4.7	4.5	4.3	3.2	2.6
10–19	4.6	4.6	3.4	3.3	2.7
20–29	3.3	4.1	4.4	4.4	3.5
30–39	1.0	1.9	2.6	3.4	4.0
40–49	1.6	1.9	2.2	4.3	5.7
50–59	2.0	1.9	1.6	2.0	2.2
60–69	3.2	2.8	3.2	3.2	3.4
70+	3.0	3.4	3.7	4.2	6.1

technique living arrangements are the product of two factors. One is the standard propensities themselves; these are shown in table D.1. The second factor is the *availability* of kin of specific types—that is, the frequency of surviving kin of each specific type available for coresidence. The figures on availability of kin are relatively unrevealing except in the context of residential propensities; virtually everyone has *some* sort of kin available for coresidence. For analyzing the figures presented in table D.3, however, the data on availability serves useful heuristic purposes.

The frequency of residence with parents as extended kin, as shown in table D.3, is relatively unaffected by changes in age at marriage. One might expect a dramatic effect; age at marriage is, after all, the chief determinant of generation length and generation length profoundly affects whether parents survive to their children's adulthood.

To see why marriage age would have so little influence on the frequency of residence with parents, let us first examine the data on *availability* of mothers, given in table D.4. This table shows the percentage of all individuals in the population who are in families in which the head has a surviving mother of the indicated characteristics.

The availability of mothers is in fact greatest when marriage occurs early, as one would expect. But because residential propensities vary with age and marital status, the *characteristics* of mothers are just as important, for family extension, as is the overall *availability* of mothers. When marriage occurs late, those mothers who do survive until their children are grown are generally older and frequently widowed. As was shown in table D.1, there is much greater propensity to reside with aged and widowed mothers than with younger married mothers. Thus, with later marriage the shifting characteristics of mothers tend to counteract the progressive drop in their overall availability.

Table D.4. Availability of Mothers (Percentage of All Individuals in the Population Who Are in Families in Which the Head Has a Surviving Mother of the Indicated Characteristics)

	M1	M2	REF	M3	M4
Median female age at first marriage	18.1	19.3	22.2	23.2	25.2
Married Mothers					
Age of mother					
30–39	0.2	0.1	0.1	0.0	0.0
40–49	5.4	4.1	2.2	1.0	0.6
50–59	11.8	13.2	7.9	7.6	3.5
60–69	9.0	8.2	7.9	6.6	7.0
70+	4.6	6.2	3.4	6.4	5.4
Widowed mothers					
Age of mother					
30–39	0.0	0.0	0.0	0.0	0.0
40–49	1.5	0.7	0.2	0.4	0.0
50–59	4.0	2.4	1.8	1.9	0.6
60–69	7.8	5.2	6.3	5.1	5.1
70+	4.5	6.6	7.0	8.0	10.0

As was the case for mothers, older and unattached siblings are more likely to reside in extended families than are younger and married siblings. Thus, the effect of marriage age on the frequency of residence with siblings and siblings-in-law also depends on their shifting characteristics. The availability of sisters of family heads is shown in table D.5. Later marriage results in a marked increase in the availability of single sisters in the older age groups where propensities are high. Understandably, if sisters marry late, more of them will be single at any given age; accordingly, delayed marriage would increase the frequency of extended families containing sisters of the head.

There is, in addition, a more subtle effect of marriage age on the availability of siblings that plays an important role in determining extended-family structure. When women marry late, their duration of childbearing is reduced. If a shortened childbearing span is coupled with constant completed fertility, then children must necessarily be more closely spaced. Accordingly, the average age difference between family heads and their sisters goes down as marriage age goes up. Later marriage

Table D.5. Availability of Sisters (Percentage of All Individuals in the Population Who Are in Families in Which the Head Has a Surviving Sister of the Indicated Characteristics)

	M1	M2	REF	M3	M4
Median female age at first marriage	18.1	19.3	22.2	23.2	25.2
Single Sisters					
Age of sister					
0–9	2.0	1.7	1.4	0.9	0.2
10–19	7.4	8.4	8.3	4.9	3.9
20–29	3.3	6.8	8.2	12.0	12.1
30–39	0.2	2.8	4.3	9.0	18.7
40–49	0.0	0.9	1.7	8.2	15.3
50–59	0.0	0.7	1.7	2.0	7.6
60–69	0.0	0.3	0.4	1.5	2.4
70+	0.0	0.1	0.1	0.1	0.4
Married sisters					
Age of sister					
0–9	0.0	0.0	0.0	0.0	0.0
10–19	2.1	1.4	1.1	0.6	0.0
20–29	21.9	20.4	15.6	10.1	8.3
30–39	33.7	33.2	29.7	23.6	21.9
40–49	28.4	29.0	29.5	27.6	28.1
50–59	17.6	16.5	16.2	15.8	19.0
60–69	7.2	6.4	6.4	6.7	8.2
70+	1.1	1.1	1.1	0.8	1.6

thus means that fewer heads have sisters who are much younger—say, under 20, whereas more heads have available sisters close to them in age—say, 30 and older. Since older sisters have higher residential propensities, the shift to older sisters that occurs with delayed marriage would encourage horizontal extension.

The mean number of available sisters is essentially unaffected by marriage age, but the age and marital status of sisters is dramatically altered. As a result, given the standard propensities from 1900, residence with sisters is closely tied to age at marriage.

Two aspects of nuptiality other than marriage age—percent never marrying and age intervals between spouses—also have the potential to influence the frequency of residence with extended kin. Runs M5 and M6 are designed to assess the influence of varying proportions never marrying on extended-family structure. The summary demographic parameters for these models appear in table D.6, and the resulting general measures of family structure are presented in table D.7. Once again, the reference run is also included for purposes of comparison.

The main effect of increasing the percent never marrying would be an increase in the frequency of residence with horizontally extended kin. The mechanism is simple: married horizontal kin have far lower residential propensities than do single ones. Thus, as the availability of single horizontal kin goes up, so does coresidence.

The relationship is reversed for vertical kin, but it is weak; a high proportion never marrying *reduces* vertical extension. The availability of ascendant kin—parents and parents-in-law—is unaffected by the proportion never marrying; people with children are by definition married.[3] Lowering the proportion married does reduce the frequency of residence with children-in-law and grandchildren, but this effect is fairly small.

Runs M7 and M8 reveal the effects of age intervals between husband and wife on family structure. Table D.8 shows the demographic conditions assumed for these runs, whereas table D.9 indicates the outcome of the experiment. Note that alteration of age intervals has a significant impact on age at marriage. Nonetheless, the influence of age intervals on extended-family structure is trivial. Once again, the different effects of demographic change cancel out. By increasing intervals between spouses, we increase the frequency of widowed female kin and single male kin. At the same time, however, the frequency of widowed male kin

3. This is because my definition of marriage is designed to reflect eligibility to conceive. See my discussion of illegitimacy in appendix C for further details.

Table D.6. Basic Demographic Parameters of Percent Marrying Runs

	REF	M5	M6
Percent of women never			
married at age 40	8.6	14.7	21.7
Median age at first marriage			
Females	22.2	22.6	22.5
Males	25.0	25.1	25.2
Mean age at childbirth for			
mothers who survive to age 45	30.7	30.8	30.9
Life expectancy at birth			
Females	48.4	47.7	47.9
Males	46.0	44.6	45.7
Total fertility rate	4.93	4.93	4.89

Table D.7. Effect of Percent Never Marrying on Family Structure, Assuming 1900 Standard Propensities

	REF	M5	M6
Percent of women never			
married at age 40	8.6	14.7	21.7
Percent of individuals residing in:			
Extended families	20.3	21.6	25.1
Vertically extended families	11.0	10.3	10.1
Horizontally extended families	11.2	13.1	16.7

Table D.8. Basic Demographic Parameters of Spouse-Interval Runs

	M7	REF	M8
Mean age interval between spouses[a]	0.7	3.7	7.0
Median age at first marriage			
Females	23.5	22.2	21.2
Males	23.6	25.0	26.6
Mean age at childbirth for			
mothers who survive to age 45	31.6	30.7	29.8
Life expectancy at birth			
Females	48.2	48.4	47.7
Males	45.4	46.0	44.8
Total fertility rate	4.92	4.93	4.90

[a]Age of husband minus age of wife.

Table D.9. Effect of Age Intervals between Spouses on Family Structure, Assuming
1900 Standard Propensities

	M7	REF	M8
Mean age interval between spouses[a]	0.7	3.7	7.0
Percent of individuals residing in:			
Extended families	20.3	20.3	20.3
Vertically extended families	11.2	11.0	11.5
Horizontally extended families	11.2	11.2	10.7

[a]Age of husband minus age of wife.

and single female kin goes down. As a result, the overall frequency of extended living arrangements would remain about the same.

The conscientious reader may have been sorely tried by this mass of detail, and a brief summary is in order. The consequences of altering marital patterns while holding residential propensities constant are dramatic for age at first marriage. Early marriage encourages vertical extension and discourages horizontal extension; late marriage has the opposite effect. In addition, if the proportion of the population never marrying increased, so would the frequency of horizontally extended families. Changes in age intervals between spouses have an insignificant effect on the expected aggregate number of extended families.

Mortality, Fertility, and Standard Propensities

Mortality has marked effects on the formation of extended families, and these effects are more straightforward than those of marriage. The runs designed to assess the influence of mortality levels are labeled D1 through D4; their corresponding demographic conditions appear in table D.10. Mortality distributions were obtained from regional model life tables, rather than through use of adjustment techniques.[4] Use of model life tables enabled me to vary life expectancy at birth over an extremely broad range—from about 18 years for model D1 up to almost 75 years for model D4.

The results from the mortality runs are given in table D.11. As might be expected, lowering life expectancy while holding propensities constant would reduce residence with extended kin, whereas raising life expectancy would increase the percentage of the population residing in ex-

4. In particular, runs D1, D2, D3, and D4 were based on levels 1, 7, 18, and 24, respectively, of Coale and Demeny's (1983) "West" series of model life tables.

Table D.10. Basic Demographic Parameters of Mortality Runs

	D1	D2	REF	D3	D4
Life expectancy at birth					
Females	18.4	34.7	48.4	62.7	76.2
Males	17.5	33.7	46.0	56.4	73.1
Mean age at childbirth for					
mothers who survive to age 45	30.9	30.4	30.7	30.6	30.5
Median age at first marriage					
Females	21.8	22.1	22.2	22.6	22.7
Males	24.7	25.0	25.0	25.2	25.2
Total fertility rate	4.95	5.02	4.93	4.84	4.82

tended families. Vertical and horizontal extension both increase, in about the same proportion.

The lower portion of table D.11 gives the frequency of residence with specific types of extended kin. Raising life expectancy would increase the frequency of residence with almost every kind of extended relative, with widows being the sole exception. Although the survival of widows is encouraged by high life expectancy, there is a countervailing pressure: high life expectancy reduces the odds of losing one's spouse.

Varying life expectancy while holding propensities constant does not have an equal effect on residence with all categories of extended kin. In particular, the frequency of residence with parents and parents-in-law is only moderately affected by life expectancy, whereas the effect on residence with grandchildren is extraordinary.

The slight effect of mortality on residence with parents is partly a result of the familiar intervening effect of widowhood. Raising life expectancy increases the *overall* supply of living parents, but it decreases the availability of *widowed* parents. Since there are higher propensities to reside with widowed parents than with married parents, the effects tend to cancel.

There are other factors operating to minimize the impact of mortality on residence with parents and maximize the consequences for residence with grandchildren. Mortality has a profound effect on age structure; in low mortality societies, the population is older. Thus, where life expectancy is high, family heads tend to be older, and older heads are more likely to have grandchildren and less likely to have living parents. Once again, the older age structure tends to counteract the greater availability of parents resulting from increased survival.

Table D.11. Mortality Runs: Measures of Family Structure, Assuming 1900 Standard Propensities

	D1	D2	REF	D3	D4
Female life expectancy at birth	18.4	34.7	48.4	62.7	76.2
Percent of individuals residing in:					
Extended families	7.4	15.0	20.3	24.2	28.6
Vertically extended families	4.2	8.1	11.0	13.7	16.6
Horizontally extended families	3.9	8.3	11.2	12.8	14.7
Percent of individuals residing with kin, by kin's relation to head:					
Siblings	1.6	3.7	4.8	5.5	6.4
Siblings-in-law	1.4	2.6	3.7	4.2	4.8
Nephews/Nieces	1.2	3.4	3.4	3.8	5.2
Uncles/Aunts	0.2	0.4	0.6	0.8	1.0
Parents	2.2	4.0	4.2	5.0	5.1
Parents-in-law	2.0	2.7	2.7	3.2	3.0
Grandchildren/Children-in-law	0.4	1.9	4.4	5.9	8.6
Percent of individuals residing with kin, by kin's sex and marital status:					
Males					
Single	2.0	4.6	7.4	8.8	10.9
Married	0.4	1.0	1.7	2.2	2.9
Widowed	1.6	1.8	1.5	1.8	1.3
Females					
Single	2.0	5.4	8.5	10.1	13.0
Married	0.4	1.3	1.7	2.7	3.6
Widowed	3.1	5.3	5.3	5.5	4.9
Percent of individuals residing with kin, by kin's age group:					
0–9	0.8	2.4	4.3	5.1	6.9
10–19	1.1	2.6	3.4	4.8	5.9
20–29	1.6	3.0	4.4	5.2	5.9
30–39	0.9	1.8	2.6	3.2	3.8
40–49	1.0	1.9	2.2	2.5	2.8
50–59	1.6	1.7	1.6	2.0	2.0
60–69	1.8	3.5	3.2	3.1	3.0
70+	0.8	2.5	3.7	5.1	6.3

Moreover, the overall availability of grandchildren is highly sensitive to mortality risks, for two reasons. First, the variation in mortality between populations is greatest for infants and children. Since parents have by definition survived to the age of childbearing, they are not so greatly affected by differences in mortality. Second, the availability of grandchildren is both directly and indirectly affected by mortality; the supply of surviving grandchildren depends not only on children's own mortality, but also on the survival of potential parents. Those members of the second generation who die in childhood obviously do not leave behind offspring. Thus, any reduction of mortality counts double for grandchildren.

The effects of variation in fertility on extended-family structure are more moderate than are those of age at marriage and mortality. The fertility runs, in which changes in the distribution of children ever born were achieved through adjustment, are labeled F1 through F4. As shown in table D.12, the total fertility rate varies from 2.5 in run F1 to 8.0 in run F4. The consequences of fertility level for family structure are indicated in table D.13. Generally speaking, under the standard-propensities technique high fertility is associated with high frequency of extended families, and low fertility leads to fewer extended families.

Moderate adjustments of fertility—from a total fertility rate of 4 in F2 to one of almost 7 in F3—have only slight effects on the frequency of our hypothetical extended families. Both vertical and horizontal extension are affected by variations in fertility, but the frequency of horizontally extended families is considerably more sensitive to such changes in fertility. In model F1—which has the lowest fertility—less than 48 percent of extended living arrangements would include horizontal kin, whereas for model F4—with high fertility—the comparable figure would be 60 percent. The smaller impact of fertility on vertical extension is understandable: the availability of ascendant kin—parents and parents-in-law—is unaffected by variation in fertility. Because everyone in the population necessarily had parents, fertility is not a factor in the supply of such kin.

Table D.12. Basic Demographic Parameters of Fertility Runs

	F1	F2	REF	F3	F4
Total fertility rate	2.51	4.06	4.93	6.88	8.06
Mean age at childbirth for					
mothers who survive to age 45	30.1	30.5	30.7	31.0	31.0
Median age at first marriage					
Females	22.3	22.5	22.2	22.3	22.4
Males	25.2	25.2	25.0	25.2	25.0
Life expectancy at birth					
Females	48.1	49.0	48.4	48.3	48.0
Males	45.4	45.8	46.0	44.8	45.8

Table D.13. Fertility Runs: Measures of Family Structure, Assuming 1900 Standard
Propensities

	F1	F2	REF	F3	F4
Total fertility rate	2.51	4.06	4.93	6.88	8.06
Percent of individuals residing in:					
Extended families	15.7	18.4	20.3	21.9	22.8
Vertically extended families	9.7	10.6	11.0	11.5	11.2
Horizontally extended families	7.4	9.6	11.2	12.4	13.6
Percent of individuals residing with kin, by kin's relation to head:					
Siblings	3.4	4.2	4.8	5.3	5.8
Siblings-in-law	2.6	3.2	3.7	4.0	4.3
Nephews/Nieces	2.0	2.8	3.4	3.8	4.2
Uncles/Aunta	0.4	0.6	0.6	0.7	0.7
Parents	4.6	4.7	4.2	4.8	4.4
Parents-in-law	3.0	3.0	2.7	3.0	3.0
Grandchildren/Children-in-law	2.8	3.4	4.4	4.2	4.8
Percent of individuals residing with kin, by kin's sex and marital status:					
Males					
Single	4.3	5.9	7.4	8.0	8.9
Married	1.4	1.6	1.7	1.7	1.8
Widowed	2.1	1.9	1.5	2.4	2.2
Females					
Single	5.4	7.2	8.5	8.8	9.9
Married	1.7	1.8	1.7	2.0	1.9
Widowed	5.3	5.4	5.3	5.4	5.4
Percent of individuals residing with kin, by kin's age group:					
0–9	2.0	3.1	4.3	4.4	5.1
10–19	2.3	3.2	3.4	4.3	4.9
20–29	2.8	3.4	4.4	4.9	5.1
30–39	1.9	2.4	2.6	3.0	3.2
40–49	1.7	1.8	2.2	2.3	2.6
50–59	1.7	1.7	1.6	1.8	1.9
60–69	3.5	3.4	3.2	3.1	3.5
70+	4.4	4.7	3.7	4.2	3.7

The insignificant influence that fertility exerts on residence with parents provides a good illustration of the limitations of the standard-propensities technique. In a real population, an increase in fertility would probably lead to a decline in the propensity to reside with parents. Elderly parents typically reside with only one of their adult children. As the *number* of children increases, the propensity of *each* child to reside with parents should decline. In other words, propensities are not really fixed, and to some extent they are bound to be influenced by changing demographic conditions. My use of standard propensities is necessarily stylized and counterfactual.

Analysis through Hypothetical Rules

For substantive as well as theoretical purposes, it is important to isolate the specific mechanisms by which demographic conditions influence the potential for formation of stem families. If we understand the reasons *why* demographic conditions shape family structure, we stand less chance of misinterpreting our aggregate results. It is particularly revealing to assess the ways in which the potential frequency of stem families differs from the frequency of vertically extended families, as obtained through the use of standard propensities.[5] To this end, I will briefly discuss how each demographic parameter can affect the frequency of stem living arrangements.

For the purpose of this appendix, I draw on the results obtained using hypothetical Rule System 1. To reiterate, according to Rule System 1, the eldest currently living married son remains in his parents' household after marriage. If no sons exist, the eldest daughter remains. All other family members leave the household upon marriage or upon reaching age 21, whichever comes first.

Use of the MOMSIM model coupled with Rule System 1 reveals the percentage of persons who could have resided in stem families if everyone acted according to these hypothetical rules. In addition, the model indicates the mean size of stem families. This statistic is not very interesting in itself, but, as we have seen in Chapter 6, it is necessary for comparing my simulation results with the observations of other researchers who have adopted household rather than individual-level measurement.[6]

5. Note that all stem families are vertically extended and vertically extended families are typically stem families. The frequency of vertically extended families obtained through the use of standard propensities yields markedly different results than are obtained through the use of hypothetical rules. This is largely because the standard propensities are based on assumptions about residential *preferences*, whereas the stem rules yield a theoretical *maximum* frequency of vertical families, assuming everyone in the population followed the rules.

6. As I point out in appendix A, family size determines the relationship between the percentage of persons living in stem families and the percentage of families that take the stem form. As stem-family size goes up, the percentage of stem families goes down, if everything else is held constant. Knowledge of stem-family size therefore helps us compare household-level historical data with individual-level figures from the simulation model.

Table D.14. Measures of Stem-Family Structure, Assuming Stem Hypothetical Rules: Marriage Runs

	M1	M2	REF	M3	M4
Median female age at first marriage	18.1	19.3	22.2	23.2	25.2
Maximum percentage of population in stem families under Rule System 1	45.1	41.2	34.5	30.1	22.5
Mean size of stem families	6.33	6.56	6.55	6.57	6.41

The effect of age at marriage on the maximum frequency and mean size of stem families under Rule System 1 is shown in table D.14. The demographic parameters for runs M1 through M4 and REF are the same as those employed above, in the analysis based on standard propensities.

In general, age at first marriage has more dramatic effects on the maximum frequency of stem families than on vertical extension calculated through standard propensities. This is because widowhood is not a factor determining stem frequencies. As noted earlier, late marriage reduces overlap between generations, but it also increases the frequency of widowed parents. Because the propensity to reside with widows is high, frequent widowhood augments vertical extension calculated through standard propensities, but it does not affect stem-family structure. The results shown in table D.14 indicate that the late marriage characteristic of the preindustrial period must have often prohibited the formation of stem families. But marriage age has no appreciable effect on stem-family size.

The effect of percent never marrying on stem frequencies is shown in table D.15. Recall that under standard propensities the proportion never marrying had virtually no effect on the frequency of vertically extended families. Under the stem rules, a high proportion never marrying significantly discourages the formation of stem families. The reason is simply that a stem family cannot be formed unless a marriage takes place.

The role of mortality in stem-family formation can be seen in table

Table D.15. Measures of Stem-Family Structure, Assuming Stem Hypothetical Rules: Percent Marrying Runs

	REF	M5	M6
Percent of women never married at age 40	8.6	14.7	21.7
Maximum percentage of population in stem families under Rule System 1	34.5	32.0	29.8
Mean size of stem families	6.55	6.30	6.52

Table D.16. Measures of Stem-Family Structure, Assuming Stem Hypothetical Rules: Mortality Runs

	D1	D2	REF	D3	D4
Female life expectancy at birth	18.4	34.7	48.4	62.7	76.2
Maximum percentage of population in stem families under Rule System 1	24.4	32.6	34.5	39.1	42.0
Mean size of stem families	5.97	6.14	6.20	7.11	7.41

D.16. The frequency of potential stem living arrangements is less sensitive to mortality than is the frequency of vertical families under standard propensities. This is because grandchildren play a less-critical role in the determination of stem-family structure; the frequency of grandchildren, you may recall, is highly sensitive to variation in mortality. From the perspective of stem-family formation, what is really important is the mortality of the eldest generation, since this dictates the extent of overlap between generations. The death of grandchildren influences the *size* of the stem group, but, so long as the married child and child-in-law are present, mortality of grandchildren will not affect the *existence* of the stem group.

A one-year difference in age at marriage has considerably more influence on stem frequencies than does a one-year difference in life expectancy. In effect, age at marriage counts twice; the extent of overlap between generations is determined equally by the marriage age of the eldest generation and the marriage age of the second generation. By contrast, since those children who survive to adulthood are likely to outlive their parents, the age at death of the second generation has little consequence for the duration of stem living arrangements; mortality of the eldest generation is much more important. Of course, both historical and contemporary evidence indicate considerably greater potential variation in life expectancy than in age at first marriage.

The authors of socsim argue that age at marriage is the only important demographic determinant of stem-family structure; they contend that the effect of life expectancy is minor. But Wachter and Hammel arrived at their conclusion partly because they measured family structure at the level of the household rather than at the level of individuals.[7] Mortality risks have a significant influence on the *size* of stem families. High life expectancy yields a high frequency of individuals in stem families, but it also results in a larger mean size of stem families. Thus, the influence of

---

7. See my discussion in chapters 4 and 5 and the comments in appendix A.

mortality on the number of stem *families* in a population is considerably smaller than the influence of mortality on the number of *individuals* residing in stem families.

The value of using stem rules as an alternative to standard propensities is clearly illustrated when we turn to fertility. Under standard propensities, low fertility *discourages* the formation of vertically extended families. This is because one's propensity to reside with a living parent does not depend on the number of one's siblings, even though, in reality, one's brothers and sisters may take over the burden of supporting a dependent parent. As table D.17 shows, the effect of low fertility on the potential frequency of individuals in stem families is the opposite: the highest frequency of stem living arrangements occurs at the lowest level of fertility.

This apparent paradox is a consequence of stem-family rules. If fertility is low, there can be few independent nuclear families formed by younger siblings, because few younger siblings exist. There is, however, a counter-vailing effect: high fertility increases the probability that at least one married child will be available to form a stem family. For the highest fertility runs, F3 and F4, the two effects cancel one another out.

As might be expected, fertility also affects the size of stem families. For run F1, stem families averaged only about five members; by contrast, for run F4 mean stem-family size reached almost eight persons.

Conclusion

Let me summarize and present, as simply as possible, the main effects of individual demographic factors on the formation of extended families. Low mortality encourages extended family structure, whereas high mortality discourages extension. Late marriage encourages horizontal extension but discourages vertical extension, including stem-family structure. High fertility tends to encourage extended-family structure, but this generalization does not hold when stem rules are followed.

Countervailing effects on extended-family structure are exerted by

Table D.17. Measures of Stem-Family Structure, Assuming Stem Hypothetical Rules: Fertility Runs

	F1	F2	REF	F3	F4
Total fertility rate	2.51	4.06	4.93	6.88	8.06
Maximum percentage of population in stem families under Rule System 1	37.8	36.4	34.5	34.0	34.0
Mean size of stem families	4.99	6.20	6.55	7.29	7.73

each category of demographic behavior. Early marriage, for example, increases the frequency of vertically extended families by reducing generation length. But since the propensity to reside with single kin is higher than that for married kin, this effect is more than counterbalanced by the reduction in the frequency of unattached individuals that results from early marriage. Similarly, the effect of high mortality in reducing the frequency of extended kin is partially counteracted by the increase in the proportion of extended kin who are widowed.

When we consider the effects of varying several demographic variables *simultaneously*, as was done in chapter 6, the tendency for different factors to cancel out is even more pronounced. In real populations, high fertility is associated with high mortality, and low fertility is associated with low mortality. Since high fertility tends to encourage the availability of extended kin and high mortality discourages extension, these two factors tend to counteract one another. The highest potential frequency of extended families would occur in a society characterized by high fertility and low mortality; by contrast, a society characterized by low fertility and high mortality would necessarily contain few extended families.

Historically, however, only the former sort of population—with relatively high fertility and relatively low mortality—*has* occurred, albeit as a brief stage in the history of most Western populations. In most countries, decline in mortality preceded fertility decline. In this phase of the demographic transition, the potential for formation of extended families is unusually high. One might expect, *ceteris paribus*, that a rise of the extended family would be associated with demographic transition. The only plausible demographic regime capable of supporting a higher frequency of extended living arrangements would be one of *extremely* low mortality, like that found in mid-twentieth-century industrial societies.

The analysis presented here is thus consistent with the figures presented in chapter 1 on the high frequency of extended living arrangements in the late nineteenth century. From a demographic perspective, the rise of the extended family from the preindustrial period to the late Victorian era makes a good deal of sense. The low frequency of extended families in the twentieth century is more anomalous; this can only be explained by a dramatic change in residential preferences. In recent years, people have shown strikingly little desire to prolong their family connections.

Appendix E
Marriage
and Class Patterns of
Extended-Family Structure

"A single man of large fortune; four or five thousand a year. What a thing for our girls!"
Mrs. Bennet, in Jane Austen, *Pride and Prejudice* (1833)

The dire statistics contained in a new demographic study confirm what everybody has suspected all along: many women who seem to have it all will never have husbands. White college-educated baby boomers in particular are victims of a "marriage squeeze"—a shortage of available men that adds up to a numbers game that women can't win.
"The Marriage Crunch," *Newsweek*, June 2, 1986

Victorian marriage patterns were strongly conditioned by economic status. In chapter 3, I stressed that there were also large class differences in the frequency of extended families in nineteenth-century Erie County and Lancashire. In both localities, extended living arrangements were far more common among the bourgeoisie than among the working class (see figures 3.1 and 3.2, chapter 3). In light of the evident sensitivity of extended-family structure to demographic conditions and especially to marriage patterns (as shown in chapter 6 and appendix D), it is appropriate to ask if class differences in the frequency of extended families can be ascribed to differing demographic experience.

Demography and Extended Families in Lancashire
My analysis of the effects of demographic factors on class patterns of family structure is confined to the Lancashire data set. This is because the demographic differences between classes were more pronounced in Lancashire than in Erie County or in the United States as a whole. In particular, the American data show much smaller class differentials in marriage patterns than the English data do. As shown in appendix C, extended-family structure is highly sensitive to age at marriage. Thus, if

208

demography can serve as explanation for the class pattern of extended-family structure in any of the data sets, it is most likely to be in Lancashire.

In order to assess the role of class differences in demographic conditions on the frequency of extended families in Lancashire, I turned to the standard-propensities technique described in chapter 5. In this case, the standard propensities were based on the population of the two Lancashire towns rather than the U.S. population in 1900. On the whole, these English standard propensities are very similar to the American ones.

My strategy was to estimate the extent to which there would have been class differences in the frequency of extended living arrangements if residential propensities had been constant across classes but demographic conditions varied. Overall, the bourgeoisie in late-nineteenth-century England experienced lower fertility and mortality than did the working class and they married later. Among these demographic differences, the most critical variable is age at marriage, and this is the only one that might plausibly explain the observed class differences in extension.

Accordingly, I focus on the effects of class differences in age at marriage. Marriage age can be directly estimated from the census itself. The Lancashire population conformed quite closely to England and Wales as a whole in this respect. In England and Wales in 1871, working-class men married at an average age of about 24, whereas women married at approximately 22. By contrast, in the higher ranks men delayed marriage until an average age of 28, whereas women married at 24.[1]

The nineteenth-century class differential in marriage age has been explained as a function of cultural and economic constraints. J. A. Banks has argued that middle-class men delayed marriage until they could afford the expense of a house and servants, as demanded by Victorian concepts of bourgeois respectability.[2] The industrial working class of the new mill towns, on the other hand, reached peak earnings early in life and had little incentive to delay marriage. The traditional pattern of late marriage among the lower ranks was eroded by the factory system and the increasing commercialization of labor.[3]

1. Glass (1973: 172).
2. Banks (1954).
3. Among the women of Manchester and Salford, where part of the Lancashire sample was taken, the proportion of young marriages (under 21) rose 307 percent between 1841 and 1871, but declined thereafter. The comparable increase for men was 344 percent. A similar pattern of declining marriage age is apparent for the Bolton area, which includes Turton, the other textile town sampled. The magnitude is slightly lower, however; there was a 158

Table E.1. Simulation Results, Assuming 1871 Standard Propensities

	Model A	Model B	Model C	Model D
Assumed Demographic Conditions				
Mean age at marriage				
Males	23.8	28.0	23.7	28.3
Females	21.6	24.1	21.7	24.3
Mean life expectancy				
Males	42.4	42.2	35.6	52.3
Females	44.7	45.9	39.5	55.7
Completed fertility,				
married women	4.4	4.4	5.1	3.7
Simulation Results				
Percent of individuals				
residing in extended families	19.7	21.6	23.8	19.9
Percent of extended-family				
members residing in				
vertically extended families	56.4	40.0	58.1	40.9
Percent of extended-family				
members residing in				
horizontally extended families	43.6	60.0	41.9	60.1

The Banks argument is not a strictly economic one, at least in a theoretical sense. If lack of material resources had been the only constraint on marriage, then we would expect that those with the greatest resources would have married soonest. It was only because of the cultural constraint of bourgeois respectability that the wealthiest class delayed marriage longest.

The demographic explanation for class differences in the frequency of extended families is tested in table E.1, which provides summary results for four runs of the MOMSIM microsimulation. The top section of the table shows the demographic assumptions employed for each run. Models A and B are designed to assess the effects of differential marriage age alone. The low mean age at marriage in model A corresponds to the low marriage ages prevailing among the working class, whereas the higher marriage ages assumed for model B approximate the bourgeois marital pattern. Fertility and mortality were held constant for these two runs.[4]

percent and a 237 percent increase in the frequency of young marriages for women and men, respectively. See Great Britain, General Register Office (1841–1881). Additional evidence on marriage age decline is cited in chapter 6.

4. The assumed levels of mortality and fertility are designed to approximate local conditions; see Great Britain, General Register Office (1871).

The results of the simulation runs appear at the bottom of table E.1. Model A yields 19.7 percent extended living arrangements, compared with 21.6 percent for model B. Thus, the effect of class differences in age at marriage—assuming constant fertility, mortality, and residential propensities—is small.[5] The effect is far too small to explain the large observed class differences in the frequency of extended families.

Models C and D are designed to assess the ways in which class differences in fertility and mortality—in combination with marriage age—could affect family structure. Although we lack reliable class-specific data on fertility and mortality for the Lancashire towns in this period, we can safely assume that the working class had more children and died younger than the bourgeoisie.[6] Thus, model C incorporates the working-class marriage pattern and assumes high fertility and early death. Model D, on the other hand—which has the bourgeois pattern of late marriage—assumes lower fertility and longer life expectancy. The differences in fertility and mortality between models C and D are deliberately exaggerated to highlight their impact.

The results of models C and D indicate that the higher observed frequency of extended living arrangements among the bourgeoisie cannot be explained in demographic terms. Indeed, the results of models C and D suggest that had propensities been constant between classes, demographic differences would have led to a *lower* overall frequency of extension among the bourgeoisie. Because the bourgeoisie were in fact far more likely to reside in extended families than were the working class, the simulation exercise provides compelling evidence that residential propensities differed radically between classes.

Vertical and Horizontal Extension

Even though demographic factors cannot explain class differences in the frequency of extended families in Victorian Lancashire, demography had substantial effects on the *types* of extended families that occurred in the

5. The sensitivity of extended-family structure to marriage age indicated here is similar to that shown in appendix C, although the absolute levels of extension differ slightly because these runs are based on a different set of standard residential propensities and employ different demographic parameters.

6. We lack reliable statistics on class differentials in adult mortality in Victorian Lancashire, but it seems fair to surmise that the poor diet, lack of sanitation, and oppressive working conditions of the working class contributed to substantially higher adult mortality than would be found among the bourgeoisie; see appendix B. It is generally accepted that fertility decline occurred first among the bourgeoisie; see, for example, Banks (1954), Habakkuk (1972: 55), Wrong (1958), Innes (1938), Stern (1979).

different economic strata. The last two rows of table E.1 indicate the hypothetical percentage of extended-family members who would reside in vertically and horizontally extended families, given the demographic assumptions of the model. Vertically and horizontally extended families are defined slightly differently here than elsewhere in this book: vertically extended families must contain parents, parents-in-law, children-in-law, or grandchildren, and all other extended families are defined as horizontally extended. Thus, according to these definitions, the two categories are mutually exclusive.

The simulation results show that the working-class marital pattern substantially favors the formation of vertically, as opposed to horizontally, extended families. This holds true whether or not we consider the effects of fertility and mortality as well as marriage.[7] According to models A and C—which assume the working-class marriage age—56 to 58 percent of extended-family members would reside in vertically extended families. In contrast, models B and D—which assume the bourgeois marriage age—show only 40 to 41 percent vertical extension.

The same pattern is evident in the real Lancashire population: working-class extended-living arrangements were primarily vertical, whereas horizontally extended relationships predominated among the bourgeoisie.[8] But the observed class difference in types of extended families is substantially greater than the difference predicted by the simulation model. This pattern is shown in table E.2.

The standard propensities model does not, then, explain the entire class difference in types of extended families, but it explains a good deal. The demographic mechanisms involved are straightforward. The high frequency of vertically extended families in the working class was encouraged by early marriage. The low age at marriage among the working class

7. High adult mortality would reduce the overlap between generations, which in turn inhibits the formation of vertically extended families. Thus, the direct effects of differential mortality cannot help to explain the class pattern of extended-family structure in Victorian Lancashire; to the extent that it had any effect at all, high mortality among the working class would tend to constrain the frequency of vertical extension, yet vertically extended families were most common among the poor. High fertility among the working class would encourage a high overall frequency of extended families, with a preponderance of horizontal extension—again, the opposite of the observed pattern. Further discussion of the potential effects of fertility, mortality, and nuptiality on vertical and horizontal extension appears in appendix D.

8. The same relationship existed in Erie County, but it was considerably weaker. In 1880, 59 percent of the working-class members of extended families resided in vertically extended families, compared with 43 percent among the bourgeoisie. The greater homogeneity of Erie County in this respect was probably a consequence of greater homogeneity with respect to marital patterns.

Table E.2. Percentage of Extended-Family Members Residing in "Vertical" and
           "Horizontal" Families, Lancashire Towns, 1871

	Unskilled	Skilled	Bourgeois
Vertically extended families	67.9	58.0	27.0
Horizontally extended families	32.1	42.0	73.0
Total	100.0	100.0	100.0
N (100%)	254	390	448

favored the formation of vertically extended families because it reduced generation length, prolonging the period during which three generations were likely to be alive simultaneously. A partial explanation for the high frequency of horizontally extended families among the bourgeoisie also hinges on marriage age. Late marriage led to a high frequency of single young adults among the bourgeoisie, and such people had a high propensity to reside with horizontally extended kin. These mechanisms are discussed at some length in appendix D.

The overwhelming majority of bourgeois horizontally extended relatives had not yet married. Those who delayed marriage had to reside somewhere and they had three possible options: they could reside without family, remain with their parents, or reside with horizontally extended kin. Few chose the first route, perhaps because of the expense. Many remained with their parents, but these cases usually appear as nuclear living arrangements. Moreover, many single persons were unable to choose the second option; a significant proportion of the older bachelors and spinsters in the upper classes had no living parents simply because late marriage in both generations meant that some parents died while their children were still unmarried.

Some unmarried young adults therefore opted to move in with relatives. Most horizontally extended kin were between the ages of 15 and 34, and they usually resided with their older married siblings. Among the bourgeoisie, horizontal extension seems to have been a transitional phase between leaving the parental home and marriage.[9]

9. The tables in appendix F show the proportion of persons residing in extended families broken down by age for each data set. In every case except for the tables restricted to adult women, there is a bulge in extended living arrangements between 15 and 34. This bulge is due to the presence of unmarried horizontally extended kin. As one would expect, the bulge is much more pronounced if we restrict our focus to the extended relatives themselves rather than looking at the population as a whole.

In general the characteristics of horizontally extended kin—their age, sex, and marital status—look a lot like the characteristics of boarders, lodgers, and servants, Like boarding,

These direct effects of late marriage among the bourgeoisie and early marriage among the working class can explain about 40 percent of the observed class difference in the relative frequency of vertically and horizontally extended families.[10] There were also, I believe, indirect consequences of class differences in marital behavior that are too subtle to be captured by the standard-propensities technique. The remainder of this appendix is devoted to an admittedly speculative discussion of the interaction of class patterns of marriage and the relative frequency of vertical and horizontal extension in Victorian Lancashire.

Hypergamy and Horizontal Extension

If late marriage alone accounted for the high frequency of horizontally extended families among the bourgeoisie, we would expect that a majority of horizontally extended relatives would be men because men married later than women. In fact, 62 percent of bourgeois horizontally extended kin were never-married women and these women tended to be older than their male counterparts. Something more complicated was going on.

Bourgeois men delayed marriage; many bourgeois women did not marry at all. The reasons for this gender difference are suggested by age intervals between spouses. In the skilled and unskilled workers' families, men were on average 1.6 and 0.9 years older than their wives, respectively. By contrast, among the bourgeoisie, men were on average 4.8 years older than their wives. Upper-class men delayed marriage, presumably—as Banks would have it—as a means of obtaining the economic security dictated by contemporary standards of social respectability. As a result of their forbearance, they were in a position to pick and choose their wives, and the evidence suggests that they preferred younger women. If middle-class women were not married by their early twenties, the chances of lifelong spinsterhood loomed large.

The desirable characteristics of a bourgeois wife were youthful beauty

---

lodging, or being a servant, horizontal extension was probably often a short-term, transitional living arrangement. But perhaps—for the bourgeoisie—living as an extended relative was more socially acceptable. Katz, Doucet, and Stern (1982) and Katz (1975) see the similarities between extended kin and boarders and lodgers as so great that they lump them together. Likewise, Berkner (1972a) and others have seen servants and other nonrelatives as substitutes for family members. In certain economic respects extended-family members and coresident nonrelatives may have filled similar roles, although we have no evidence for this in the nineteenth century. But I find it hard to believe that they were equivalent in emotional terms.

10. The maximum observed class difference in the percentage of vertical as opposed to horizontal extension is 40.9 percent; the simulated class difference is 16.4 to 17.2 percent.

and household-management skills.[11] There was a broader class of women who possessed these attributes than there was of men who were capable of supporting them in proper bourgeois fashion. In other words, the criteria of suitability for wives were mainly noneconomic, whereas the primary criterion for suitability of husbands was their financial resources. Because of this, women were more likely than men to make economically advantageous marriages.

Another factor may have augmented the possibilities for women to marry men of higher economic status. Some women toward the top of the economic hierarchy, who had independent means, may have chosen to remain unmarried in order to escape the subjugation of matrimony.[12] To the extent that such women removed themselves from the marriage market, they increased the opportunities for other women to marry upward.

Thus, Victorian society was apparently characterized by hypergamy, which is the tendency for women to marry above their station. The result was that the group of women competing for bourgeois husbands was larger than the supply of qualified husbands. This phenomenon can partly explain the much-heralded "surplus of women" among the Victorian middle class.[13] In the Lancashire towns, the sex ratio was 109.8 women for 100 men among the bourgeoisie; in the population as a whole, the sex ratio was nearly even. A contemporary observer described the problem as

> an uncomfortably great fact—it is thrust into our brain like a fat thirteenth into an omnibus—we are alarmingly overstocked with lovely women; there is a perfect glut of angel purity . . . And what is the consequence? Our youths are pursued by clever mammas, and hemmed in by desperate daughters. Embroidered braces, worked cigar cases, and beaded pen-wipers are showered down upon them. Still the ladies cannot be married! Bountiful nature has provided two and a half wives for each Briton; but selfish Parliament denies them more than one; and no Englishman—however sanguine—can expect to be a widower more than twice.[14]

11. Gordon and Bernstein (1971); also, many of the items cited by Kanner (1977) are revealing on the criteria for mate selection.

12. Freeman and Klaus (1984).

13. Additional explanations include higher rates of emigration and higher mortality among men than among women. Moreover, fewer men would survive to the mean age at marriage even if males experienced the same mortality as women, simply because men married later.

14. Cruikshank et al. (1912: 330). The passage was first published in 1851. Also see Cobbe (1862). For additional contemporary literature on the surplus of women, see Kanner

The figure of two and a half wives for every man is obviously unrealistic if it is taken to mean the overall ratio of women to men, but it may not be too far off from the ratio of eligible women to eligible men among the highest ranks of society. The results of the surplus of women can be seen in table E.3, which shows the marital status of women over 35. The table was restricted to older women in an attempt to eliminate the effects of class differences in marriage age. A much larger proportion of bourgeois women than working-class women remained single for their entire lives, and of those who had ever married, many more were widows in 1871.[15]

In sum, a large group of middle-class Victorian women were either unable to marry or chose not to do so. Hypergamy seems to have resulted in a concentration of women in the upper economic strata, and this in turn meant that there was a high proportion of spinsters and widows.

Some of these unattached women lived alone, and some remained in their parents' households for their entire lives. But others, whether from financial pressure or simply out of personal preference, chose to reside with their horizontally extended relatives.[16]

Headship and Vertical Extension

Three-generation families can be formed in either of two ways. First, the elderly can move into households that have been independently established by their children. Second, the children can move into their parents' household or simply remain in their parents' household after they marry.

Headship patterns offer a clue as to who moved in with whom. I refer here to household headship as listed in the census, not family headship as generally employed in this book (see appendix A). It seems improbable that a dependent parent who was taken into an established household would assume the headship of that household. By the same token, it

(1972: 182–85). For discussions of spinsterhood by historians, see Anderson (1984), Watkins (1984). England's changing sex ratio is analyzed by Hajnal (1947a). Burn (1964: 251) views the dependent grown-up daughter as one of the fundamentals of the middle-class Victorian home.

15. In view of the presumably lower mortality among the bourgeoisie, it may seem surprising that widows were most common among the bourgeoisie. There are three explanations for this anomaly: first, age intervals between spouses were substantially greater among the bourgeoisie, which would lengthen the average duration of widowhood; second, there was a surplus of unmarried women—especially older ones—among the bourgeoisie, which reduced the opportunities for remarriage of bourgeois widows; and third, bourgeois widows had less financial need to remarry.

16. The relationship between spinsterhood and residence in extended families was pointed out by Anderson (1984: 393).

Table E.3. Marital Status of Women over Age 35, Lancashire Towns, 1871

	Unskilled	Skilled	Bourgeois
Married	81.6	65.8	59.6
Single	7.3	13.2	15.8
Widowed	11.2	21.0	24.5
Total	100.0	100.0	100.0
N (100%)	265	272	179

seems unlikely that a child would assume headship in the parental household as long as his or her parents remained alive. Although these certainly are not hard and fast rules, the generational pattern of headship may nevertheless be a useful indicator of how vertically extended families are formed.

Table E.4 gives the headship patterns of three-generation families in the Lancashire towns in 1871. Among the working class, the headship of the family was generally retained by the eldest generation, whereas among the bourgeoisie most heads were members of the second generation. These data suggest that working-class vertically extended families were usually formed when a resident child married and brought his or her spouse into the family fold. In the upper classes, the three-generation family may have functioned more like a nursing home: the elderly parents probably moved in with their married children when they were widowed or no longer capable of caring for themselves.

These class differences in vertically extended family formation have implications for the duration of vertically extended families. If working-class vertically extended families were formed upon the marriage of a child, they could potentially remain intact as vertically extended families

Table E.4. Headship Patterns for Persons in Three-Generation Families, Lancashire Towns, 1871

	Unskilled	Skilled	Bourgeois
Head in eldest generation	72.6	57.8	29.2
Head in middle generation	27.4	42.2	70.8
Total	100.0	100.0	100.0
N (100%)	168	225	120

for the entire period that all three generations were alive. In many cases, however, the working-class pattern of vertical extension may have been a short-term arrangement, which lasted only until the second generation gained sufficient resources to set up a household of its own. Nonetheless, early formation of three-generation families would at least create the possibility of long duration. By contrast, if the bourgeois three-generation families were formed only after the parents and children had resided separately for a number of years, the duration of extended living arrangements would necessarily be brief and a smaller proportion of the population could reside in such families at any one time.

Evidence on age patterns supports the interpretation that working-class vertically extended families were formed early in life. The second generation in unskilled laborers' families was on average 9.7 years younger than the second generation in bourgeois families, and the second generation in skilled workers' families was an average of 7.0 years younger than in bourgeois families. Among the bourgeoisie, the eldest generation consisted primarily of elderly widows.

The working-class pattern of vertical extension seems to be similar to the stem-family model. As described in chapter 4, according to the stem-family hypothesis, it was common in preindustrial Western society for one child to remain in his or her parents' household after marriage, while any other children left home to establish new households. The stem family is supposed to have operated as a means of transmitting property between generations and of assuring a stable supply of agricultural labor.

While the *form* of the working-class three-generation family may have resembled the stem-family model, the reasons underlying the adoption of that form must have been different. Inheritance was probably not a major reason for the adoption of stem-family forms in nineteenth-century working-class Lancashire; as noted in chapter 3, few parents had substantial enough assets to serve as incentive for their children to remain at home. Moreover, although the need for labor on the family farm may have encouraged the formation of stem families in rural areas, the economy of industrial Lancashire did not necessitate such living arrangements among the working class.

The divergence between classes in vertically extended family formation brings us back to the issue of differential marriage behavior. If Banks is correct, bourgeois youth postponed marriage precisely because they wished to begin married life in establishments of their own and could eventually afford to do so. By contrast, young working-class men could not expect dramatically improved earnings in later years, and they were not constrained by notions of bourgeois respectability. So working-class males married early, and often moved in with their parents.

Conclusion

I have offered four explanations for the class patterns of vertically and horizontally extended family structure in Victorian Lancashire. First, the low age at marriage among the working class led to a longer period during which three generations were alive simultaneously; this encouraged a high frequency of vertically extended families. Second, late marriage among the upper classes led to a high frequency of spinsters and bachelors, and these groups have a high propensity to reside with horizontally extended kin. Third, there was a surplus of unmarried women among the bourgeoisie because marriage decisions were dictated by the economic power of men; this led to hypergamy. Many of the unmarried women from the upper classes spent their adult lives in their siblings' households. Finally, the vertically extended families in the working class, unlike those of the bourgeoisie, were most often formed when young people remained in their parents' households after marriage or moved in with their spouses' parents. This pattern of household formation maximizes the potential frequency of extended families because it reduces the period during which parents and children reside in independent nuclear families.

These four mechanisms can plausibly explain the predominance of vertically extended families among the working class and horizontally extended families among the bourgeoisie. But they do not explain everything.

The evidence indicates that demographic factors—including marital patterns—had little effect on class differentials in the *overall* frequency of extended living arrangements. Indeed, when class differences in mortality, fertility, and nuptiality are all included in the simulation runs, the results suggest that demographic conditions actually favored extended-family structure among the working class to a greater extent than among the bourgeoisie.

The fact that demography fails to explain class differences in the *overall frequency* of extended living arrangements is ultimately a more significant finding than the successful explanation of class differences in *types* of extended families. As pointed out in chapter 2, historians have generally seen the nineteenth-century extended family as a functional adaptation to economic hardship and industrial working conditions. The concentration of family extension among the bourgeoisie is a fundamental challenge to the hardship interpretation. Because the Victorian class pattern of extended-family structure contradicts prevailing social theory and the assumptions of many historians, it is important to know that this pattern was not merely an indirect consequence of prevailing demographic conditions.

Appendix F
Multivariate Analyses

With a rule and a pair of scales, and the multiplication table always in his pocket, Sir, ready to weigh and measure any parcel of human nature, and tell you exactly what it comes to. It is a mere question of figures, a case of simple arithmetic.

Charles Dickens, *Hard Times* (1854)

Charlie Brown: "Where do you think the source of this security lies—in your thumb, in that blanket, or in the pose you assume?"
Linus: "I would say it's a combination of ingredients—not unlike a Doctor's Prescription!"

Charles Schultz, *Peanuts* (1962)

It is obligatory these days for social scientists to try to disentangle the "combination of ingredients" that makes society tick. In the course of the research for this study, I employed a variety of techniques to fulfill this obligation, including logit, probit, ordinary least squares regression, Multiple Nominal Analysis, decomposition techniques, and Multiple Classification Analysis. Each technique, I have found, reveals essentially the same thing: strong relationships between any two variables—that is, relationships strong enough to have *historical* as well as statistical significance—are generally somewhat diminished but rarely disappear when we control for the effects of intervening variables.

An example may clarify this point. In chapter 3, I noted that members of the bourgeoisie resided with extended kin far more frequently than did members of the working class in both Lancashire and Erie County. Part of this class difference is a by-product of the fact that bourgeois people were far more frequently natives than were working-class persons; migration discourages residence in extended families. However, the class difference in extension is not entirely a function of birthplace; when we examine the native and foreign born separately, the class pattern of extension is apparent within each group.

The least problematic means of assessing the effects of several variables simultaneously is to create multidimensional tables that break the results down several ways at once. As soon as we incorporate more than three or four variables, however, tables become unwieldy. In fact, one can easily create a table with more cells than the number of cases in the sample.

Thus, we turn to regression. I have included several Multiple Classification Analysis (MCA) runs to support the generalizations I made in chapter 3. MCA has two advantages over alternative regression techniques. First, it is relatively easy to interpret MCA results; second, MCA does not impose linearity on the relationships between variables.

In MCA, all independent variables are "dummied," regardless of whether or not they are categorical. In other words, each value or category of each variable is treated as though it were a separate variable with a value of either zero or one. Because each category is treated separately, MCA can isolate and describe nonlinear relationships.

The dependent variable for the runs presented here is a dichotomy— whether or not an individual resides with his or her extended kin. It can be argued that MCA is not ideally suited to the use of a dichotomous dependent variable, but in practice it works just fine.[1]

The MCA coefficients are expressed as deviations from the grand mean of the dependent variable. In this case, the grand mean is simply the percentage of the entire population that resided with extended kin.

Tables F.1 through F.10 each contain three columns of figures. The first column shows the number of cases for each category of each variable. Since the Erie County data sets from 1855, 1900, and 1915 employ complicated weighting schemes, these numbers should be viewed as approximate for those years.

The second column shows the "unadjusted deviation" of each category of each variable. The unadjusted deviation is the difference between the percent residing with extended kin within the category and the percent residing with extended kin in the entire population. For example, the unadjusted deviation for persons over 75 in table F.1 is 45.01. This figure is the difference between the percentage of persons over 75 residing with extended kin and the corresponding percentage for the entire population. The percentage of those in the 75 and older age group residing with extended kin is 45.01 *plus* the overall percent extended, 19.94. Thus, 65.95 percent of these elderly people resided in extended families.

The third column shows the "adjusted deviations" for each category.

---

1. See Andrews et al. (1973: 10), who defend the use of MCA with dichotomous dependent variables. Problems mainly arise when the mean of the dichotomous dependent variable is close to zero or one, for two reasons. First, this will lead to heteroscedasticity. Second, extreme values of the dependent variable may lead to predicted values of less than zero or greater than one. Obviously, it would be impossible for *less* than zero percent or more than 100 percent of the population to reside in extended families.

These figures are identical to the coefficients that would be obtained by ordinary regression with dummy variables, except that they are adjusted so that the weighted mean of the coefficients for each variable equals zero.

Under ordinary regression with dummy variables, one category of each variable must always be omitted from the equation. The resulting coefficients tell us the predicted deviation of each category from the omitted category. Another way of looking at it is that the coefficient gives the amount of change in the dependent variable resulting from one unit of change in the independent variable, with all else held constant. Since the independent variables are dummied, they only *have* one unit; their value is either zero or one. Thus, the "slope" associated with each dummied category is identical to the *deviation* of that category from the category omitted from the equation.

The MCA coefficients are slightly different, since they represent the predicted deviation of each category from the grand mean. No categories are omitted. The conversion from ordinary regression (OLS) coefficients to MCA coefficients is straightforward. The omitted category of each variable is first assigned an OLS coefficient of zero, since it of course has no deviation from itself. Then the weighted average of the coefficients for all categories of the variable is calculated. This weighted average is then subtracted from the OLS coefficient for each category, including the category that was previously omitted; this yields the MCA coefficients. The weighted average of the MCA coefficients is then equal to zero.

This format for the coefficients is convenient and intuitively accessible. The MCA coefficients—labeled "adjusted deviation" in table F.1—are intended to show what the deviation of the category from the grand mean would be if all of the other variables included in the run were controlled. By comparing the unadjusted deviation with the adjusted deviation, we can estimate the extent to which holding the other variables constant would affect the percent extended within each category.

The relationships indicated in the tables presented in chapter 3 are reproduced here, in the form of unadjusted deviations. The same patterns emerge in the adjusted deviations, although the strength of the relationships is generally somewhat diminished. Since the relationships persist when we control for the effects of intervening variables, it is clear that the patterns described in chapter 3 are not merely a by-product of correlated structural conditions.

Two tables are shown for each data set. The two runs for Erie County in 1855 are based on roughly the same population, but they include somewhat different independent variables. For the rest of the census files, the two runs look at different populations: the first run for each data set includes the main variables available for all individuals in the file, whereas the second focuses on adult women. The tables on adult women are designed to assess Michael Anderson's "working mothers" hypothesis.

Table F.1. Multiple-Classification Analysis of the Probability of Residing in an Extended Family, Erie County, 1855
Grand Mean = 19.94 Percent Extended
Total N = 123,350
Multiple R Squared = 0.063

Variable and Category	N	Unadjusted Deviation	Adjusted Deviation
Age			
0–4	19,318	−0.90	0.33
5–9	14,843	−2.61	−2.31
10–14	13,152	−2.17	−2.16
15–19	12,008	−1.93	−1.53
20–24	12,316	1.14	2.48
25–29	11,782	−0.32	1.46
30–34	10,364	−1.78	−0.60
35–39	7,900	−1.27	−0.98
40–44	6,259	−1.02	−1.89
45–49	4,454	−3.08	−5.09
50–54	3,946	2.64	−0.35
55–59	2,489	5.96	1.36
60–64	2,019	14.09	6.43
65–69	1,140	26.90	16.14
70–74	721	45.94	32.96
75+	639	45.01	28.67
Occupational class			
With servant	5,010	14.73	12.23
Other bourgeois	5,999	2.30	2.23
Skilled	32,676	−1.17	−0.55
Unskilled	20,583	−8.90	−6.52
Agricultural	34,889	2.93	2.53
Unclassified	24,193	1.30	−0.39
Birthplace of family head			
Native	43,685	5.08	2.85
Irish	15,412	−0.47	0.92
Other U.K.	2,733	0.48	0.22
German	42,801	−3.47	−1.76
Eastern Europe	215	−1.33	0.02
Italian	73	−14.46	−13.42
Other	18,431	−3.57	−3.42

Continued on the following page

Table F.1. (*continued*)

Variable and Category	N	Unadjusted Deviation	Adjusted Deviation
Marital status			
Single	71,555	−1.63	−0.76
Married	47,056	−0.91	−1.53
Widowed	4,741	33.70	26.67
Gender*			
Male	62,986	−0.55	−0.13
Female	60,364	0.57	0.14
Urban/Rural			
Urban	68,200	−0.39	1.20
Rural	55,150	0.48	−1.49
Years spent locally			
0–1	21,304	−5.92	−3.85
2–5	30,771	−3.73	−2.84
6–10	25,975	0.46	0.66
11–19	20,882	2.74	2.43
20–29	18,436	6.65	4.44
30+	5,982	8.25	3.31

*Not significant at the 0.01 level.

Table F.2. Multiple-Classification Analysis of the Probability of Residing in an
Extended Family, Erie County, 1855
Grand Mean = 19.92 Percent Extended
Total N = 126,595
Multiple R Squared = 0.050

Variable and Category	N	Unadjusted Deviation	Adjusted Deviation
Age			
0–4	19,503	−1.06	−0.28
5–9	15,206	−2.64	−3.06
10–14	13,605	−2.15	−2.91
15–19	12,445	−1.83	−2.30
20–24	12,581	1.00	1.65
25–29	11,919	−0.30	1.03
30–34	10,491	−1.90	−1.08
35–39	8,044	−1.40	−1.33
40–44	6,529	−1.02	−1.39
45–49	4,668	−2.70	−3.85
50–54	4,096	2.63	1.71
55–59	2,679	6.32	4.83
60–64	2,134	13.91	12.28
65–69	1,217	27.16	24.84
70–74	778	43.31	41.08
75 +	700	42.93	39.73
Occupational class			
Upper bourgeois	6,722	11.45	8.91
Lower bourgeois	4,563	2.54	1.21
Skilled	33,221	−1.22	−0.65
Unskilled	20,558	−8.97	−6.79
Agricultural	37,384	3.04	2.25
Unclassified	24,147	0.93	−0.48
Birthplace of family head			
Native	46,365	4.98	2.52
Irish	15,243	−0.49	1.38
Other U.K.	2,866	2.58	1.79
German	42,516	−3.74	−1.61
Eastern Europe	214	−1.23	−0.76
Italian	73	−14.45	−13.69
Other	19,408	−3.63	−3.75
Urban/Rural			
Urban	68,577	−0.47	2.47
Rural	58,018	0.55	−2.92

Continued on the following page

Table F.2. (*continued*)

Variable and Category	N	Unadjusted Deviation	Adjusted Deviation
Years spent locally			
0–1	21,231	−6.06	−3.68
2–5	30,726	−3.81	−2.59
6–10	26,138	−0.03	0.22
11–19	20,853	2.48	1.98
20–29	18,422	6.60	4.36
30–35	5,976	8.29	3.61
36+	3,249	7.19	2.68
Number of households in dwelling			
One	99,771	1.54	1.35
Two	13,176	−5.09	−4.69
Three	5,860	−5.97	−5.24
Four or more	7,788	−6.61	−5.45

Table F.3. Multiple-Classification Analysis of the Probability of Residing in an
            Extended Family, Erie County, 1880
            Grand Mean = 23.82 Percent Extended
            Total N = 13,581
            Multiple R Squared = 0.062

Variable and Category	N	Unadjusted Deviation	Adjusted Deviation
Age			
0–4	1,502	0.81	1.94
5–9	1,588	−1.78	0.22
10–14	1,425	−5.43	−3.28
15–19	1,387	−4.93	−2.85
20–24	1,494	−0.33	−0.08
25–29	1,176	4.33	3.55
30–34	945	1.68	0.41
35–39	820	−1.14	−1.57
40–44	689	−0.16	−0.63
45–49	623	−3.60	−4.95
50–54	546	−4.59	−5.94
55–59	467	−0.91	−3.82
60–64	372	8.71	4.58
65–69	218	13.34	6.84
70–74	164	22.52	15.99
75+	165	38.60	29.85
Occupational class			
Upper bourgeois	906	8.52	7.38
Lower bourgeois	1,355	5.48	4.25
Skilled	4,541	−0.43	0.52
Unskilled	3,810	−6.71	−5.89
Agricultural	1,708	4.04	4.57
Unclassified	1,261	4.89	0.48
Birthplace of family head			
Native	5,440	7.01	5.93
Irish	1,213	−4.45	−3.30
Other U.K.	566	2.15	2.25
German	4,931	−5.95	−5.04
Eastern Europe	72	5.35	9.54
Italian	54	−23.82	−18.15
Other	1,305	−2.93	−3.44
Race*			
White	13,487	−0.06	−0.05
Nonwhite	94	9.16	6.82
Unemployment			
Listed as unemployed	71	−9.74	−13.12
Other	13,510	0.05	0.07

Continued on the following page

Table F.3. (*continued*)

Variable and Category	N	Unadjusted Deviation	Adjusted Deviation
Marital status			
Single	7,861	−2.19	−1.43
Married	4,960	−0.37	−0.98
Widowed	760	25.13	21.19
Gender*			
Male	7,085	−1.38	−0.60
Female	6,496	1.50	0.65
Urban/Rural*			
Urban	10,701	−0.53	0.41
Rural	2,880	1.98	−1.53

*Not significant at the 0.01 level.

Table F.4. Multiple-Classification Analysis of the Probability of Residing in an
Extended Family for Women Aged 18 or Older, Erie County, 1880
Grand Mean = 26.83 Percent Extended
Total N = 4,201
Multiple R Squared = 0.094

Variable and Category	N	Unadjusted Deviation	Adjusted Deviation
Age			
15–19	422	−7.16	−4.26
20–24	789	−3.13	−3.56
25–29	566	2.15	0.06
30–34	463	−3.28	−4.73
35–39	381	−2.42	−2.73
40–44	349	−2.76	−2.38
45–49	283	−4.57	−3.91
50–54	255	−5.26	−3.87
55–59	211	3.03	4.55
60–64	165	11.35	12.04
65–69	99	18.63	18.34
70–74	76	33.70	33.78
75+	76	44.23	41.58
Occupational class			
Upper bourgeois	295	9.11	6.68
Lower bourgeois	408	7.24	6.16
Skilled	1,229	1.73	2.77
Unskilled	1,184	−9.51	−6.54
Agricultural	515	5.42	3.29
Unclassified	570	0.89	−3.49
Birthplace of family head			
Native	1,868	6.79	6.78
Irish	402	−8.92	−6.76
Other U.K.	180	1.51	2.83
German	1,300	−5.90	−6.31
Eastern Europe	15	−6.83	−4.07
Italian	13	−26.83	−17.37
Other	419	−3.20	−4.92
Mother's work			
Working mother, children under 5	373	−9.94	−8.44
Working woman, no children under 5	1,384	−7.75	−5.42
Nonworking mother, children under 5	544	5.34	7.06
Other woman, 18 or older	1,900	6.07	3.59
Urban/Rural			
Urban	3,314	−0.64	0.61
Rural	887	2.38	−2.30

Table F.5. Multiple-Classification Analysis of the Probability of Residing in an
Extended Family, Erie County, 1900
Grand Mean = 20.52 Percent Extended
Total N = 40,067
Multiple R Squared = 0.052

Variable and Category	N	Unadjusted Deviation	Adjusted Deviation
Age			
0–4	4,613	− 1.79	− 1.56
5–9	4,563	− 3.66	− 3.41
10–14	4,210	− 3.39	− 3.26
15–19	3,593	− 1.88	− 2.00
20–24	3,570	− 0.54	1.09
25–29	3,606	2.70	3.70
30–34	3,429	0.10	1.55
35–39	3,212	− 0.32	1.10
40–44	2,520	− 2.59	− 1.88
45–49	1,929	− 0.31	0.01
50–54	1,420	0.24	− 0.52
55–59	1,074	3.26	1.16
60–64	792	5.85	2.10
65–69	659	17.52	10.43
70–74	415	21.64	11.86
75 +	461	28.41	18.07
Occupational class			
Upper bourgeois	2,257	5.78	4.98
Lower bourgeois	4,775	5.01	4.06
Skilled	12,085	− 1.12	− 0.08
Unskilled	9,077	− 5.44	− 3.79
Agricultural	3,053	7.36	7.69
Unclassified	8,820	0.49	− 1.98
Birthplace of family head			
Native	20,030	4.13	3.28
Irish	2,051	− 0.04	− 0.71
Other U.K.	1,865	0.56	0.25
German	8,869	− 5.22	− 4.93
Eastern Europe	3,693	− 6.27	− 2.61
Italian	903	− 4.22	− 1.09
Other	2,656	− 3.90	− 3.39
Marital status			
Single	22,391	− 1.73	0.09
Married	15,364	− 1.76	− 3.73
Widowed	2,312	28.49	23.91
Gender*			
Male	20,042	− 0.41	0.11
Female	20,026	0.41	− 0.11
Urban/Rural*			
Urban	32,621	− 0.55	0.26
Rural	7,446	2.43	− 1.16

*Not significant at the 0.01 level.

Table F.6. Multiple-Classification Analysis of the Probability of Residing in an
            Extended Family for Women Aged 18 or Older, Erie County, 1900
            Grand Mean = 22.58 Percent Extended
            Total N = 12,960
            Multiple R Squared = 0.061

Variable and Category	N	Unadjusted Deviation	Adjusted Deviation
Age			
15–19	1,129	−6.51	−6.22
20–24	1,957	−2.94	−2.88
25–29	1,887	−0.59	−0.74
30–34	1,687	−2.41	−2.21
35–39	1,599	−1.21	−1.15
40–44	1,187	−3.62	−4.17
45–49	931	−2.32	−2.68
50–54	710	−1.44	−1.77
55–59	536	6.81	6.85
60–64	392	9.83	9.81
65–69	355	20.32	21.32
70–74	229	26.09	26.73
75+	234	32.92	33.34
Occupational class			
Upper bourgeois	755	7.47	6.06
Lower bourgeois	1,526	7.79	6.88
Skilled	3,335	−0.67	0.49
Unskilled	2,939	−7.19	−5.42
Agricultural	862	15.90	18.61
Unclassified	3,543	−0.66	−2.46
Birthplace of family head			
Native	6,685	4.76	4.27
Irish	799	−1.49	−1.96
Other U.K.	705	−1.41	−0.44
German	2,728	−6.27	−6.92
Eastern Europe	850	−6.53	−1.95
Italian	223	−7.84	−2.45
Other	970	−5.44	−5.77
Mother's work			
Working mother, children under 5	94	0.75	2.45
Working woman, no children under 5	2,898	−2.48	1.39
Nonworking mother, children under 5	2,955	−4.68	−3.04
Other woman, 18 or older	7,013	2.99	0.68
Urban/Rural*			
Urban	10,653	−0.72	0.46
Rural	2,307	3.33	−2.10

*Not significant at the 0.01 level.

Table F.7. Multiple-Classification Analysis of the Probability of Residing in an
           Extended Family, Erie County, 1915
           Grand Mean = 18.6 Percent Extended
           Total N = 63,389
           Multiple R Squared = 0.089

Variable and Category	N	Unadjusted Deviation	Adjusted Deviation
Age			
0–4	7,502	−0.53	3.94
5–9	7,584	−3.74	0.57
10–14	6,910	−4.28	−0.61
15–19	7,031	−3.16	0.43
20–24	6,470	1.57	2.95
25–29	5,345	2.99	2.52
30–34	4,543	1.67	−0.88
35–39	4,353	0.37	−2.43
40–44	3,714	−2.28	−6.07
45–49	3,166	−1.17	−5.80
50–54	2,498	1.23	−4.57
55–59	1,706	3.95	−5.23
60–64	1,049	10.73	−1.68
65–69	660	15.26	1.87
70–74	371	26.35	8.48
75+	487	41.15	16.53
Occupational class			
Upper bourgeois	3,736	4.97	3.76
Lower bourgeois	9,450	4.82	2.89
Skilled	26,925	−1.27	−0.42
Unskilled	13,772	−4.89	−1.33
Agricultural	3,792	6.63	2.95
Unclassified	5,714	3.31	−2.98
Birthplace of family head			
Native	25,656	6.92	5.48
Irish	1,454	0.85	1.13
Other U.K.	2,037	5.71	5.42
German	5,683	−5.47	−4.89
Eastern Europe	21,447	−7.63	−6.21
Italian	3,363	1.17	2.12
Other	3,749	−0.32	−0.18
Marital status			
Single	39,826	−3.08	−3.63
Married	20,899	0.19	1.44
Widowed	2,663	44.60	42.91
Gender			
Male	33,166	−0.52	0.46
Female	30,223	0.57	−0.50
Urban/Rural*			
Urban	53,650	−0.70	−0.11
Rural	9,739	3.85	0.61

*Not significant at the 0.01 level.

Table F.8. Multiple-Classification Analysis of the Probability of Residing in an
Extended Family for Women Aged 18 or Older, Erie County, 1915
Grand Mean = 21.76 Percent Extended
Total N = 18,449
Multiple R Squared = 0.093

Variable and Category	N	Unadjusted Deviation	Adjusted Deviation
Age			
15–19	2,502	−5.58	−0.62
20–24	2,892	−1.51	−0.90
25–29	2,417	−0.58	−1.93
30–34	2,132	−1.86	−3.52
35–39	2,055	−3.56	−5.49
40–44	1,800	−5.33	−6.49
45–49	1,425	−1.87	−2.10
50–54	1,067	2.98	2.79
55–59	777	5.05	4.41
60–64	489	15.46	14.67
65–69	318	19.78	19.61
70–74	181	38.72	37.65
75+	258	47.34	46.90
Occupational class			
Upper bourgeois	1,174	8.11	6.80
Lower bourgeois	2,863	5.60	3.76
Skilled	7,292	−0.52	0.55
Unskilled	3,629	−7.76	−3.52
Agricultural	1,000	5.99	0.31
Unclassified	2,491	0.46	−3.83
Birthplace of family head			
Native	8,734	7.02	6.14
Irish	456	−1.79	−0.28
Other U.K.	755	4.69	4.69
German	1,823	−7.30	−7.82
Eastern Europe	4,922	−9.82	−8.21
Italian	689	1.52	2.04
Other	1,070	−3.39	−3.75
Mother's work			
Working mother, children under 5	156	48.06	49.72
Working woman, no children under 5	5,356	−5.23	−3.58
Nonworking mother, children under 5	4,673	−1.72	2.48
Other woman, 18 or older	8,261	3.44	−0.03
Urban/Rural*			
Urban	15,722	−0.70	0.03
Rural	2,727	4.02	−0.17

*Not significant at the 0.01 level.

Table F.9. Multiple-Classification Analysis of the Probability of Residing in an
Extended Family, Turton and Salford, Lancashire, 1871
Grand Mean = 20.82 Percent Extended
Total N = 9,247
Multiple R Squared = 0.051

Variable and Category	N	Unadjusted Deviation	Adjusted Deviation
Age			
0–4	1,034	2.10	3.31
5–9	935	−0.07	0.87
10–14	912	−2.29	−1.01
15–19	1,067	−2.35	0.18
20–24	1,057	−0.86	2.23
25–29	826	−3.87	−2.35
30–34	718	−0.48	−0.11
35–39	547	−4.36	−5.87
40–44	502	−3.89	−6.98
45–49	460	−1.47	−4.04
50–54	350	0.33	−3.86
55–59	247	7.93	1.11
60–64	226	13.25	6.33
65–69	143	25.34	17.34
70–74	65	16.11	5.13
75+	158	13.99	9.94
Occupational class			
Bourgeois	1,688	9.92	10.48
Skilled	2,282	1.05	−0.44
Unskilled	2,391	−9.02	−7.86
Unclassified	2,886	0.84	0.76
Birthplace of family head			
Born locally	3,225	2.62	2.35
Born in Lancashire	2,663	0.81	0.65
Born in Ireland	2,059	−5.32	−4.67
Born elsewhere in U.K.	702	−0.59	1.59
Born outside U.K.	298	−0.01	−5.09
Marital status			
Single	5,987	−2.13	−2.25
Married	2,749	0.83	1.78
Widowed	511	20.47	16.79
Gender*			
Male	4,051	0.29	−0.30
Female	5,196	−0.22	0.23

*Not significant at the 0.01 level.

Table F.10. Multiple-Classification Analysis of the Probability of Residing in an
Extended Family for Women Aged 18 or Older, Turton and Salford,
Lancashire, 1871
Grand Mean = 18.67 Percent Extended
Total N = 2,491
Multiple R Squared = 0.147

Variable and Category	N	Unadjusted Deviation	Adjusted Deviation
Age			
15–19	325	−4.51	0.19
20–24	446	−2.97	0.34
25–29	352	−4.75	−3.55
30–34	313	−1.41	−2.09
35–39	233	−1.07	−2.52
40–44	164	−2.20	−7.39
45–49	154	−0.16	−3.33
50–54	113	−0.80	−3.81
55–59	77	16.40	10.32
60–64	71	17.95	11.39
65–69	44	38.15	30.62
70–74	18	42.44	34.29
75+	47	17.50	11.93
Occupational class			
Bourgeois	526	18.41	14.23
Skilled	759	2.81	1.02
Unskilled	1,206	−9.79	−6.85
Birthplace of family head			
Born locally	873	5.96	4.08
Born in Lancashire	609	−0.28	−1.59
Born in Ireland	738	−7.29	−3.89
Born elsewhere in U.K.	189	1.44	4.97
Born outside U.K.	82	0.84	−8.02
Mother's work			
Working mother, children under 5	89	12.79	14.71
Working woman, no children under 5	1,404	−8.48	−4.72
Nonworking mother, children under 5	345	1.33	0.48
Other woman, 18 or older	653	15.79	7.88

Bibliography

Achenbaum, A., and P. N. Stearns.
1978.   "Old Age and Modernization." *The Gerontologist* 18.307–12.

Agresti, B. F.
1979.   "Household Composition, the Family Cycle, and Economic Hardship in a Postbellum Southern County: Walton County, Florida, 1870–1885." *International Journal of the Sociology of the Family* 9.245–58.

Åkerman, S., H. C. Johanson, and D. Gaunt, eds.
1978.   *Chance and Change: Social and Economic Studies in Historical Demography in the Baltic Area.* Odense, Denmark.

Allen, L. F.
1896.   "The Cholera in Buffalo in the 1830s and 1840s." *Publications of the Buffalo Historical Society* 4.245–56.

Angel, R., and M. Tienda.
1982.   "Determinants of Extended Household Structure: Cultural Pattern or Economic Need?" *American Journal of Sociology* 87.1360–83.

Anderson, M.
1971.   *Family Structure in Nineteenth Century Lancashire.* Cambridge.
1972a.   "The Study of Family Structure." *In*: E. A. Wrigley, ed.
1972b.   "Household Structure in the Industrial Revolution: Mid-Nineteenth Century Preston in Comparative Perspective." *In*: P. Laslett and R. Wall, eds.
1976.   "Sociological History and the Working Class Family: Smelser Revisited." *Social History* 1.317–43.
1977.   "The Impact on Family Relationships of the Elderly on Changes Since Victorian Times in Governmental Income Maintenance Provi-

sion." *In*: E. Shanas and M. B. Sussman, eds., *Family, Bureaucracy, and the Elderly*. Durham, N.C.
1978.   "Family, Household, and the Industrial Revolution." *In*: M. Gordon, ed., *The American Family in Social-Historical Perspective*. 2d ed. New York.
1980.   *Approaches to the History of the Western Family*. London.
1984.   "The Social Position of Spinsters in Mid-Victorian Britain." *Journal of Family History* 9.377–93.
1985.   "Stability and Change in Urban Communities." *Journal of Family History* 10.196–205.

Andrews, F. M., et al.
1973.   *Multiple Classification Analysis: A Report on a Computer Program for Multiple Regression Using Categorical Predictors*. Ann Arbor, Mich.

Anshen, R. N., ed.
1959.   *The Family: Its Function and Destiny*. New York.

Aries, P.
1962.   *Centuries of Childhood*. New York.

Armstrong, A.
1972a.   "The Use of Information about Occupation." *In*: E. A. Wrigley, ed.
1972b.   "A Note on the Household Structure of Mid-Nineteenth Century York in Comparative Perspective." *In*: Laslett and Wall, eds.
1974.   *Stability and Change in an English Country Town: A Study of York, 1801–51*. Cambridge.
1978.   "The Census Enumerators Books: A Commentary." in R. Lawton, ed.

Ashcroft, P. F.
1898.   *The English Poor Law System*. Trans. H. Prestion-Thomas. London.

Ashenfelter, O.
1974.   "Comment." *In:* T. W. Schultz, ed.

Ashworth, H.
1842.   "Statistics on the Present Depression of Trade at Bolton." *Journal of the Statistical Society* 5.74–81.

Atwood, M.
1976.   *The Edible Woman*. New York.

Auerbach, N.
1978.   *Communities of Women: An Idea in Fiction*. Cambridge, Mass.
1982.   *The Woman and the Demon: The Life of a Victorian Myth*. Cambridge, Mass.

Bane, M. J.
1976.   *Here to Stay: American Families in the Twentieth Century.* New York.

Banks, J. A.
1954.   *Prosperity and Parenthood.* London.
1978.   "The Social Structure of Nineteenth Century England as Seen through the Census." *In*: R. Lawton, ed.
1981.   *Victorian Values: Secularism and the Size of Families.* London.

Banks, J. A., and Banks, O.
1964.   *Feminism and Family Planning in Victorian England.* New York.

Barnes, H. E.
1925.   *The New History and the Social Studies.* New York.

Barrett, J. C.
1977.   "Criteria for Choosing Between Analytical Methods and Simulation." *International Population Conference, Mexico, 1977.* IUSSP. Vol. 1.

Barry J. F., and R. W. Elmes, eds.
1924.   *Buffalo's Text Book.* Buffalo, N.Y.

Barrie, J. M.
1911.   *Peter Pan: The Story of Peter and Wendy.* New York.

Basch, F.
1974.   *Relative Creatures: Victorian Women in Society and the Novel.* New York.

Beauvoir, S. de
1970.   *The Coming of Age.* Trans. P. O'Brian. New York.

Becker, G. S.
1964.   *Human Capital.* New York.
1965.   "A Theory of the Allocation of Time." *Economic Journal* 71.493–517.
1974.   "A Theory of Marriage." *In* T. W. Schultz, ed.
1976.   *The Economic Approach to Human Behavior.* Chicago.

Becker, G. S., and H. G. Lewis.
1974.   "Interaction Between Quantity and Quality of Children." *In* T. W. Schultz, ed.

Beeton, I.
1861.   *Book of Household Management.* London.

Bell, N. W., and E. F. Vogel.
1960.   "Towards a Framework for Functional Analysis of Family Behavior." *In*: N. W. Bell and E. F. Vogel, eds., *A Modern Introduction to the Family.* New York.

Bellamy, J. M.
1978.   "Occupation Statistics in the Nineteenth Century." *In*: R. Lawton, ed.

Bendix, R.
1967.   "Comparative Analysis of Historical Change." *In*: T. Burns and S. B. Saul, eds., *Social Theory and Economic Change*. London.

Bengston, V., D. H. Dowd, and A. Inkeles.
1975.   "Modernization, Modernity, and Perceptions of Aging: A Cross-Cultural Study." *Journal of Gerontology* 30.688–95.

Ben-Porath, Y.
1974.   "Economic Analysis of Fertility in Israel." *In*: T. W. Schultz, ed.
1977.   "The Economic Value and Costs of Children in Different Economic and Social Settings." *International Population Conference, Mexico, 1977*. IUSSP, 77–92.

Benson, L.
1966   "Quantification, Scientific History, and Scholarly Innovation." *American Historical Association Newsletter* 4.11–16.

Berkner, L. K.
1972a.   "Rural Family Organization in Europe: A Problem in Comparative History." *Peasant Studies Newsletter* 1.145–56.
1972b.   "The Stem Family and the Developmental Cycle of the Peasant Household: An Eighteenth Century Austrian Example." *American Historical Review* 77.398–418.
1973.   "Recent Research on the History of the Family in Western Europe." *Journal of Marriage and the Family* 35.395–405.
1975.   "The Use and Misuse of Census Data in the Historical Study of Family Structure." *Journal of Interdisciplinary History* 5.721–38.
1976.   "Inheritance, Land Tenure, and Peasant Family Structure: A German Regional Comparison." *In*: J. Goody, J. Thirsk, and E. P. Thompson, eds.
1977a.   "Household Arithmetic: A Note." *Journal of Family History* 2.159–63.
1977b.   "Peasant Household Organization and Demographic Change in Lower Saxony (1689–1766)." *In*: R. D. Lee, ed.

Berkner, L. K., and F. F. Mendels.
1978.   "Inheritance Systems, Family Structure, and Demographic Patterns in Western, Europe, 1700–1900." in C. Tilly, eds., *Historical Studies of Changing Fertility*. Princeton, N.J.

Berkner, L. K., and J. W. Shaffer.
1978.   "The Joint Family in the Nivernais." *Journal of Family History* 3.150–62.

Blake, J.
1968.   "Are Babies Consumer Durables?" *Population Studies* 22.5–25.

Blau, P. M.
1964.   *Exchange and Power in Social Life.* New York.

Blaug, M.
1963.   "The Myth of the Old Poor Law and the Making of the New."
           Journal of Economic History 23.151–84.

Blumberg, R. L., and R. F. Winch.
1972.   "Social Complexity and Family Complexity: Evidence for the Curvi-
           linear Hypothesis." *American Journal of Sociology* 77.898–920.

Blumin, S. M.
1977.   "Rip Van Winkle's Grandchildren: Family and Household in the
           Hudson Valley, 1800–1860." *In*: T. K. Hareven, ed., *Family and Kin
           in Urban Communities 1700–1930.* New York.

Bolton Free Press.
1844.   21 December.

Bongaarts, J.
1981.   "Simulation of the Family Life Cycle." Working Papers, Center for
           Policy Studies, Population Council. New York.

Boyson, R.
1970.   *The Ashworth Cotton Enterprise: The Rise and Fall of a Family Firm,
           1818–1880.* Oxford.

Bradley, B., and F. Mendels.
1978.   "Can the Hypothesis of a Nuclear Family Be Tested Empirically?"
           Population Studies 32.381–94.

Branca, P.
1975   *Silent Sisterhood.* Pittsburgh.

Brayshay, M.
1980.   "Depopulation and Changing Household Structure in the Mining
           Communities of West Cornwall, 1851–1871." *Local Population
           Studies* 25.26–41.

Brooks, M.
1978.   "Love and Possession in a Victorian Household: The Example of the
           Ruskins." *In*: A. Wohl, ed.

Brumbaugh, G. M.
1928.   *Maryland Records: Colonial, Revolutionary, County, and Church.*
           Vol. II. Baltimore.

Buckley, J. H.
1951.   *The Victorian Temper.* Cambridge, Mass.

Buckley, W.
1968.   "Society as a Complex Adaptive System." *In*: W. Buckley, ed.,
          Modern Systems of Research for the Behavioral Scientist. Chicago.

Buffalo Board of Health
1855.   *Sanitary Reports*. Buffalo, N.Y.

Buffalo Chamber of Commerce
1911–1914. *The Live Wire*. Buffalo, N.Y.

Burch, T. K.
1967.   "The Size and Structure of Families: A Comparative Analysis of
          Census Data." *American Sociological Review* 32.347–63.
1970.   "Some Demographic Determinants of Average Household Size: An
          Analytic Approach." *Demography* 7.61–70.
1979.   "Household and Family Demography: A Bibliographic Essay."
          Population Index 47.173–96.
1980.   "The Index of Overall Headship: A Simple Measure of Household
          Complexity Standardized for Age and Sex." *Demography* 17.25–37.

Burch, T. K., and M. Gendall.
1970.   "Extended Family Structure and Fertility: Some Conceptual and
          Methodological Issues." *Journal of Marriage and the Family* 32.227–
          36.

Burgess, E. W.
1960.   *Aging in Western Societies*. Chicago.
1963.   "The Transition from Extended Families to Nuclear Families." *In*:
          R. H. Williams, et al., eds., *The Process of Aging: Social and
          Psychological Perspectives*. Vol II. New York.

Burn, W. L.
1964.   *The Age of Equipoise*. New York.

Burton, E.
1971.   *The Early Victorians at Home, 1837–1861*. London.

Butler, S.
1936.   (1903). *The Way of All Flesh*. New York.
1912.   (ca. 1885). *Note-Books*. New York.

Calhoun, A. W.
1917–1919. *A Social History of the American Family from Colonial Times to the
          Present*. 3 vols. Cleveland.

Calman, A. L.
1875.   *Life and Labours of John Ashworth*. Manchester.

Carpenter, N.
1927.   *Nationality, Color, and Economic Opportunity in the City of Buffalo*.
          New York.

Chadwick, D.
1860.   "On the Rate of Wages in Manchester and Salford, and the Manufac-
           turing Districts of Lancashire, 1839–59." *Journal of the Statistical
           Society* 23.1–36.

Chaytor, M.
1980.   "Household and Kinship: Ryton in the Late 16th and Early 17th
           Centuries." *History Workshop Journal* 10.26–51.

Chevalier, L.
1973.   *Laboring Classes and Dangerous Classes*. Princeton, N.J.

Chudacoff, H. P.
1978.   "Newlyweds and Family Extension: The First Stage of the Family
           Cycle in Providence, Rhode Island, 1864–65, 1879–80." *In*: T. K.
           Hareven and M. A. Vinovskis, eds.

Chudacoff, H. P., and T. K. Hareven.
1978.   "Family Transitions into Old Age." *In*: T. K. Hareven, ed.
1979.   "From the Empty Nest to Family Dissolution: Life Course Transi-
           tions into Old Age." *Journal of Family History* 4.69–83.

Cleaver, E.
1968.   *Soul on Ice*. New York.

Coale, A. J.
1965.   "Estimates of Average Size of Household." *In*: M. J. Levy, ed.,
           Aspects of the Analysis of Family Structure. Princeton, N.J.
1972.   "Age Patterns of Marriage." *Population Studies* 25.193–214.

Coale, A. J., and P. Demeny.
1983.   *Regional Model Life Tables and Stable Populations*. 2d ed. Prince-
           ton, N.J.

Coale, A. J., and T. J. Trussell.
1974.   "Model Fertility Schedules: Variations in the Age Structure of Child-
           bearing in Human Populations." *Population Index* 42.185–258.

Coale, A. J., and M. Zelnik.
1963.   *New Estimates of Fertility and Population in the United States*. Prince-
           ton, N.J.

Cobbe, F. P.
1862.   "What Shall We Do with Our Old Maids." *Frasers Magazine*
           66.594–610.

Cohen, P. S.
1967.   "Economic Analysis and Economic Man." *In*: R. Firth, ed., *Themes
           in Economic Anthropology*. London.

Cohn, R. M.
1982.   "Economic Development and Status Change of the Aged." *American Journal of Sociology* 87.1150–61.

Collier, F.
1965.   (1921). *The Family Economy of the Working Classes in the Cotton Industry 1784–1833*. Manchester.

Condran, G., and R. Cheney.
1982.   "Mortality Trends in Philadelphia: Age and Cause-Specific Death Rates, 1870–1930." *Demography* 19.97–123.

Cornford, F. M.
1908.   *Microcosmographia Academica*. London.

Cowgill, D.
1974a.   "The Aging of Populations and Societies." *American Academy of Political and Social Sciences* 415.
1974b.   "Aging and Modernization: A Revision of the Theory." *In*: J. Gubrum, ed., *Late Life: Communities and Environmental Policies*. New York.

Cowgill, D., and L. D. Holmes, eds.
1972.   *Aging and Modernization*. New York.

Crafts, N. F. R., and N. J. Ireland.
1975.   "The Role of Simulation Techniques in the Theory and Observation of Family Formation." *Population Studies* 29.75–95.

Cruikshank, G., et al.
1912.   *The Comic Almanack: An Ephemeris in Jest and Earnest, Containing Merry Tales, Humorous Poetry, Quips and Oddities*. London.

Czap, P.
1978.   "Marriage and the Peasant Join Family in the Era of Serfdom." *In*: D. L. Ransel, ed., *The Family in Imperial Russia*. Urbana, Ill.

Dahlin, M.
1980.   "Perspectives on the Family Life of the Elderly in 1900." *The Gerontologist* 20.99–107.

Darroch, A. G., and M. Ornstein.
1983.   "Family Coresidence in Canada in 1871: Family Life Cycles, Occupations and Networks of Mutual Aid." Paper presented at the Canadian History Association Meetings, Vancouver.
1984.   "Family and Household in Nineteenth-Century Canada: Regional Patterns and Regional Economies." *Journal of Family History* 9.158–77.

Davidoff, L.
1976.   "Landscape with Figures: Home and Community in English Soci-
           ety." *In*: J. Mitchell and A. Oakley, eds., *The Rights and Wrongs of
           Women*. New York.

Deane, P.
1965.   *The First Industrial Revolution*. Cambridge.

Deane, P., and W. A. Cole.
1968.   *British Economic Growth, 1688–1959: Trends and Structure*. Cam-
           bridge.

De Bono, E.
1971.   *Practical Thinking*. London.

Degler, C. N.
1980.   *At Odds: Women and the Family in America from the Revolution to
           the Present*. Oxford.

DeMause, L., ed.
1974.   *The History of Childhood*. New York.

Demos, J.
1965.   "Notes on Life in Plymouth Colony." *William and Mary Quarterly*
           22.279–85.
1968.   "Families in Colonial Bristol, Rhode Island: An Exercise in Histori-
           cal Demography." *William and Mary Quarterly* 25.40–45.
1970.   *A Little Commonwealth: Family Life in Plymouth Colony*. New
           York.
1978.   "Old Age in Early New England." *In*: M. Gordon, ed., *The Amer-
           ican Family in Social-Historical Perspective*. 2d ed. New York.

Demos, J., and S. S. Boocock, eds.
1978.   *Turning Points: Historical and Sociological Essays on the Family*.
           Chicago.

De Vos, S., and A. Palloni.
1984.   "Formal Methods and Models for Analyzing Kinship and Household
           Organization." CDE Working Paper No. 84-30, Center for De-
           mography and Ecology, University of Wisconsin-Madison.

De Vos, S., and S. Ruggles.
1986.   "The Demography of Kinship and the Life Course." *In*: P. B.
           Baltes, D. L. Featherman, and R. M. Lerner, eds., *Life Span De-
           velopment and Behavior*, vol. 8. New York.

De Quincy, T.
1822.   *Confessions of an English Opium Eater*. London.

Dickens, C.
1967.   (1854). *Hard Times*. London.

Dodd, W.
1842.   *The Factory System Illustrated in a Series of Letters to Lord Ashley*.
          London.

Douglas, M.
1970.   *Natural Symbols*. New York.

Doyle, A. C.
1976.   (1891–1892). *The Adventures of Sherlock Holmes*. New York.

Duncan, O. D.
1974.   "Comment." *In*: T. W. Schultz, ed.

Dupaquier, J., et al., eds.
1981.   *Marriage and Remarriage in Populations of the Past*. New York.

Dupree, M.
1977.   "The Family and the Industrial Revolution: A Case Study from the
          Staffordshire Potteries." Unpublished.

Dyke, B., and J. W. MacCluer, eds.
1973.   *Computer Simulation in Human Population Studies*. New York.

Edwards, J. N.
1969.   "Familial Behavior as Social Exchange." *Journal of Marriage and the
          Family* 31.518–36.

Edwards, J. N., and M. B. Brauburger.
1973.   "Exchange and Parent-Youth Conflict." *Journal of Marriage and the
          Family* 35.101–7.

Edwards, M. M., and R. L. Jones.
1973.   "N. J. Smelser and the Cotton Factory Family: A Reassessment." *In*:
          N. B. Harte and K. G. Ponting, eds., *Textile History and Economic
          History: Essays in Honor of J. de Lacy Mann*. London.

Ekeh, R.
1974.   *Social Exchange Theory*. Cambridge, Mass.

Elder, G. H.
1975.   "Age Differentiation and the Life Course." *Annual Review of
          Sociology* 1.165–90.
1978a.   "Approaches to Social Change and the Family." *In*: J. Demos and
          S. S. Boocock, eds.
1978b.   "Family History and the Life Course." *In*: T. K. Hareven, ed.
1981.   "History and the Family: the Discovery of Complexity." *Journal of
          Marriage and the Family* 43.508–14.

Engels, F.
1958.   (1844). *The Condition of the Working Class in England*. Trans. W. O.

Henderson and W. H. Chaloner. Oxford.
1884.   *The Origin of the Family, Private Property, and the State*. London.

Fallers, L. A.
1965.   "The Range of Variation in Actual Family Size: A Critique of
             Marion Levy's Argument." *In*: A. J. Coale et al., eds., *Aspects of the
             Analysis of Family Structure*. Princeton, N.J.

Farber, B.
1972.   *The Guardians of Virtue: Salem Families in 1800*. New York.

Farnie, D. A.
n.d.   "The Establishment of the New Poor Law in Salford, 1835–50."
             Unpublished, Salford Central Library.

Faucher, L. J.
1844.   *Manchester in 1844, Its Present Condition and Future Prospects*.
             London.

Fisher, H. A. L.
1936.   *A History of Europe*. Boston.

Fitch, N.
1980.   Review of "Statistical Studies of Historical Social Structure." *Histor-
             ical Methods* 13.127–37.

Flandrin, J.-L.
1979.   *Families in Former Times*. Trans. R. Southern. Cambridge.

Fletcher, R.
1963.   "The Making of the Modern Family." *In*: K. Eliot, ed., *The Family
             and Its Future*. New York.

Foster, J. O.
1974.   *Class Struggle in the Industrial Revolution: Early Industrial Capital-
             ism in Three English Towns*. London.

Foucault, M.
1980.   *History of Sexuality*. Vol. 1. New York.

Fourastie, J.
1959.   "De la vie traditionelle a la vie 'tertiere': recherches sur le calandrier
             démographique de l'homme moyen." *Population* 14.417–32.

Frankle, B. S.
1969.   "The Genteel Family: High Victorian Conceptions of Domesticity
             and Good Behavior." Ph.D. dissertation, University of Wisconsin-
             Madison.

Freeman, R., and P. Klaus.
1984.   "Blessed or Not? The New Spinster in England and the United States

in the Late Nineteenth and Early Twentieth Centuries." *Journal of Family History* 9.394–414.

French, G. J.
1859.   *Life and Times of Samuel Crompton.* London.

Furstenberg, F. F.
1966.   "Industralization and the American Family: A Look Backward." *American Journal of Sociology* 31.326–37.

Gardiner, P.
1961.   *The Nature of Historical Explanation.* Oxford.

George, P. M., and E. T. Pryor.
1971.   "Some Theoretical and Methodological Suggestions for Reconceptualization of Family Nuclearization." *International Journal of the Sociology of the Family* 1.201–6.

Gilbert, J. P., and E. A. Hammel.
1966.   "Computer Simulation and Analysis of Problems in Kinship and Social Structure." *American Anthropologist* 68.71–93.

Glasco, L. A.
1973.   "Ethnicity and Social Structure: Irish, Germans, and Native-Born of Buffalo, New York, 1850–1860." Ph. D. thesis, SUNY-Buffalo.
1978.   "Migration and Adjustment in the Nineteenth Century City: Occupation, Property, and Household Structure of Native-Born Whites, Buffalo, New York, 1855." *In*: T. K. Hareven and M. Vinovskis, eds.

Glass, D. V.
1951.   "A Note on the Under-Registration of Births in Britain in the Nineteenth Century." *Population Studies* 5.70–88.
1965.   "Introduction." in D. V. Glass and D. E. C. Eversley, eds., *Population in History: Essays in Historical Demography.* Chicago.
1966.   "London Inhabitants Within the Walls 1695." *London Record Society.* Vol. 2, introduction.
1973.   *Numbering the People.* Farnborough, Hants.

Glass, D. V., and D. E. C. Eversley, eds.
1965.   *Population in History.* London.

Glick, P.
1957.   *American Family: A Volume in the Census Monograph Series.* New York.
1977.   "Dimensions of the Fields of Family Demography." *International Population Conference, Mexico, 1977.* IUSSP 1.389–404.

Glick, P., and R. Parke.
1965.   "New Approaches in Studying the Life Cycle of the Family." *Demography* 2.187–202.

Goldfield, E. D.
1948.   "Appendix B: Methods of Analyzing Labor Force Change." *In*: J. D. Durand, ed., *The Labor Force in the United States: 1890–1960*. New York.

Goldin, C.
1981.   "Family Strategies and the Family Economy in the Late Nineteenth Century." *In*: T. Hershberg, ed., *Philadelphia: Work, Space, Family, and Group Experience in the Nineteenth Century: Towards an Interdisciplinary History of the City*. New York.

Goldman, N.
1977.   "The Demography of Kin." Unpublished D.Sc. dissertation, Harvard University.

Goode, W. J.
1963a.   *World Revolution and Family Patterns*. New York.
1963b.   "Industrialization and Family Change." *In*: B. F. Hoselitz and W. E. Moore, eds., *Industrialization and Society*. Mouton.
1964.   *The Family*. New York.
1973.   *Explorations in Social Theory*. Oxford.
1974.   "The Economics of Non-Monetary Variables." *In*: T. W. Schultz, ed.

Goodman, L. A., N. Keyfitz, and T. W. Pullum.
1974.   "Family Formation and the Frequency of Various Kinship Relationships." *Theoretical Population Biology* 5.1–27.
1975.   "Addendum." *Theoretical Population Biology* 8.376–81.

Goody, J.
1983.   *The Development of the Family and Marriage in Europe*. Cambridge.

Goody, J., J. Thirsk, and E. P. Thompson, eds.
1976.   *Family and Inheritance: Rural Society in Western Europe, 1200–1800*. Cambridge.

Goose, N.
1980.   "Household Size and Structure in Early Stuart Cambridge." *Social History* 5.347–88.

Gordon, M.
1969.   "The Ideal Husband as Depicted in the 19th Century Marriage Manual." *Family Coordinator* 18.226–31.

Gordon, M., ed.
1978.   *The American Family in Social-Historial Perspective.* 2d ed. New York.

Gordon, M., and M. C. Bernstein.
1970.   "Mate Choice and Domestic Life in the 19th Century Marriage Manual." *Journal of Marriage and the Family* 32.665–74.

Goubert, P.
1977.   "Family and Province: A Contribution to the Knowledge of Family Structures in Early Modern France." *Journal of Family History* 2.179–95.

Gouldner, A. W.
1960.   "The Norm of Reciprocity: A Preliminary Statement." *American Sociological Review* 25.161–78.

Grabill, W. H., C. V. Kiser, and P. W. Whelpton.
1958.   *The Fertility of American Women.* New York.

Graham, S. N.
1980.   *1900 Public Use Sample: User's Handbook.* Seattle.

Grahame, K.
1908.   *The Wind in the Willows.* London.

Great Britain, General Register Office.
1841–1901. *The Registrar-General's Annual Reports of Births, Deaths, and Marriages* (title varies). London.
1968.   *Sample Census, 1966. Household Composition Tables.* London.

Greenall, R. L.
1974.   "The Making of the Borough at Salford." *In:* S. P. Bell, ed., *Victorian Lancashire.* Manchester.

Greenfield, S. S.
1961.   "Industrialization and the Family in Sociological Theory." *American Journal of Sociology* 67.312–22.

Greven, P. J.
1966.   "Family Structure in Seventeenth Century Andover, Massachusetts." *William and Mary Quarterly*, 3d series, 23.234–56.
1970.   *Four Generations: Population, Land, and Family in Colonial Andover, Massachusetts.* Ithaca, N.Y.

Grew, R.
1978.   "Modernization and Its Discontents." *American Behavioral Scientist* 21.289–309.

Grieco, M. S.
1982.   "Family Structure and Industrial Employment: The Role of In-

formation and Migration." *Journal of Marriage and the Family* 44.701–07.

Griffin, W. T.
1886.   *The Homes of Our Country: Or The Centers of Moral and Religious Influence; The Crystals of Society; The Nuclei of National Character.* Des Moines, Iowa.

Griliches, Z.
1974.   "Comment." *In*: T. W. Schultz, ed.

Habakkuk, H. J.
1953.   "English Population in the Eighteenth Century." *Economic History Review*, 2nd ser., 6.117–33.
1960.   "Family Structure and Economic Change in Nineteenth Century Europe." *In*: N. W. Bell and E. F. Vogel, eds., *A Modern Introduction to the Family.* New York.
1972.   *Population Growth and Development since 1750.* Leicester.

Hague, W.
1855.   *Home Life: Twelve Lectures.* New York.

Haines, M.
1979.   "The Use of Model Life Tables for the United States in the Late Nineteenth Century." *Demography* 16.289–312.
1981.   "Poverty, Stress, and the Family in a Late Nineteenth Century City: Philadelphia 1880." *In*: T. Hershberg, ed., *Philadelphia: Work, Space, Family, and Group Experience in the Nineteenth Century: Towards an Interdisciplinary History of the City.* New York.

Hajnal, J.
1947a.   "Aspects of Recent Trends in Marriage in England and Wales." *Population Studies* 1.72–98.
1947b.   "The Analysis of Birth Statistics in Light of the Recent International Recovery of the Birth Rate." *Population Studies* 1.137–64.
1965.   "European Marriage Patterns in Perspective." *In*: D. V. Glass and D. E. C. Eversley, eds., *Population in History. Essays in Historical Demography.* London.
1982.   "Two Kinds of Pre-Industrial Household Formation Systems." *Population and Development Review* 8.449–94.

Halpern, J. M.
1972.   "Town and Countryside in Serbia in the Nineteenth Century." *In*: P. Laslett and R. Wall, eds.

Hammel, E. A., et al.
1976.   *The Socsim Demographic-Sociological Microsimulation Program Operating Manual.* Berkeley.

Hammel, E. A., and R. Z. Deuer.
1977.   *Five Classy Programs*. Research Series no. 33, Institute for International Studies. Berkeley.

Hammel, E. A., and P. Laslett.
1974.   "Comparing Household Structure across Time and between Cultures." *Comparative Studies in History and Society* 16.73–109.

Hammel, E. A., and K. W. Wachter.
1977.   "Primonuptiality and Ultimonuptiality: Their Effects on Stem Family Household Frequencies." *In*: R. Lee, ed.

Hammel, E. A., K. W. Wachter, and C. K. McDaniel.
1981.   "The Kin of the Aged in the Year 2000: The Chickens Come Home to Roost." *In*: S. B. Kiesler, J. N. Morgan, and V. K. Oppenheimer, eds., *Aging and Social Change*. New York.

Hammersley, J. M., and D. C. Handscomb.
1964.   *Monte-Carlo Methods*. London.

Hansard.
1844   3d series, vol. 73.

Hareven, T. K.
1975.   "Family Time and Industrial Time: Family and Work in a Planned Corporation Town, 1900–1924." *Journal of Urban History* 1.365–89.
1978.   "The Last Stage: Historical Adulthood and Old Age." *Daedalus* 105.13–28.
1982.   *Family Time and Industrial Time: The Relationship Between the Family and Work in a New England Industrial Community*. Cambridge.

Hareven, T. K., ed.
1977.   *Family and Kin in Urban Communities*. New York.
1978.   *Transitions: The Family and Life Course in Historical Perspective*. New York.

Hareven, T. K., and M. A. Vinovskis, eds.
1978.   *Family and Population in Nineteenth Century America*. Princeton, N.J.

Harris, C. C.
1967.   *The Family: An Introduction*. New York.

Hecht, I. W.
1973.   "The Virginia Muster of 1624/5 as a Source for Demographic History." *William and Mary Quarterly*, 3d ser., 30.65–92.

Henry, L.
1968.   "Historical Demography." *Daedalus* 97.385–96.

Hershberg, T.
1973.   "A Method for the Computerized Study of Family and Household
            Structure Using the Manuscript Schedules of the U.S. Census
            of Population, 1850–1880." *The Family in Historical Perspective*
            1.6–20.

Hershberg, T., et al.
1974.   "Occupation and Ethnicity in Five Nineteenth Century Cities: A
            Collaborative Inquiry." *Historical Methods Newsletter* 7.174–216.

Higgs, R., and H. L. Stettler.
1970.   "Colonial New England Demography: A Sampling Approach." *William and Mary Quarterly* 27.282–94.

Holman, T. B., and W. R. Burr.
1980.   "Beyond the Beyond: The Growth of Family Theories in the 1970s."
            Journal of Marriage and the Family 42.729–41.

Homans, G. C.
1941.   *English Villagers of the Thirteenth Century.* Cambridge, England.
1961.   *Social Behavior: Its Elementary Forms.* New York.
1964.   "Bringing Man Back In." *American Sociological Review* 29.809–18.

Horvitz, D. G., et al.
1969.   "POPSIM, a Demographic Microsimulation Model." *International
            Population Conference, London, 1969.* IUSSP. 1.95–106.

Houghton, W. E.
1957.   *The Victorian Frame of Mind 1830–1870.* New Haven, Conn.

Houlbrooke, R. A.
1984.   *The English Family, 1450–1700.* New York.

Howell, N.
1979.   *Demography of the Dobe !Kung.* New York.

Howells, W. D., M. Twain, and N. S. Shaler.
1901.   *The Niagra Book.* New York.

Howlett, N. M.
1983.   "Family and Household in a Nineteenth Century Devon Village."
            Local Population Studies 30.42–48.

Huesmann, L. R., and G. Levinger.
1976.   "Incremental Exchange Theory: A Formal Model for Progression in
            Dyad Social Interaction." *In*: L. Berkowitz and E. Walster, eds.,
            Advances in Experimental Social Psychology 9.191–229.

Hunt, D.
1970.   *Parents and Children in History.* New York.

Imhof, A.
1981.   "Women, Family, and Death: Excess Mortality of Women of Child-
           bearing Age in Four Communities in Nineteenth-Century Ger-
           many." *In*: R. Evans and W. R. Lee, eds., *The German Family:*
           Essays on the Social History of the Family in Nineteenth and Twen-
           tieth Century Germany. New York.

Immerwahr, G. E.
1967.   "Survivorship of Sons under Conditions of Improving Mortality."
           Demography 9.710–20.

Inkeles, A., and D. M. Smith.
1974.   *Becoming Modern: Individual Change in Six Developing Countries.*
           Cambridge, Mass.

Innes, J. W.
1938.   *Class Fertility Differentials in England and Wales, 1876–1934.* Prince-
           ton, N.J.

Jacquard, A., and H. Leridon.
1974.   "Simulating Human Reproduction: How Complicated Should a
           Model Be?" *In*: B. Dyke and J. W. MacCluer, eds.

James, J. A.
1832.   *The Family Monitor, or a Help to Domestic Happiness.* Concord,
           N.H.

Jones, C. E.
1918.   "A Geneological Study of Population." *Publications of the American*
           Statistical Association 16.201–21.

Joplin, J.
1969.   "Me and Bobby McGee," on the album *Pearl.* Columbia KC 30322
           (1970).

Kaestle, C. F., and M. A. Vinovskis.
1978.   "From Fireside to Factory: School Entry and School Leaving in
           Nineteenth Century Massachusetts." *In*: T. K. Hareven, ed.

Kanner, S. B.
1972.   "The Women of England in a Century of Social Change, 1815–1914:
           A Select Bibliography." *In*: M. Vinicus, ed., *Suffer and Be Still:*
           Women in the Victorian Age. Bloomington, Ind.
1977.   "The Women of England in a Century of Social Change, 1815–1914:
           A Select Bibliography, Part II." *In*: M. Vinicus, ed., *A Widening*
           Sphere: Changing Roles of Victorian Women. Bloomington, Ind.

Kasakoff, A. B.
1974.   "How Many Relatives?" *In*: P. Ballonoff, ed., *Geneological Mathe-*
           matics. Paris.

Katz, M.
1972.   "Occupational Classification in History." *Journal of Interdisciplinary History* 3.63–88.
1975.   *The People of Hamilton, Canada West: Family and Class in a Mid-Nineteenth Century City.* Cambridge, Mass.
1981.   "Social Class in North American Urban History." *Journal of Interdisciplinary History* 11.579–605.
1983.   *Poverty and Policy in American History.* New York.

Katz, M., M. Doucet, and M. Stern.
1978.   "Migration and the Social Order in Erie County, New York, 1855–1915." *Journal of Interdisciplinary History* 8.669–702.
1982.   *The Social Organization of Early Industrial Capitalism.* Cambridge, Mass.

Kertzer, D. I.
1984.   *Family Life In Central Italy, 1880–1910: Sharecropping, Wage Labor, and Coresidence.* New Brunswick, N.J.

Keyfitz, N.
1968.   *An Introduction to the Mathematics of Population.* Reading, Mass.

Knodel, J.
1968.   "Infant Mortality and Fertility in Three Bavarian Villages." *Population Studies* 22.297–318.

Kobrin, F. E.
1976.   "The Fall in Household Size and the Rise of the Primary Individual in the United States." *Demography* 13.127–38; also in M. Gordon, ed.

Koller, M. R.
1954.   "Studies of Three Generation Households." *Marriage and Family Living* 16.205–6.

Kousser, J. M.
1984.   "The Revival of Narrative: A Response to Recent Criticisms of Quantitative History." *Social Science History* 8.133–49.

Kreps, J. M.
1969.   "The Economics of Retirement." *In:* E. Busse and E. Pfeffer, eds., *Behavior and Adaptation in Later Life.* Boston.

Kyvig, D. E., and M. A. Marty.
1978.   *Writing Your Family History: A Handbook for Research and Writing.* Arlington Heights, Ill.

Kunstadter, P., et al.
1963.   "Demographic Variability and Preferential Marriage Patterns." *American Journal of Physical Anthropology* 21.511–19.

Lafferty, R. A.
1970.   *Nine Hundred Grandmothers*. New York.

Landers, A.
1975.   Syndicated column, 12 October.

Lantz, H. R., J. Keyes, and M. Schultz.
1975.   "The American Family in the Preindustrial Period: From Base Lines in History to Change." *American Sociological Review* 40.21–36.

Lasch, C.
1977.   *Haven in a Heartless World*. New York.

Laslett, B.
1973.   "The Family as a Public and Private Institution: A Historical Perspective." *Journal of Marriage and the Family* 35.480–92.
1977.   "Social Change and the Family: Los Angeles, California 1850–1870." *American Sociological Review* 42.268–91.
1982.   "Rethinking Household Structure: A New System of Classification." *Historical Methods* 15.3–10.

Laslett, P.
1965a   *The World We Have Lost*. London.
1965b.   "The History of Population and Social Structure." *International Social Science Journal* 27.582–94.
1966.   "New Light on the History of the English Family." *The Listener* 75.233–34.
1970.   "The Comparative History of Household and Family." *Journal of Social History* 4.75–87.
1972a.   "Introduction." *In*: P. Laslett and R. Wall, eds.
1972b.   "Mean Household Size in England Since the Sixteenth Century." *In*: P. Laslett and R. Wall, eds.
1977a.   *Family Life and Illicit Love in Earlier Generations*. New York.
1977b.   "Societal Development and Aging." *In*: R. H. Binstock and E. Shanas, eds., *Handbook of Aging and the Social Sciences*. New York.
1978.   "The Stem Family and Its Privileged Position. " *In*: K. Wachter, E. A. Hammel, and P. Laslett, eds.
1984.   "The Significance of the Past in the Study of Aging." *Ageing and Society*, vol. 4.

Laslett, P., and J. Harrison.
1963.   "Clayworth and Cogenhoe." in H. E. Bell and R. L. Ollard, eds., *Historical Essays 1600–1750: Presented to David Ogg*. London.

Laslett, P., and R. Wall, eds.
1972.   *Household and Family in Past Time*. Cambridge.

Lawton, R., ed.
1978.   *The Census and Social Structure: An Interpretive Guide to Nineteenth Century Censuses of England and Wales.* London.

LeBras, H.
1973.   "Parents, grand-parents, biseaux." *Population* 28.9–38.

Lebsock, S. H.
1984.   *The Free Women of Petersberg: Status and Culture in a Southern Town, 1784–1860.* New York.

Lee, G. R.
1980.   "Kinship in the Seventies: A Decade Review of Research and Theory." *Journal of Marriage and the Family* 42.923–34.

Lee, R. D., ed.
1977.   *Population Patterns in the Past.* New York.

Le Play, P. G. F.
1855.   *Les ouvriers Européens.* Paris.
1864.   *La réforme sociale.* Paris.
1871.   *L'organisation de la famille selon le vrai modèle signalé par l'histoire de toutes les races et tous les temps.* Paris.

Leeuwen, L. T.
1981.   "Early Family Sociology in Europe: Parallels to the United States." *In*: R. L. Howard, *A Social History of American Family Sociology, 1865–1940.* Westport, Conn.

Lescohier, J.
1935.   "Working Conditions." *In*: J. R. Commons, ed., *The History of Labor in the United States.* Madison, Wis.

Levine, D.
1977.   *Family Formation in an Age of Nascent Capitalism.* New York.
1982.   " 'For their Own Reasons': Individual Marriage Decisions and Family Life." *Journal of Family History* 7.255–64.

Levy, M.
1965.   "Aspects of the Analysis of Family Structure." *In:* M. Levy et al., *Aspects of the Analysis of Family Structure.* Princeton, N.J.
1970.   "Some Hypotheses about the Family." *Journal of Comparative Family Studies* 1.119–31.

Levy, M., and L. A. Fallers.
1973.   "Some Aspects of Sex, Generation, and Modernization." *Journal of the National Sociology Honor Society* 41.73–84.

Liebenstein, H.
1974.   "An Interpretation of the Economic Theory of Fertility: Promising Path or Blind Alley?" *Journal of Economic Literature* 12.457–79.
1977.   "The Economic Theory of Fertility—Survey, Issues, and Considerations." *International Population Conference, Mexico, 1977.* IUSSP 2.49–64.

Linder, F. E., and R. D. Grove.
1947.   *Vital Statistics Rates on the United States 1900–1940.* Washington, D.C.

Litwak, E.
1965.   "Extended Kin Relations in an Industrial Democratic Society." *In*: E. Shanas and G. F. Streib, eds., *Social Structure and the Family: Generational Relations.* Englewood Cliffs, N.J.
1970.   "Geographic Mobility and Extended Family Cohesion." *In*: T. R. Ford and G. F. DeJong, eds., *Social Demography.* Englewood Cliffs, N.J.

Lloyd, C., ed.
1975.   *Sex, Discrimination, and the Divison of Labor.* New York.

Lockhead, M.
1964.   *The Victorian Household.* London.

Lockridge, K.
1968.   "Land, Population, and the Evolution of New England Society 1630–1790." *Past and Present* 39.62–80.
1970.   *A New England Town: The First Hundred Years, Dedham, Massachusetts, 1636–1736.* New York.

Lotka, A. J.
1931.   "Orphanhood in Relation to Demographic Factors: A Study in Population Analysis." *Metron* 9.37–109.

MacDonald, G. W.
1981.   "Structural Exchange and Marital Interaction." *Journal of Marriage and the Family* 43.825–59.

MacFarlane, A.
1978.   *Origins of English Individualism.* Cambridge.

Manchester Statistical Society.
1836.   *Report of a Committee of the Manchester Statistical Society, on the State of Education in the Borough of Salford in 1835.* London.

Marcuse, H.
1970.   *Five Lectures.* Berkeley.

Marshall, D.
1926.   *The English Poor in the Eighteenth Century.* London.

Mathias, P.
1968.   *The First Industrial Nation*. London.

McArdle, F.
1974.   "Another Look at 'Peasant Families East and West'." *Peasant Studies Newsletter* 3.11–14.

McClelland, P. D., and R. J. Zeckhauser.
1982.   *Demographic Dimensions of the New Republic: American Interregional Migration, Vital Statistics, and Manumissions, 1800–1860*. Cambridge.

McCloskey, D. N.
1983.   "The Rhetoric of Economics." *Journal of Economic Literature* 21.481–517.

McCusker, J. J., and R. R. Menard.
1985.   *The Economy of British America, 1607–1789*. Chapel Hill, N.C.

McDaniel, C. K.
1983.   "Kin Based Demographic Measures." Ph.D. dissertation, University of California, Berkeley.

McEvedy, C., and R. Jones.
1978.   *Atlas of World Population History*. London.

McKinley, C., and R. W. Frase.
1970.   *Launching Social Security 1935–1937*. New York.

Medick, H.
1976.   "The Proto-Industrial Family Economy: The Structural Function of Household and Family during the Transition from Peasant Society to Industrial Capitalism." *Social History* 1.291–315.

Medick, H., and D. W. Sabean.
1984.   "Interest and Emotion in Family and Kinship Studies: A Critique of Social History and Anthropology." *In*: H. Medick and D. W. Sabean, eds., *Interest and Emotion: Essays in the Study of Family and Kinship*. Cambridge.

Menard, R.
1973.   "Immigration to the Chesapeake Colonies in the Seventeenth Century: A Review Essay." *Maryland Historical Magazine* 68.323–29.

Mendels, F. F.
1978.   "Notes on the Age of Maternity, Population Growth, and Family Structure in the Past." *Journal of Family History* 3.236–50.

Menken, J.
1981.   "Models for the Analysis of Fertility Change." *International Population Conference, Manila, 1981*. IUSSP 3.435–47.

Michael, R. T., V. R. Fuchs, and S. R. Scott.
1980.   "Changes in the Propensity to Live Alone: 1950–1976." *Demography* 17.39–56.

Mindel, C. H.
1979.   "Multigenerational Family Households: Recent Trends and Implications for the Future." *The Gerontologist* 19.456–63.

Mineau, G. P., and J. Trussell.
1982.   "A Specification of Marital Fertility by Parents' Age, Age at Marriage, and Marital Duration." *Demography* 19.335–50.

Mintz, S.
1983.   *A Prison of Expectations: The Family in Victorian Culture*. New York.

Mitchell, B. R., and P. Deane.
1962.   *Abstract of British Historical Statistics*. Cambridge.

Mitterauer, M., and A. Kagan.
1982   "Russian and Central European Family Structures—A Comparative View." *Journal of Family History* 7.103–31.

Mitterauer, M., and R. Sieder.
1982.   *The European Family: Patriarchy to Partnership from the Middle Ages to the Present*. Chicago.

Modell, J.
1978.   "Patterns of Consumption, Acculturation, and Family Income Strategies in Late Nineteenth Century America." *In*: T. K. Hareven and M. Vinovskis, eds.
1979.   "Changing Risks, Changing Adaptations." *In*: J. Challinor and A. J. Lichtman, eds., *Kin and Communities*. Washington, D.C.

Modell, J., and T. K. Hareven.
1973.   "Urbanization and the Malleable Household: An Examination of Boarding and Lodging in American Families." *Journal of Marriage and the Family* 35.467–79.

Moller, H.
1945.   "Sex Composition and Correlated Culture Patterns of Colonial America." *William and Mary Quarterly*, 3d series, 2.115–17.

Mogey, J. M.
1955.   "Contribution of Frederic Le Play to Family Research." *Marriage and Family Living* 17.310–24.

Morgan, E.
1944.   *The Puritan Family*. Boston.

Mount, F.
1982.   *The Subversive Family: An Alternative History of Love and Marriage*. London.

Neal, S.
1851.   *Special Report on the State of Juvenile Delinquency in the Borough of Salford*. Manchester.

Nerlove, M.
1974.   "Toward a New Theory of Population and Economic Growth." *In*: T. W. Schultz, ed.

Nerlove, M., and T. W. Schultz.
1970.   *Love and Life between the Censuses: A Model of Family Decision-Making in Puerto Rico, 1950–1960*. Santa Monica, Calif.

Nimkoff, M.
1962.   "Changing Family Relationships of Older People in the United States During the Last Fifty Years." *In*: C. Tibbitts and W. Donahue, eds., *Social and Psychological Aspects of Aging*. New York.

Nimkoff, M., and R. Middleton.
1960.   "Types of Family and Types of Economy." *American Journal of Sociology* 66.215–25.

Nisbet, R.
1967.   *The Sociological Tradition*. New York.

Norton, S. L.
1971.   "Population Growth in Colonial America: A Study of Ipswich, Massachusetts." *Population Studies* 25.433–52.

Nugent, W.
1981.   *Structures of American Social History*. Bloomington, Ind.

Nye, F. I.
1978.   "Is Choice and Exchange Theory the Key?" *Journal of Marriage and the Family* 40.219–33.
1979.   "Choice, Exchange, and the Family." *In*: W. R. Burr, R. Hill, F. I. Nye, and I. L. Reiss, eds., *Contemporary Theories about the Family*. Vol. 2. New York.

Nye, F. I., and F. M. Berando.
1966.   *Emerging Conceptual Frameworks in Family Analysis*. New York.

Ohlin, G.
1961.   "Mortality, Marriage, and Growth in Pre-Industrial Populations." *Population Studies* 14.190–97.

Ogburn, W. F., and M. K. Nimkoff.
1955.   *Technology and the Changing Family*. Boston.

Olinick, M.
1978.   *An Introduction to Mathematical Models in the Social and Life Sciences*. New York.

Orcutt, G.
1961.   *Microanalysis of Socioeconomic Systems: A Simulation Study*. New York.

Orcutt, G., et al.
1976.   *Policy Exploration through Microanalytic Simulation*. Washington, D.C.

Orcutt, G., and J. D. Smith
1979.   "Toward a Theory of Wealth Accumulation and Distribution: A Model of U.S. Wealth Accumulation." *Annales de L'Insee* 33–34.5–56.

Ormerod, F.
n.d.   *Lancashire Life and Character*. Manchester.

Orshansky, M.
1965.   "Counting the Poor: Another Look at the Poverty Profile." *Social Security Bulletin* 28 (January): 3–29.

Osmond, M. W.
1978.   "Reciprocity: A Dynamic Model and Method to Study Family Power." *Journal of Marriage and the Family* 40.49–61.

Osterud, N., and J. Fulton.
1976.   "Family Limitation and Age of Marriage: Fertility Decline in Sturbridge, Massachusetts, 1730–1850." *Population Studies* 30.481–94.

Outhwaite, R. B.
1973.   "Age at Marriage in England from the Late Seventeenth to the Nineteenth Centuries." *Transactions of the Royal Historical Society*, 5th series, vol. 23.

Outhwaite, R. B., ed.
1981.   *Marriage and Society. Studies in the Social History of Marriage*. New York.

Oxley, G. W.
1974.   *Poor Relief in England and Wales, 1601–1834*. London.

Paillot, P.
1979.   "Influences of Demographic Trends in Family Building and Elderly People's Role." *In*: G. Doogh and J. Helander, eds., *Family Life and Old Age*. The Hague.

Palmer, J. A.
1967.   "Some Antecedents of Progressivism: Buffalo in the 1890s." Ph.D. thesis, SUNY-Buffalo.

Palmore, E.
1975.   *The Honorable Elders: A Cross-Cultural Analysis of Aging in Japan.*
           Durham, N.C.

Palmore, E., and K. Manton.
1974.   "Modernization and the Status of the Aged: International Correla-
           tions." *Journal of Gerontology* 29.205–10.

Parke, R.
1969.   "Changes in Household and Family Structure in the U.S.A." *Inter-*
           national Population Conference, London, 1969. IUSSP, 2244–59.

Parliamentary Papers.
1833.   450 XX.
1834.   167 XX and XIX.
1840.   384 XI.
1860.   455 XXII.

Parsons, T.
1942.   "Age and Sex in the Social Structure of the United States." *American*
           Sociological Review 7.604–19.
1952.   *The Social System.* Glencoe, Ill.
1959.   "The Social Structure of the Family." *In*: R. Anshen, ed., *The*
           Family: Its Functions and Destiny. Chicago.

Parsons, T., and R. F. Bales.
1965.   *Family, Socialization, and the Interaction Process.* Glencoe, Ill.

Pasternak, B., C. R. Ember, and M. Ember.
1976.   "On the Conditions Favoring Extended Family Households." *Jour-*
           nal of Anthropological Research 32.109–23.

Perkin, H.
1969.   *The Origins of Modern English Society.* London.

Phelps-Brown, E. H., and S. V. Hopkins.
1956.   "Seven Centuries of Prices of Consumables Compared with Build-
           ers' Wage Rates." Economica, new series, 23.296–314.

Pinchbeck, I., and M. Hewitt.
1969.   *Children in English Society.* Toronto.

Piovesana, G.
1974.   "The Aged in Chinese and Japanese Cultures." *In*: W. Bier, ed.,
           Aging: Its Challenge to the Individual and to Society. New York.

Pitts, J. R.
1964.   "The Structural-Functional Approach." *In*: H. T. Christenson, ed.,
           Handbook of Marriage and the Family. Chicago.

Plakans, A.
1973.   "Peasant Families East and West: a Comment on Lutz K. Berkner's
           'Rural Family Organization in Europe: A Problem in Comparative
           History'." *Peasant Studies Newsletter* 2.11–16.

1975.   "Peasant Farmsteads and Households in the Baltic Littoral, 1797."
            Comparative Studies in History and Society 17.2–35.

Poole, M. F.
1905.   "Social Life of Buffalo in the 1830s and 1840s." *Publications of the
            Buffalo Historical Society* 8.439–94.

Poster, M.
1979.   *Critical Theory of the Family*. New York.

Potter, J.
1965.   "The Growth of Population in America, 1700–1860." in D. V. Glass
            and D. E. C. Eversley, eds., *Population in History: Essays in Histor-
            ical Demography*. London.

Press, I., and P. McKool.
1972.   "Social Structure and the Status of the Aged: Toward Some Valid
            Cross-Cultural Comparisons." *Aging and Human Development*
            3.297–306.

Pressat, R.
1972.   *Demographic Analysis: Methods, Results, Applications*. Trans.
            J. Matras. Chicago.

Preston, S. H.
1977.   "Mortality Trends." *Annual Review of Sociology* 3.163–78.

Preston, S. H., and M. Haines.
1984.   "New Estimates of Child Mortality at the Turn of the Century."
            Journal of the American Statistical Association 79.272–81.

Preston, S. H., N. Keyfitz, and R. Schoen.
1972.   *Causes of Death: Life Tables For National Populations*. New York.

Preston, S. H., and J. M. MacDonald.
1979.   "The Incidence of Divorce within Cohorts of American Marriages
            Contracted since the Civil War." *Demography* 16.1–26.

Pryor, E. T.
1972.   "Rhode Island Family Structure, 1875 and 1960." *In*: P. Laslett and
            R. Wall, eds.

Pullum, T. W.
1982.   "The Eventual Frequencies of Kin in a Stable Population." *De-
            mography* 19.549–65.

Pythian-Adams, C.
1979.   *Desolation of a City: Coventry and the Urban Crisis of the Late
            Middle Ages*. Cambridge.

Quadagno, J. S.
1981.   "The Modernization Controversy: A Socio-Historical Analysis of

Retirement in Nineteenth Century England." Paper delivered at the American Sociological Association Meeting, New York.

1982.   *Aging in Early Industrial Society: Work, Family and Social Policy in Nineteenth Century England*. New York.

Razzell, P. E., and R. W. Wainwright, eds.
1973.   *The Victorian Working Class: Selections from Letters to the Morning Chronicle 1849–1851*. London.

Reyna, S. P.
1976.   "The Extending Strategy: Regulation of Household Dependency Ratio." *Journal of Anthropological Research* 32.182–97.

Roach, J.
1978.   *Social Reform in England, 1780–1880*. London.

Roberts, R.
1971.   *The Classic Slum: Salford Life in the First Quarter of the Century*. Manchester.

Robins, J. B.
1896.   *The Family: A Necessity of Civilization*. Chicago.

Roe, F. G.
1959.   *The Victorian Child*. London.

Rose, M. E.
1971.   *The English Poor Law*. London.

Rosenzweig, M., and K. Wolpin.
1985.   "Specific Experience, Household Structure, and Intergenerational Transfers: Farm, Family, Land and Labor Arrangements in Developing Countries." *Quarterly Journal of Economics*, vol. 100, suppl., 961–88.

Rosser, C., and C. Harris.
1965.   *The Family and Social Change: A Study of Family and Kinship in a South Wales Town*. London.

Rossi, F.
1975.   "Un modello di simulazione per lo studio del ciclo di vita della famiglia." *Genus* 31.34–94.

Rowntree, B. S.
1902.   *Poverty: A Study of Town Life*. London.

Ruggles, N., and R. Ruggles.
1970.   *The Design of Economic Accounts*. New York.

Ruggles, S.
1984.   "Prolonged Connections: Demographic Change and the Rise of the Extended Family in Nineteenth Century England and America." Ph.D. dissertation, University of Pennsylvania.

Ruskin, J.
1865.   *Sesame and Lilies*. London.

Russell, J. C.
1948.   *British Medieval Population*. Albuquerque, N.M.

Ryan, M.
1976.   *Cradle of the Middle Class*. Cambridge.

Ryder, N. B.
1974.   *"Comment." In*: T. W. Schultz, ed.
1975.   "Reproductive Behavior and the Family Life Cycle." *In The Population Debate: Dimensions and Perspectives: Papers of the World Population Conference, Bucharest, 1974*. Vol. 2. New York.

Salford Weekly News.
1877.   (Letter to the editor, 31 March.) Salford, England.

Santow, G.
1978.   *A Simulation Approach to the Study of Human Fertility*. Leiden.

Sawhill, I. V.
1978.   "Economic Perspectives on the Family." *In*: A. S. Rossi, J. Kagan, and T. K. Hareven, eds., *The Family*. New York.

Schultz, C.
1962.   *Peanuts*. New York.

Schultz, T. W.
1981.   *Economics of Population*. Reading, Mass.

Schultz, T. W., ed.
1974.   *Economics of the Family: Marriage, Children, and Human Capital*. Chicago.

Senior, N. W.
1837.   *Letters on the Factory Act, as it affects the Cotton Manufacturer*. London.

Sennett, R.
1970.   *Families against the City: Middle Class Homes of Industrial Chicago, 1872–1890*. Cambridge, Mass.

Seward, R. R.
1978.   *The American Family: A Demographic History*. Beverly Hills, Calif.

Shanas, E., et al.
1968.   *Old People in Three Industrial Societies*. New York.

Sharlin, A. N.
1977.   "Historical Demography as History and Demography." *American Behavioral Scientist* 21.249–62.

Sheldon, H. D.
1958.   *The Older Population of the United States.* New York.

Shelton, B. K.
1976.   *Reformers in Search of Yesterday: Buffalo in the 1890s.* Albany, N.Y.

Sheps, M.
1969.   "Simulation Methods and the Use of Models in Fertility Analysis." *International Population Conference, London, 1969.* IUSSP, 1.53–64.

Shorter, E.
1976.   *The Making of the Modern Family.* New York.
1982.   *Women's Bodies.* New York.

Showalter, E.
1977.   *A Literature of Their Own: British Women Novelists from Brontë to Lessing.* New York.

Shryock, H. S., and J. S. Siegel.
1973.   *The Methods and Materials of Demography.* New York.

Sieder, R., and M. Mitterauer.
1983.   "The Reconstruction of the Family Life Course: Theoretical Problems and Empirical Results." *In*: R. Wall, ed.

Simmons, L.
1945.   *The Role of the Aged in Primitive Society.* New Haven, Conn.
1960.   "Aging in Preindustrial Societies." *In*: *Handbook of Social Gerontology*, ed. C. Tibbitts. Chicago.

Smelser, N.
1959.   *Social Change in the Industrial Revolution.* London.
1967.   "Sociological History: The Industrial Revolution and the British Working Class Family." *Journal of Social History* 1.18–35.
1968.   *Essays in Sociological Explanation.* Englewood Cliffs, N.J.

Smith, D. B.
1978.   "Mortality and Family in the Colonial Chesapeake." *Journal of Interdisciplinary History* 8.403–27.
1982.   "The Study of the Family in Early America: Trends, Problems, and Prospects." *William and Mary Quarterly*, 3d series, 39.3–28.

Smith, D. S.
1972.   "The Demographic History of Colonial New England." *Journal of Economic History* 32.166–74.
1973a.   "Population, Family, and Society in Hingham, Massachusetts." Ph.D. thesis, University of California.
1973b.   "Parental Power and Marriage Patterns: An Analysis of Historical

Trends in Hingham, Massachusetts." *Journal of Marriage and the Family* 35.419–28.

1978a.   "A Community Based Sample of the Older Population from the 1880 and 1980 United States Manuscript Census." *Historical Methods* 11.67–74.

1978b.   "A Homeostatic Demographic Regime: Patterns in West European Family Reconstitution Studies." *In*: R. D. Lee, ed.

1979a.   "Life Course, Norms, and the Family System of Older Americans in 1900." *Journal of Family History* 4.285–98.

1979b.   "Averages for Units and Averages for Individuals within Units: A Note." *Journal of Family History* 4.84–86.

1981.   "Historical Change in the Household Structure of the Elderly." *In*: V. T. Openheimer et al., eds., *Stability and Change in the Family*. New York.

1983.   "Differential Mortality in the United States Before 1900." *Journal of Interdisciplinary History* 8.735–59.

1984.   "Modernization and the Family Structure of the Elderly in the United States." *Zeitschrift fur Gerontologie* 17.

Smith, F. N.
1979.   *The People's Health, 1830–1900*. New York.

Smith, R.
1961.   "Japan, the Later Years of Life, and the Concept of Time." *In*: R. Kleemier, ed., *Aging and Leisure: A Research Perspective into the Meaningful Use of Time*. New York.

Smith, R. M.
1979.   "Kin and Neighbors in a 13th Century Suffolk Community." *Journal of Family History* 4.219–56.

1981.   "Fertility, Economy, and Household Formation in England Over Three Centuries." *Population and Development Review* 7.595–622.

Smith, Roger.
1970.   "Early Victorian Household Structure." *International Review of Social History* 15.69–84.

Smith-Rosenberg, C.
1971.   "Beauty, the Beast, and the Militant Woman: A Case Study in Sex Roles and Social Stress in Jacksonian America." *American Quarterly* 23.562–84.

1972.   "The Hysterical Woman: Sex Roles and Role Conflict in 19th Century America." *Social Research* 39.652–78.

1975.   "The Female World of Love and Ritual: Relations between Women in Nineteenth-Century America." *Signs: Journal of Women in Culture and Society* 1.1–29.

1978.   "Sex as Symbol in Victorian Purity." *In*: J. Demos and S. S. Boocock, eds.

1985.   *Disorderly Conduct: Visions of Gender in Victorian America.* New
             York.

Smuts, R. W.
1959.   *Women and Work in America.* New York.

Spencer, A. G.
1923.   *The Family and Its Members.* Philadelphia.

Stern, M. J.
1979.   "The Demography of Capitalism: Industry, Class, and Fertility in
             Erie County New York, 1855–1915." Ph.D. thesis, York University.

Stevenson, A.
1965.   *The Wit and Wisdom of Adlai Stevenson.* Compiled by E. Hanna
             et al. New York.

Stone, L.
1977a.   *The Family, Sex, and Marriage in England 1500–1800.* New York.
1977b.   "Walking Over Grandma." *New York Review of Books* 24 (12 May):
             10–16.

Sundin, J., et al., eds.
1979.   *Time, Space, and Man.* Uppsala.

Sussman, M. B.
1959.   "The Isolated Nuclear Family: Fact or Fiction?" *Social Problems*
             6.333–40.

Sweet, J. A.
1972.   "The Living Arrangements of Separated, Widowed, and Divorced
             Mothers." *Demography* 9.143–57.
1977.   "Demography and the Family." *Annual Review of Sociology* 3.363–
             405.

Taueber, I. B.
1958.   *The Population of Japan.* Princeton, N.J.
1971.   "Change and Transition in Family Structures." *In*: A. A. Campbell,
             et al., eds., *The Family in Transition.* Washington, D.C.

Taylor, A. J., ed.
1975.   *The Standard of Living in the Industrial Revolution.* London.

Taylor, W. C.
1842.   *Notes of a Tour in the Manufacturing Districts of Lancashire.*
             London.

*Tenth Annual Report on the Health of Salford with Statistical Abstracts for the
Decennium.*
1880.   Manchester.

Thibault, J. W., and H. H. Kelly.
1959.   *The Social Psychology of Groups*. New York.

Thirsk, J., ed.
1967.   *The Agrarian History of England and Wales, 1500–1640*. Cambridge.

Thomas, K.
1976.   "Age and Authority in Early Modern England." *Proceedings of the British Academy* 62.205–48.

Thomlinson, R.
1975.   *Demographic Problems: Controversy Over Population Control*. Belmont, Calif.

Thompson, E. P.
1977.   "Happy Families." *New Society* (8 September): 499–501.

Thompson, W. S., and P. K. Whelpton.
1933.   *Population Trends in the United States*. New York.

Tillott, P. M.
1972.   "Sources of Inaccuracy in the 1851 and 1861 Censuses." *In*: E. A. Wrigley, ed.

Tilly, L. A.
1979a.   "The Family Wage Economy of a French Textile City: Roubaix, 1872–1906." *Journal of Family History* 4.381–94.
1979b.   "Individual Lives and Family Strategies in the French Proletariat." *Journal of Family History* 4.137–52.

Tilly, L. A., and J. Scott.
1978.   *Women, Work, and Family*. New York.

Tönnies, F.
1957.   *Community and Society*. New York.

Tranter, N. L.
1967.   "Population and Social Structure in a Bedfordshire Parish: The Cardington List of Inhabitants, 1782." *Population Studies* 21.261–82.
1973.   "The Social Structure of a Bedfordshire Parish in the Mid-Nineteenth Century," *International Review of Social History* 18.90–106.
1973.   *Population since the Industrial Revolution*. New York.

Trudeau, G. B.
1973.   *I Have No Son*. New York.

Trumbach, R.
1978.   *The Rise of the Egalitarian Family*. New York.

Uhlenberg, P.
1969.   "A Study of Cohort Life Cycles: Cohorts of Native Born Mas-

sachusetts Women, 1830–1920." *Population Studies* 23.407–20.
1978.   "Changing Configurations of the Life Course." *In*: T. K. Hareven, ed.

U.S. Bureau of the Census.
1905.   *Special Reports. Mortality Statistics, 1900–1904*. Washington, D.C.
1921.   *United States Life Tables, 1890, 1901, 1910, and 1901–10*, by James W. Glover. Washington, D.C.
1949.   *Historical Statistics of the United States: 1789–1945*. Washington, D.C.
1963.   *Census of Population: 1960*. Subject Reports. Final Report. PC (2)-4A. Family Composition. Washington, D.C.
1973.   *Census of Population: 1970*. Subject Reports. Final Report, PC (2)-4A. Family Composition. Washington, D.C.
1975.   *Historical Statistics of the United States: Colonial Times to 1970*. Washington, D.C.
1985.   *Current Population Reports*. Series P-20, No. 398.

U.S. Public Health Service.
1967.   *Vital Statistics of the United States*. Washington, D.C.

Van de Walle, E.
1976.   "The Current State of Historical Demography." *Review of Public Data Use* 4.8–11.

Vinovskis, M. A.
1971.   "The 1789 Life Table of Edward Wigglesworth." *Journal of Economic History* 31.570–90.
1972.   "Mortality Rates and Trends in Massachusetts before 1860." *Journal of Economic History* 32.184–213.
1978.   "From Household Size to the Life Course: Some Observations on Recent Trends in Family History." *American Behavioral Scientist* 21.263–87.
1981.   *Fertility in Massachusetts from the Revolution to the Civil War*. New York.

Von Neumen, J.
1961.   *The Computer and the Brain*. New Haven, Conn.

Wachter, K. W.
1980.   "The Sister's Riddle and the Importance of Variance When Guessing Demographic Rates from Kin Counts." *Demography* 17.103–14.

Wachter, K. W., E. A. Hammel, and P. Laslett.
1978.   *Statistical Studies of Historical Social Structure*. New York.

Wall, R.
1972.   "Mean Household Size in England from Printed Sources." *In*: P. Laslett and R. Wall, eds.

1982.   "Regional and Temporal Variations in the Structure of the British Household since 1851." *In*: T. Barker and M. Drake, eds., *Population and Society in Britain 1850–1980*. New York.
1983a.   "Introduction." *In*: R. Wall, ed.
1983b.   "The Household: Demographic and Economic Change in England, 1650–1970." *In*: R. Wall, ed.

Wall, R., ed.
1983c.   *Family Forms in Historic Europe*. Cambridge.

Walling, W. H.
1904.   *Sexology*. Philadelphia.

Walsh, L., and R. Menard.
1974.   "Death in the Chesapeake: Two Life Tables for Men in Early Colonial Maryland." *Maryland Historical Magazine* 69.211–27.

Watkins, S. C.
1980.   "On Measuring Transitions and Turning Points." *Historical Methods* 13.181–87.
1984.   "Spinsters." *Journal of Family History* 9.310–25.

Watkins, S. C., and J. Menken.
1984.   "Continuities and Change in the American Family." Paper presented at the Annual Meeting of the American Psychiatric Association.

Wells, R. V.
1971.   "Demographic Change and the Life Cycle of American Families." *Journal of Interdisciplinary History* 2.273–82.
1975.   *The Population of the British Colonies of America before 1776: A Survey of Census Data*. Princeton, N.J.
1978.   "Family History and the Demographic Transition." *In*: M. Gordon, ed., *The American Family in Social-Historical Perspective*. 2d ed. New York.

Wheaton, R.
1975.   "Family and Kinship in Western Europe: The Problem of the Joint Family Household." *Journal of Interdisciplinary History* 5.601–28.

Whittle, P. A.
1885.   *Bolton-le-moors, and the Townships in the Parish, an Historical, Statistical, Civil, and Moral Account*. Bolton, England.

Winch, R. F., and R. L. Blumberg.
1968.   "Societal Complexity and Family Organization." *In*: R. F. Winch and L. W. Goodman, eds., *Selected Studies in Marriage and the Family*. New York.

Wohl, A. S., ed.
1978.   *The Victorian Family*. London.

Wolfenden, H. H.
1962.   "On the Theoretical and Practical Considerations Underlying the
         Direct and Indirect Standardization of Death Rates." *Population
         Studies* 16.188–90.

Wright, C. D.
1900.   *The History and Growth of the United States Census*. Washington,
         D.C.

Wrightson, K.
1981.   "Household and Kinship in Sixteenth Century England." *History
         Workshop Journal* 12.151–58.
1982.   *English Society 1580–1680*. London.

Wrightson, K., and D. Levine.
1979.   *Poverty and Piety in an English Village: Terling 1525–1700*. New
         York.

Wrigley, E. A.
1968.   "Family Limitation in Pre-Industrial England: The Example of Coly-
         ton, Devon, Over Three Centuries." *Daedalus* 97.546–80.
1969.   *Population in History*. London.
1978.   "Fertility Strategy for the Individual and the Group." *In*: C. Tilly,
         ed., *Historical Studies of Changing Fertility*. Princeton, N.J.

Wrigley, E. A., ed.
1972.   *Nineteenth Century Society. Essays in the Use of Quantitative
         Methods for the Study of Social Data*. Cambridge.
1973.   *Identifying People in the Past*. London.

Wrigley, E. A., and R. S. Schofield.
1981.   *The Population History of England, 1541–1871: A Reconstruction*.
         Cambridge, Mass.

Wrong, P. H.
1958.   "Class Fertility Differentials before 1850." *Social Research* 25.70–
         86.

Yans-McLaughlin, V.
1977.   *Family and Community: Italian Immigrants in Buffalo, 1880–1930*.
         Ithaca, N.Y.

Yasuba, Y.
1961.   *Birth Rates of the White Population of the United States, 1800–1860:
         An Economic Study*. Baltimore.

Young, G. M.
1964.   *Victorian England: Portrait of an Age*. New York.

Young, M., and P. Wilmott.
1957.   *Family and Kinship in East London*. London.
1973.   *The Symmetrical Family*. New York.

Zaretsky, E.
1976.   *Capitalism, the Family, and Personal Life*. New York.

Zitomersky, J.
1985.   "Family Residence and Support for the Elderly in Pre-Industrial Swedish Agrarian Society: Shared Evidence and Varying Interpretations." Paper presented at the Annual Meetings of the Social Science History Association. Chicago.

Index

Adventures, racy, 106
Age: and dependence, 45–47; of heads, 64, 195, 217; intervals between spouses, 70, 110n, 161, 162–63, 168, 171, 172–73, 196–98, 214, 216n; structure, 50n, 67, 69, 147–48, 181–82, 187, 199, 213n, 223–35. *See also* Old Age
Agresti, B., 26
Agricultural Census, 36, 152
Agricultural inheritance, 27n, 56–57, 62, 91, 122n, 127, 128, 218
Altruism, 19, 20, 28
Ambush, 72n
Analytic models, 65–71
Anderson, M., 6n, 10n, 20–23, 26n, 30, 45n, 47–57 *passim*, 75n, 76n, 132n, 216n, 223
Ashworth family, 152
Atwood, M., 129n
Austin, J., 208

Babysitting, 47
Banks, J. A., 209, 214
Barnes, H. E., 28n
Barry, J. M., 21n
Becker, G., 13, 16n, 17–18
Beeton, I., 35n
Ben-Porath, Y., 19n
Benson, L., 28n
Berkner, L. K., 3n, 62–65, 68, 74, 75, 114n, 119, 122, 147, 214n

Birthplace, and extended family structure, 54, 220, 223–35
Blake, J., 16n
Boarders, 12, 31, 53n, 120n, 140, 214n
Bongaarts, J., 74, 75n
Bourgeoisie, defined, 32, 35
Boxes, statistical, 129n
Bradley, B., 68n
Brumbaugh, G. M., 4n
Buffalo, N.Y. *See* Erie County, N.Y.
Burch, T. K., 66n
Business class, 32n
Butler, S., 3, 130

Cambridge Group for the History of Population and Social Structure, 3n, 62, 80, 95n, 111n, 121n
Camsim, 72n
Capitalist mentality, 27
Catch-22, 83n
Causal analysis, 135n
Census data: Erie County, N.Y., 1855–1915, 30, 151; Lancashire, England, 1871, 30, 151; United States, 1900, 93, 110, 151, 154–55, 160
Children: in analytic models, 67; and economic dependence, 45–46; and elderly, 56, 148, 194; and headship patterns, 216–18; influence in residence decisions, 22; and inheritance, 56, 62; in Macrosimulation, 74; in momsim, 88,

Children *(Continued)*
103, 104, 123*n*, 157, 158, 161, 163–82 *passim*, 196; mortality of, 153*n*, 200; in New Home Economics, 16, 19; relationship with parents, 9–10, 28, 57*n*, 130–33; in SOCSIM, 77–78, 123*n*; status of, 25; and stem family hypothesis, 62, 63, 64, 82, 91, 97–98*n*, 205–6; in textile industry, 35*n*; and working mothers, 21–22, 47–49, 56, 153*n*. *See also* Fertility
Choosiness index, 79
Christie, A., 139, 150
Chudacoff, H. P., 4*n*
Clayworth, Nottinghamshire, 3
Cleaver, E., 184*n*
Coale, A., 66, 68*n*, 70*n*, 76*n*, 107*n*
Colonial America: demographic conditions, 108*n*, 109*n*; extended families, 3–4; peculiarities of, 109; regional demographic variations in, 108*n*
Contradiction, 127
Critical life situations, 21, 47, 56, 128
Crowding, 50–54

Darling, Mr., 21*n*
De Quincey, T., 156
Decay, moral, 3
Demographic models. *See* Analytic models; Macrosimulation; Microsimulation
Demographic Transition, effects on family structure, 11, 106, 207
Demography: class differences, 126, 208–19; colonial America, 108*n*, 109*n*; effects on family structure, 60–64, 110–25, 191–207, 209–19; English conditions, eighteenth–nineteenth centuries, 106, 107*n*–9*n*; narrowly defined, 85, 159*n*; quicksand of, 59; theory on extended families, 60–65; U.S. conditions, nineteenth century, 107*n*–8*n*. *See also* Fertility; Marriage; Mortality
Dependence, 21, 25, 42–47, 49, 50, 57–58, 132*n*, 141, 148, 206, 216
Developing countries, family structure in, 15*n*, 61, 115–18, 124
DEV population, defined, 115, 117
Dickinson, E., 139
Dodd, W., 152

Doucet, M., 43*n*, 214*n*
Douglas, M., 16*n*
Doyle, A. Conan, 84
Dunn, R. S., 60
Dwelling value, 36–40, 52
DYNASIM, 158*n*

Eastern Europe, 125
Economic analysis of the family: assumptions of, 18, 19*n*, 20, 22, 24–25; and demographic factors, 208–19 *passim*; exchange theory, 20–22, 26, 47–58; and historical interpretations, 25–27; and levels of analysis, 22–23; limitations of, 24–25, 27–29, 58–59; new home economics, 16–20; and nonmaterial factors, 23–24, 27; role of poverty, 21, 26–27, 40–42; sociological interpretations, 13–16, 20–22
Economic dependency ratio, 42–47
Economics, thicket of, 59
Eggs, fried, 156
Elderly. *See* Old age
Engels, F., 13, 153*n*
Entrepreneurial class, 32*n*
Erie County, N.Y., 8*n*, 30–54 *passim*, 151–55, 208
Exchange theory, 20–22, 26, 47–58
Extended family: and age, 187, 213*n*, 223–35; bimodal distribution of, 33*n*, 41–42; and birthplace, 223–35; colonial America, 3–4, 4*n*; defined, 3*n*; and economic dependence, 42–47; and economic status, 31–42; effects of demographic change on, 60–64, 110–25, 191–207, 209–19; evidence on increase of, 4–9; and occupational status, 31–37, 208–18, 223–35; twentieth-century, 6, 8*n*, 33, 40, 44–45, 47, 61, 115, 124, 128, 207; urban-rural differences, 36, 53, 224–33. *See also* Horizontally extended family; Stem family; Vertically extended family

Family: cultural interpretations, 9, 61, 112, 129–34; defined, 139–40; developmental cycle, 62; headship, 12, 32*n*, 45, 93*n*, 99*n*–100*n*, 113*n*–14*n*, 140–42, 187, 196, 199, 216–18; interactions among members, 19; measurement of, 11, 31n, 81n; power relations in, 18, 19, 20, 22–23, 25, 58, 147n, 219; as psychological unit, 10, 24; sociological theories of, 13–16, 60–62; strategies, 17, 23, 25–26, 47, 58; structure, defined, 11; Victorian idealization of, 9. *See also* Extended family; Horizontally extended family; Nuclear family; Stem family; Vertically extended family

Farm families, 17n, 36, 38, 56–57, 127, 218. *See also* Agricultural inheritance; Rural family structure

Female labor force participation, 49. *See also* Women and work; Working mothers

Fertility: childspacing, 166, 195; class differences in, 211; data on, 154; DEV population, 115, 117; and economic status, 211, 213; effects on extended family structure, 63, 64, 82, 110–25 *passim*, 201–2, 206; MOD population, 114–15; in MOMSIM, 104, 163–69, 171, 173, 174–77; nineteenth century, 107n, 166; PRE and STD populations, 110–11; preindustrial, 109n; REF population, 191; in SOCSIM, 80n, 82, 104, 164; and stem family hypothesis, 63, 64; U.S. and England compared, 106, 107n–9n. *See also* Demographic transition

Fisher, H. A. L., 134n

Fitch N., 75n, 78n

Flandrin, J. L., 8

Foster, J., 27

Fox, Captain, 71, 72

Free will, 133

Fulton, J., 107n

Functional analysis, functionalism, 11, 13–16, 24–25, 26, 49, 57, 64, 133–35, 219

Furniture, inheritance of, 56

Furstenburg, F., 4n

Gender, 50n, 169–70, 187, 214, 223–35

Generation length, 63, 64, 72n, 110n, 194, 207, 213

Generational relations, 14, 21, 24, 56, 57n, 62, 217

Glasco, L., 150, 151n

Glass, D., 61n, 66–67, 68, 76n

Glover, J. W., 110n

Goodman, L. A., 70n

Goubert, P., 3n

Grahame, K., 106

Grandchildren: in analytic models, 66; in census listings, 113n–14n, 140; effects of demographic factors on, 178, 192, 196, 199–200, 205; and hypothetical rules, 104, 119; in MOMSIM, 87, 88, 93, 101, 104, 113, 119, 178; and residential propensities, 87, 88, 93, 101, 113; role in family, 131; and Whopper Assumption, 90. *See also* Vertically extended family

Grandparents: in analytic models, 66–68; in MOMSIM, 88, 178; and mortality, 60, 72n; and residential propensities, 87, 93. *See also* Old age; Parents; Vertically extended family

Greed, 27–28

Griffin, W. T., 130, 131

Guilt, 20, 132n, 133

Hammel, E. A., 65, 74–83, 111, 119n, 123n, 158n, 164, 205

Hareven, T., 25–26

Harris, C. C., 14n

Harris, Z., 135n

Harrison, J., 3

Hawn, G., 158n

Holmes, S., 84

Home ownership, 56

Home, idealization of, 29, 129–33

Horizontally extended family: and analytic models, 69–70; defined, 69, 113, 192, 212; effects of demography on, 69–70, 110–19 *passim*, 191–207 *passim*, 211–19 *passim*; in preindustrial England, 113; and residential propensities, 114. *See also* Siblings

Horrors, burthen of, 156

Hot deck imputation, 33n, 43n, 167

Houghton, W., 29n, 131–32, 133

Household: classifications, 139n–40n, 141; definitions, 6n, gods, 29, 133; headship, 12, 31, 32n, 64, 93n, 99n, 113n–14n, 140–42, 187n, 216–18; size, 120n–21n; utility functions, 19; vs. family, 139–40

Household hypotheses. *See* Hypothetical residence rules
Housing shortage, and extended family, 8*n*, 21, 50–54
Huddling, 27, 49, 128
Hypothetical residence rules: in analytic models, 68–69, 70; compared with residential propensities, 86, 100–1, 206; in MOMSIM, 88, 102–5, 119–25, 123*n*, 159, 203–6; problems of complexity, 79, 103; in SOCSIM, 76–83, 123*n*; and Whopper Assumption, 92

Ideal family type, 60–62
Immigration. *See* Migration
Imputation of missing data, 33*n*, 43*n*, 167
Individual-level measurement. *See* Levels of measurement
Industrialization: and age at marriage, 209–10; in Erie County, N.Y., and Lancashire, England, 151–53; theoretical effects on family structure, 3, 14–16, 21, 26–27, 31, 49, 55, 56, 61, 128, 134
Inheritance. *See* Agricultural inheritance

Jacquard, A., 80
Jail, 86*n*
Jealousy, 28
Jones, R., 185
Joplin, J., 132*n*

Katz, M., 20*n*, 32*n*, 43*n*, 45*n*, 68, 150, 151*n*, 214*n*
Kelly, W., 106
Keyfitz, N., 70*n*
Kin: demographic availability of, 84–89, 98*n*, 117*n*, 195–207 *passim*; groups, 85, 87, 89–90, 178–80, 184; outside household, 6*n*, 39, 87; types, in MOMSIM, 88. *See also* Extended family; Family; Grandchildren; Grandparents; Parents; Siblings
Kipling of the Economic Empire, 17*n*
Knight, F. H., 13
Kousser, J. M., 28*n*

Laborers, 32, 35
Lafferty, R. A., 156

Lancashire, England, 20–21, 30, 35–59 *passim*, 151–55, 208–19 *passim*
Laslett, B., 109*n*, 139*n*
Laslett, P., 3, 6*n*, 61, 62*n*, 66, 74–75, 81, 111, 113*n*, 119, 121*n*, 122, 123, 139*n*
Laterally extended family. *See* Horizontally extended family
LeBras, H., 72*n*
Le Play, F., 13, 14*n*, 62*n*
Leridon, H., 80
Levels of measurement and analysis: and historians' interpretations, 25–26; and hypothetical rules, 102–3, 205–6; and measurement of family structure, 11, 31*n*, 81*n*, 142–49, 203*n*; and residential propensities, 84–89; and social theory, 16*n*, 22–23, 26
Levine, D., 27*n*, 91*n*
Levy, M., 60–61, 63, 65, 66*n*, 116*n*, 124, 125
Liebenstein, H., 17*n*
Life course: and economic dependence, 45–47; in economic theory, 16–17; and extended family structure, 27, 125, 213*n*; and levels of measurement, 142*n*; in MOMSIM, 158, 169–71. *See also* Age; Children; Old age
Life expectancy. *See* Mortality
Literacy, 14, 57, 130*n*, 152, 153
Lodgers. *See* Boarders
Lotka, A. J., 65
Love, 17, 19*n*, 28, 131

McEvedy, C., 185
Macrosimulation, 73–74, 181–82
Madness, 12
Maimonides-conditioned third-aspect numbers, 156
Maltravers, M., 129*n*
Mammon, mighty, 30
Marcuse, H., 132*n*
Marriage: age at, 63, 69, 91*n*, 107*n*, 109*n*, 125; changes in, 63, 107*n*, 109*n*, 209*n*–10*n*; class differences in, 208–19; crunch, 208; DEV population, 115, 117; in Eastern and Southern Europe, 125*n*; economic models of, 17–18; effects on extended family structure, 63–64, 82, 93, 110–25 *passim*, 187, 190–98, 204,

205, 208–19, 223–35; MOD population, 114–15; in MOMSIM, 103–4, 161–63, 171, 172; and parental longevity, 91n; PRE and STD populations, 110–11; preindustrial European pattern of, 63n, 91n, 110–11; proportion never marrying, 111, 196, 204, 214–16, 219; REF population, 191; and SOCSIM hypothetical rules, 77–79, 82; and stem-family hypothesis, 63, 91, 97, 124–25, 204–5, 206–7; U.S. and England compared, 106, 107n–9n

Mate selection. *See* Marriage

Medick, H., 27, 132n

Mendels, F., 68n

Methodology, Byzantine, 105

Microsimulation: closed vs. open models, 78, 159; defined, 71, 72–73; problems of complexity in, 79, 158–59; random error in, 73, 95, 158, 192; techniques for minimizing error, 92, 101; Whopper Assumption of, 89–92. *See also* MOMSIM; SOCSIM

Migration, 21, 51n, 54–55, 78, 85n, 148, 151, 152, 159n, 215n, 220

Milne, A. A., 127

Modell, J., 25

Modernization, 3, 13–16, 57, 60, 61, 134

MOD population, defined, 114–15

MOMSIM: accuracy of, 174–77; adjustment technique, 182–84, 190–91; adultery in, 180n; allocation of deaths, 169, 171, 172, 183; assumptions of, 100n, 172–74; compared with SOCSIM, 102–4, 123n; description of model, 156–84; duration of childbearing period, 165; fertility allocation, 163–69, 171; flowchart, 169–70; general characteristics, 157–60; illegitimacy in, 167; input data and allocation procedures, 160–69; main table of, 180; marriage allocation, 161–63, 171; Maximum age at childbirth, 165; organization, 175, 178–81; piggyback projection model, 181–82; remarriage in, 168–69, 173; results, 94–95, 110–25, 186–207, 210–11; role of female ancestors in, 178; size of runs, 180; stable fertility option, 111n, 167, 191; strategy for assigning characteristics, 169; use of

hypothetical rules, 88, 102–5, 114n, 119–25; use of model life tables, 111n, 183, 198; widowhood in, 168, 174. *See also* Standard propensities

Monte-Carlo simulation. *See* Microsimulation

Morbidity. *See* Sickness

Mortality: class differences in, 211; DEV population, 115, 116n, 117; effects on extended family structure, 60–64, 110–25 *passim*, 198–201, 204–5; in Lancashire, 153; and marriage age, 91n; MOD population, 114–15; in MOMSIM, 169, 171, 172, 183; PRE and STD populations, 110–11; REF population, 191; regional model life tables, 111n; in social theory, 60–61; and stem-family hypothesis, 63, 64; U.S. and England compared, 106, 107n–9n; and widowhood, 82. *See also* Demographic transition

Mothers. *See* Parents; Working mothers

Multifamily dwellings, 6n, 52

Multigeneration families. *See* Vertically extended family

Multiple Classification Analysis. *See* Multivariate Analysis

Multivariate analysis, 148, 220–35

Mumps, 13n

Neighborhood residence patterns, 39

New England, demographic conditions in, 108n, 109n

New home economics, 16–20, 22; problems of optimal sorting, 18–19n

Newlyweds, 21, 218

Nuclear family: as basis for extended family, 9, 131; classification problems of, 141; defined, 3n; and headship, 141; in sociological theory, 3, 13–14; and stem-family hypothesis, 63, 206

Nuptiality. *See* Marriage

Occupational listings, 32–37, 42, 43n, 49n, 50

Occupational status, and extended family structure, 31–37, 208–18, 223–35

Old age: and economic dependence, 47; and exchange theory, 21, 56–57; and marriage, 162n; and residence in ex-

Old Age *(Continued)*
tended family, 56, 93, 98*n*, 202, 216–
17, 218, 221; role in modernization
theory, 13, 14*n*–15*n*; in sociological
theory of the family, 14–16, 25, 57, 62.
See also Grandparents
Orwell, G., 127
Osterud, N., 107*n*
Overcrowding, 50–54
Owl, Howland, 106

Parents: in analytic models, 66–68; in
census listings, 113*n*–14*n*, 140; demographic effects on, 72*n*, 91*n*, 192, 194,
196, 199–202, 204, 205, 206, 213; and
economic status, 213, 219; in economic
theory, 19; and fertility, 158*n*; and
headship, 216–18; and household classifications, 140, 141; and housing shortage, 21; in momsim, 88, 98*n*, 178; in old
age, 57; relationships with children, 6,
28, 130, 131, 132, 133; and residential
propensities, 96, 107*n*–8*n*, 114*n*, 187;
and stem family, 62–63, 64, 77–78, 82,
103–4, 119, 123*n*, 203; and Whopper
Assumption, 90; widowed, 67, 96,
114*n*. *See also* Children; Working
mothers
Parsons, T., 14*n*
Peter Pan, 21*n*
Photosynthesis, 71
Piggyback projection model, 104, 181–82
Pitts, J. R., 14*n*
Poe, E. A., 150
Pogo, 106
Polygyny, 17*n*
Pooh, Winnie the, 127
Poor law, 57*n*
Popsim, 76
Poverty, and extended family structure,
21, 26–27, 30–32, 40–42, 43*n*, 45, 128,
153. *See also* Standard of living
Pre population, defined, 110
Preston, S., 160*n*
Primonuptial rules, 78
Primoreal rules, 78, 122, 123*n*
Propensity. *See* Residential propensities
Propinquity. *See* Neighborhood residence
patterns

Psychic profit, 20, 25
Puddletown, Dorset, 7, 8*n*
Pullum, T. W., 70*n*
Puppeteers, 129

Race, 85*n*, 159*n*, 227
Random error, in microsimulation, 73,
95, 158, 192
Reference persons, 12, 31, 32*n*, 93*n*, 99*n*,
141
Ref population, defined, 191
Refrigerator, 18
Rent, 50–52
Residential preferences, defined, 85–86
Residential propensities, 86–88, 92–102,
121. *See also* Standard propensities
Results, shocking, 122
Riehl, W., 14*n*
Robins, J. B., 84
Rosenzweig, M., 17*n*
Ruggles, N. and R. Ruggles, 22, 72
Rural family structure, 26, 27, 36, 53,
218, 223–33
Ruskin, J., 29, 129*n*, 133*n*
Ryder, N., 19

Sabean, D. W., 132*n*
Sailing, easy, 105
Salford, England, 152–53, 209*n*
Sanitation, 55, 152, 153
Santow, G., 72
Sasgraph, 6*n*, 39*n*
Satisfaction, 16–17, 18, 19*n*, 25; defined,
20. *See also* Utility
Sawhill, I., 17*n*
Schofield, R. S., 110
Scientific history, 28*n*, 88
Servants, 31, 33, 35*n*, 36*n*, 120*n*–21*n*,
122*n*, 140, 214*n*, 223
Seward, R. R., 8*n*
Sex ratios, 17*n*, 109, 215, 216*n*
Shorter, E., 13, 132*n*
Siblings: in analytic models, 66, 69; de-
mographic effects on, 192, 195, 206;
and economic status, 213, 219; and
horizontal extension, 69; and household
classifications, 141; and hypothetical
rules, 103*n*; in momsim, 88, 178–80; relationships among, 9, 28, 130, 131, 133;

and residential propensities, 93, 114n, 187; and stem family hypothesis, 63, 103; and Whopper Assumption, 92. *See also* Horizontally extended family

Sickness, 21, 54–56, 132

Simulation models, defined, 71–74. *See also* Macrosimulation; Microsimulation

Skilled workers, defined, 32, 35n, 36n

Smelser, N., 14n

Smiles, S., 132

Smith, D. S., 86, 87, 98n, 107n, 175n

Smith-Rosenberg, C., 132n

Social Darwinism, and economic theories of the family, 25

Social norms, 16n, 57n, 83n, 85, 129

Social welfare, effects on family, 57n

Socsim, 72n, 74–83, 92, 99n, 102–4, 111, 122, 123, 164, 205

Southern Europe, 125

Spinsterhood, 69, 93 131, 213, 214, 216n, 219. *See also* Unattached individuals

Standard of living, 51, 58. *See also* Poverty

Standard propensities: adjustment for kin combinations, 100n; compared with hypothetical residence rules, 100–1, 206; defined, 96; and economic status, 209–11; of headship, 99n–100n; limitations of, 97, 98n, 99n, 101–2, 112–13, 117n, 186, 202–3; results, 110–19, 186–203. *See also* Residential propensities

Standardization: of age, 50, 148; comparison with standard propensities, 97, 101; of dwelling values, 39

Status anxiety, 27

STD population, defined, 110

Stem family: in analytic models, 66–67; findings of momsim, 114n, 119–25, 203–6; in momsim, 102–4; and 19th century working class, 218; preindustrial preference for, 121–22, 127–28; and residential propensities, 87n, 97n, 203–6; in socsim, 75–78, 80–81, 82, 102–3, 122–23; theory of, 62–64; and Whopper Assumption, 91–92. *See also* Vertically extended family

Sterling, J., 30

Stern, M., 43n, 150, 151n, 214n

Stevenson, A., 182n

Stone, L., 68

Structural-functionalist, 13–16, 57, 61

Technology, theoretical effects on family of, 14, 57

Textile workers, 35n–36n, 49, 152–53

Thinking, clear, 13

Third World, family structure in. *See* Developing countries, family structure in

Thompson, E. P., 132n

Thoughts, Grand, 127

Three generation family. *See* Vertically extended family

Tilly, L., 25–26

Toad, 106

Turton-near-Bolton, England, 152–53, 209n

Ultimonuptial rules, 78

Unattached individuals: defined, 69; effects on family structure, 187, 192, 195, 207, 216. *See also* Spinsters; Widowhood

Unemployment, 21, 48, 49–50, 227

Unskilled workers, defined, 32, 35n, 36n

Urban family structure, 26, 31, 36, 53, 55, 223–33

Utility, 23, 25, 27, utility functions, 19

Vertically extended family: and analytic models, 69–70; defined, 69, 113, 192, 212; effects of demography on, 110–25 *passim*, 191–207 *passim*, 211–19 *passim*; in preindustrial England, 113; and residential propensities, 114, 124n; R. R. Seward on 8n; and Whopper Assumption, 91–92. *See also* Extended family; Grandchildren; Grandparents; Parents; Stem family

View, Received, 28

Wachter, K. W., 65, 74–83, 111, 119n, 123n, 158n, 164, 205

Wall, R., 6n, 8, 62n, 113n, 120n, 122n

Walling, W. H., 162n

Ward density, 52

Weighting, of census samples, 221

Wells, R., 4, 107n

Wheaton, R., 68n

Whopper Assumption, 89–92, 104, 105, 122, 158n, 172, 175n, 184
Widowhood: in analytic models, 67, 69; and economic dependence, 21; and economic status, 216, 218; and extended family, 114n, 192, 194, 196, 199, 204, 207, 218; and hypothetical rules, 82; in MOMSIM, 161, 165, 168, 171, 173, 174, 178; and residential propensities, 93, 96, 187; unattached individuals, 69
Willis, R. J., 19
Wodehouse, P. G., 185
Wolpin, K., 17n
Women: and extended family, 187, 214–16, 219, 224, 228, 230, 232, 234; surplus of, 215–16; and work, 47–49. *See*

also Gender; Spinsters; Working mothers
Work/consumption index, 43n
Workhouses, 57n
Working class, occupations defined, 32, 35, 36n
Working mothers: and extended family, 21–22, 47–49, 56, 153n, 223, 229, 231, 233, 235; in Lancashire, 153n
Wrigley, E. A., 66–68, 76n, 110

Yasuba, Y., 107n
York, England, 27
Yorkshire, England, 27

Zelnik, M., 107n
Zinsser, H., 60
Zitomersky, J., 59n

COMPOSED BY MODERN TYPE & DESIGN, INC., CLEARWATER, FLORIDA
MANUFACTURED BY THOMSON-SHORE, INC., DEXTER, MICHIGAN
TEXT IS SET IN TIMES ROMAN, DISPLAY LINES IN GILL SANS

Library of Congress Cataloging-in-Publication Data
Ruggles, Steven.
Prolonged connections.
(Social demography)
Bibliography: pp. 237–274.
Includes index.
1. Family size—England—History—19th century—Case
studies.   2. Family size—United States—History—19th
century—Case studies.   3. Family—Economic aspects—
England—History—19th century—Case studies.   4. Family
—Economic aspects—United States—History—19th century—
Case studies.   5. Family demography—Mathematical models.
I. Title.   II. Series.
HQ762.G72E57   1987   306.8′57′0942   87-6079
ISBN 0-299-11030-3
ISBN 0-299-11034-6 (pbk.)